# Menstruation and Psychoanalysis

# Menstruation and Psychoanalysis

*Mary Jane Lupton*

University of Illinois Press
Urbana and Chicago

© 1993 by the Board of Trustees of the University of Illinois
Manufactured in the United States of America
1  2  3  4  5  C  P  5  4  3  2  1

*This book is printed on acid-free paper.*

Library of Congress Cataloging-in-Publication Data
Lupton, Mary Jane.
    Menstruation and psychoanalysis / Mary Jane Lupton.
        p. cm.
    Includes bibliographical references and index.
    ISBN 0-252-02012-X (cl : acid-free paper).—ISBN 0-252-06315-5
(pb : acid-free paper)
    1. Menstuation—Psychological aspects.   2. Women and
psychoanalysis. I. Title.
RG161.L87 1993
155.3'33—dc20                                              92-39668
                                                                CIP

*To Kenneth Huntress Baldwin*

# Contents

# Acknowledgments

Without Janice Delaney and Emily Toth, my investigation of menstruation would not have materialized. As co-authors of *The Curse*, we encouraged and critiqued each others' work, meeting periodically in Janice's red dining room in Washington, D.C. At many points in writing *Menstruation and Psychoanalysis*, I have missed their deadlines, their commentary, their suggestions, their wit, their companionship. I thank both Emily and Janice for their past inspiration and for their immediate enthusiasm for this project.

My husband, Kenneth Huntress Baldwin, assumed most of Emily's and Janice's critical functions, in addition to shopping for groceries, planning the meals, handling computer repairs, mailing manuscripts, locating obscure books, and performing countless other chores during the past three years. His critical reading of *Menstruation and Psychoanalysis* at every stage has been invaluable, as have been his love and encouragement.

I am especially grateful to my daughter Julia Reinhard Lupton, who translated Claude Dagmar Daly for me and who co-authored the "Annotated Bibliography of Claude Dagmar Daly (1884–1950)," which appeared in 1990 in *American Imago*. Julia's critique of the Freud chapters and her understanding of psychoanalytic feminism were indispensable to my concepualization of menstruation's place in theory.

I am indebted to my daughter Ellen Lupton for her loving support of this project, especially during hard times, and for her clarity and directness of style, qualities that I have held before me in writing this book.

I want to thank my son-in-law, Kenneth Reinhard, for having provided me with the Bollas paper, "CUTTING," and for being a dependable source of information throughout this project. I also thank Lawrence Padgett, former reference librarian at Morgan State University, for information on menstruation, always humorously presented, over the years.

Of the many other people whom I wish to thank, I would include the following: the referees who supported my (unsuccessful) grant proposals on menstruation and psychoanalysis, J. Leeds Barroll, Jonathan Crewe, Sharon Golub, and Sandra Harding; the editor of *American Imago*, Martin Gliserman, who showed strong and immediate enthusiasm for Claude Dagmar Daly and the menstruation complex; my editor for this book, Ann Lowry, who acted at every stage in a timely, intelligent, and caring way; my readers for *Menstruation and Psychoanalysis*, particularly Diana Hume George. Additionally, numerous people have given information, answered questions, loaned books, sent references, clarified issues, helped with theory, offered encouragement. The following are but a few: Chandra Agrawal, Carolyn A. Durham, Jill Duncan, Carol Ann Hohman, John D. Hohman, Shirley Landon, J. Abbott Miller, Joan Moore, Wendy Owen, Judith Pike, Ellie Ragland-Sullivan, Rosalind Reinhard, Stuart Schneiderman, Jane Venable, Aimee Wiest, and Linda Zakarin. I wish to thank as well the reference librarians at the Johns Hopkins University, the University of Maryland School of Medicine, and the National Library of Medicine.

Lastly, I am grateful to the Board for Research and the Press of Morgan State University for granting me a course reduction for two semesters during the research and writing of *Menstruation and Psychoanalysis*.

# Introduction

# Menstruation as Difference

*Menstruation and Psychoanalysis* was born from chapter 8 of *The Curse: A Cultural History of Menstruation*, the book on which I collaborated in 1976 with Janice Delaney and Emily Toth.[1] Owing to its kaleidoscopic scale, *The Curse* confined the psychoanalytic response to women's bleeding to a few chapters. We assessed Freudian theory, but not within the historical setting of the Freud-Fliess relationship, with its repressed treatment of menstruation in the correspondence and in Freud's dreams. Nor did we unravel the complex entanglement between menstruation and female sexuality, as I do in *Menstruation and Psychoanalysis*. What I present here is a new book rather than a sequel, a book that fully examines, for the first time, the impact of menstruation on a theory of sexual difference.

After *The Curse* was published, I presented a number of lectures on women's bleeding that had a psychoanalytic orientation. Often the speaking engagement dramatically confirmed the tabooed status of menstruation explored in our book. Midway through a lecture on the psychological origins of menstrual taboo at a meeting of the Baltimore NOW, a television crew arrived and taped a few of my remarks, scheduled for the 11 o'clock news. The news that night showed my mouth talking, but the audio track consisted of a male voiceover announcing the meeting and saying that Professor Lupton had "spoken about a subject of great interest to women." No one mentioned menstruation or menstrual taboo, which had been tabooed right off the air.

On another occasion, a doctor attending a lecture that I presented to a regional psychoanalytic association complained (privately, of course) that I should not have referred to my *own* menstruation in public: "Why, my own wife doesn't tell me when she is menstruating."[2] Had this statement come from a lawyer or a mechanic or a real estate agent, it would have been less disturbing; in its medical context the doctor's objection seemed anecdotally to verify the century-old gap between menstruation and psychoanalysis, between women's blood and male avoidance.

Despite an otherwise noticeable attention to Freud in psychoanalytic-feminist interpretations over the past two decades, the handful of books on menstruation published since the mid-1970s demonstrate a minimal interest in menstruation as a phenomenon in psychoanalytic writing—either as a specific theory or as an image in Freud's dream interpretation or in his analytic practice. *Menstruation and Menopause*, for example, takes a strong, feminist position on the female processes, mentioning Freud's views on castration anxiety and the menstrual taboo as instances of the persistent male fear of menstruation but without close attention to related Freudian texts.[3] *The Wise Wound*, a dream excursion that in its tone approaches menstrual alchemy, employs Jungian rather than Freudian perceptions in its discussions of theory. The comments on Freud are brief and disparaging.[4] Only two other recent books, neither of them concerned with psychoanalytic theory, treat menstruation in detail. *Blood Relations* assumes a Marxist-anthropological perspective in arguing for the female origins of the menstrual taboo, whereas *Images of Bleeding* stresses cultural history, physiology, and the politics of menstruation, dismissing Freud in half a sentence.[5] In *Menstruation and Psychoanalysis* I address the gaps in critical and psychoanalytic theory and examine the reluctance, among Freud and his followers, to recognize menstruation as a psychically relevant aspect of female sexuality.

*Menstruation and Psychoanalysis* begins with the correspondence between Sigmund Freud and Wilhelm Fliess in the 1890s and ends with the disintegration of the Freudian circle prior to World War II. While there are substantial references to menstruation in psychoanalysis, especially among women analysts, one observes a general avoidance of that topic in psychoanalytic theory, an avoidance that reflects larger cultural attitudes, not only toward menstruation but toward female sexuality. Because menstruation has been consistently silenced by institutions such as the family, the educational system, and the church, it is apt to be silenced in a theoretical work—called by another name or otherwise disguised. The "veiled" nature of menstruation makes it necessary to read a given text on at least four levels: for what is actually said about menstruation, for what is merely inferred about menstruation, for symbolic representations of menstrual blood (as in dreams), and for what is omitted or repressed about menstruation.

Certain problems related to the veiled nature of the subject arise in doing research on menstruation. Because of the arbitrariness of index systems and indexers, cumulated references to menstruation are rarely accurate; often *menstruation* is completely omitted, while at times the word appears in the text with far greater frequency than indicated in the index.[6] Menstrual omissions of this nature illustrate the difficulty of researching a topic about which even the indexer observes the menstrual taboo. Another difficulty, one that mirrors the problem of the index, is the complicity of one's own repression, of one's own failure to recognize the presence of menstrual blood. Such omissions will be detected, I am sure, by readers of *Menstruation and Psychoanalysis;* as I have pointed to menstrual gaps in Freud's interpretation of the Language of Flowers Dream or in Daly's reading of Poe or in Marie Bonaparte's accounts of excision, so I have unavoidably left breaches in my own analyses, it being the nature of menstrual imagery to elude interpretation.

Throughout this book I argue that menstrual blood is *gendered blood*— blood that separates and defines women, that has made them the subject of taboo, of exclusion, of *difference*—whether among the Kolosh Indians of Alaska or among subtle discourse communities like the Vienna Psychoanalytic Society. In either situation the male body is privileged, the female body excluded. Hidden from sight, menstruation represents what is most lacking or concealed in the culture, whereas the phallus, in its dominance, perpetually signifies its self. To recognize women's bleeding is to assess the consequence of gender in its biological, societal, and psychological representations; it is also to affirm female productivity and renewal against such traditionally negative psychoanalytic concepts as female castration anxiety and female masochism.

In writing *Menstruation and Psychoanalysis* I have focused on ideas specifically concerned with menstruation and with psychoanalytic theories associated either positively or antagonistically with Freudian precepts. I have thus omitted a number of major analysts. Carl Jung, although he is mentioned, plays no major role in this book; while concerned with feminine psychology, he leaned toward a spiritual approach to women that did not warrant an intense scrutiny of their menstrual blood.[7] As with Jung, so I have for the most part eliminated from this book the work of other major analysts who advocated theories of semiotics or maturation or ego defense, where menstruation would have no relevance: Alfred Adler, Erich Fromm, Anna Freud, Jacques Lacan, Harry Stack Sullivan.[8]

I have also excluded a discussion of the menopause, except when that phase is intrinsic to a theory of menstrual representation. The menopause is the *end* of female genital bleeding, the once and future absence, when the threat of cultural contamination recedes. In a February 1992 paper presented to a Baltimore menopause support group, I argued that the primary reason for the cross-cultural inattention to the menopause lies in the invisibility of the menopausal process, whereas most female initiation rites are based on the physical recognition of menstrual blood. Menopausal absence is not generally noted in the way that a woman's menarche is discovered, observed, and ritualized. My concern in *Menstruation and Psychoanalysis* is with the menstrual presence and with how it is frequently veiled or symbolically represented as absence, as the disguising of sexual difference.

When Freud's colleague Fritz Wittels lectured on menstruation and the sexual inferiority of women at a meeting of the Vienna Psychoanalytic Society in 1908, he was taunted for dwelling on "the otherwise insignificant phenomenon of the menses," to which Wittels responded: "Menstruation is the most important difference between man and woman."[9] Although there are admittedly numerous other factors that separate women from men, the idea of menstruation as "the most *important* difference" is the concept that guides my course of inquiry throughout this book. Within the Freudian framework, sexual difference occurs at the moment the child acknowledges the girl's castration, her absent penis. The process of sexual differentiation between boys and girls is invariably hinged to the concept of penis envy. Boys fear girls because girls lack a penis; the boy is then threatened, fearing castration—fearing to become a girl. The girl, on the other hand, always wants the penis that she realizes she lacks. Always desiring, she can only be fulfilled by giving birth to a male child—a child with a penis.[10] In the vast psychoanalytic literature on sexual development, there is barely any attention given to what the *girl* has that the boy definitely lacks, namely, an internal reproductive cycle. Freudians, who tended to undervalue motherhood and reproduction, viewed menstruation as peripheral to the formation of the psyche; the menstrual process would only reinforce distinctions made earlier, in the oedipal phase.[11]

Nonetheless, some analysts, in their revision of Freud, argued that sexual difference was transmitted not through the absence of a penis but through the mother's sexual presence, epitomized by her menstruation. The menstrual distinction is what Melanie Klein called a "fact": "Sooner or later every child discovers the fact that the sexes differ and women menstruate." [12] Claude Dagmar Daly theorized that menstruation was at the root of the Oedipus complex and the key to a concept of sexual difference, while Karen Horney used the term *specific difference* to indicate a distinction in the development of men and women. Based on her recognition of specific sexual difference, she argued that the male fear of women is greater than the female wish to be a man and that a prime object of male dread is menstrual blood.[13]

According to these theorists, menstruation achieves visibility not only during puberty but far earlier, in childhood perceptions of the mother. To examine how it functions within psychoanalytic theory requires that menstruation be examined within and against the Freudian view of female sexuality, where concepts such as penis envy, castration anxiety, passivity, hysteria, and female masochism have served to define menstrual difference. That difference tends to be expressed culturally through confinement and denial and psychoanalytically through omissions, misreading, or phallocentric bias. The historic isolation and denial of menstruous women as "polluted" or "unclean" mark a fundamental distinction between the sexes, one so emphatic that it inspires enormous cultural and psychological barriers.[14]

Certain French feminists, in approaching the question of sexual difference, include women's blood and fluid as factors distinguishing female reproductivity from the phallus. In their redefining of female sexuality, they have reclaimed the theory of *difference*, using the body distinctions between male and female in an effort to pose a female discourse against the lack (castration) projected onto the female body. Luce Irigaray, Hélène Cixous, Catherine Clément, and other psychoanalytic feminists, desiring to separate the masculine from the feminine, have questioned the dominant phallocentrism of French psychoanalysis as derived from Freud and Lacan: the woman as mirror of maleness, the little girl as little man, the clitoris as little penis.[15] Within this endeavor they have reclaimed menstruation as an emblem of sexual difference, innovatively using images of flow and bleeding to represent cycles, flexibility, rhythm, *jouissance*, "the eternal recurrence of a biological rhythm which conforms to that of nature."[16] The French feminist discussion of sexual difference is complex, involving Lacanian analysis, semiotics, deconstruction, the history of philosophy, and other disciplines; my concern in this text is with the fluid/blood metaphor as a menstrual verification of sexual difference.

Luce Irigaray, in "The 'Mechanics' of Fluids," constructs a metaphysics of fluidity, a philosophy of flow. Women's property is "milk, luminous flow, acoustic waves, . . . not to mention the gasses inhaled, emitted, variously perfumed, of urine, saliva, blood, even plasma, and so on."[17] Elsewhere she refers to *sang rouge* (red blood/women's blood), although she gives the phrase no menstrospecific reading.[18] The blood/fluid image occurs as well in the controversial "When Our Lips Speak Together," where she celebrates, with other women and with herself, their flow of blood as emblem of love and language: "Blood is familiar, close. You are all red. And so very white. Both at once. . . . Words are mute, when they are uttered once and for all. Neatly wrapped up so that their meaning— their blood—won't escape."[19] With a note of chastisement, Simone de Beauvoir has cautioned the French feminists against too much enthusiasm for speaking the female body, fearing that in reversing gender, they might erroneously force the menstrual cycle into the same dominant position as the penis: "It would be ridiculous and absurd, it would be like constructing a counter-penis."[20]

In the 1960s, the American analyst Clara Thompson expressed comparable concern about the dangers of embracing a doctrine of sexual difference, feeling that gender would be used to derogate women as skin color is used to segregate African Americans: "Sexual difference is an obvious difference, and obvious differences are especially convenient marks of derogation in any competitive situation in which one group aims to get power over the other."[21] Thompson's point of view is pervasive among American socialist feminists, who have downplayed the concept of sexual difference and of menstruation's place within feminist discourse. Many socialist feminists construe the emphasis on male/female differences as an invitation to oppression, in their belief that differences in gender derive from the patriarchal structure of society and that to call attention to them would be disastrous. In a survey of the American feminist response to sexual difference, Carolyn Burke comments: "Frequently we sought to demonstrate that significant differences between the sexes did not exist, so that these imagined differences could no longer be used against us." [22]

Feminists who protest the concept of sexual difference frequently attack their opponents with the labels *essentialist* or *biologist*.[23] Such critics would be particularly wary of a theory of *menstrual* difference, where female sexuality is encumbered with the biological awesomeness of the blood taboo. Janet Sayers, for example, strongly objected to the biological emphasis of *The Curse*. Women's differences among ourselves, she wrote, "cannot simply be wished away by glorifying and wallowing in our shared biology." [24] I would answer that our menstrual biology cannot be "shared," let alone "wallowed in," until it becomes articulated, admissible, conscious. In a theory of menstruation, the cultural attitude toward women is inseparably tied to the biological-psychological recognition of their blood. Therefore, to read menstruation as gendered blood is simultaneously to recognize the ritualization of difference through cleansing practices, psychoanalytic stereotyping, and other constructs that affect the status of all women as a class. In its assessment of women's bleeding, *Menstruation and Psychoanalysis* takes into account both the biological difference inherent in the menstrual flow as well as the cultural injunctions that oppress tabooed women, among them genital mutilation; the regulatory laws of Judaism; the taboo against incest; the psychoanalytic disparagement of the menstruating woman as witch or masochist; and the discouragement of women, on the basis of their periods, from full participation in the professions. My emphasis on the control of menstruation by taboo avoids the polarities of biological difference versus cultural construction, since taboo is precisely what demarcates the difference between "nature" and "culture." As the ground and condition of their very differentiation, the menstrual taboo thus infolds both.

Part 1, "Freud," concentrates on those aspects of his writing that either specifically concern menstruation or that suggest representations of bleeding women as veiled or disguised in his psychoanalytic interpretation. Freud, as the founder of psychoanalysis, was not only the theorist most accountable for a concept of female sexuality but also the one who initially repressed menstruation in the formulation of that theory. This section of the book begins with his reactions to a patient, Emma Eckstein, who had hemorrhaged after Freud's colleague, Wilhelm Fliess, performed nose surgery but neglected to remove a piece of gauze. I argue that Freud associated Emma Eckstein's uncontrollable nasal eruptions with menstrual flow; her issue of blood generated in him an initial horror, followed by a need to exonerate Fliess for his role in her bleeding. Her menstruation, with which he identified, continued to infiltrate Freud's work on a symbolic level, especially in *The Interpretation of Dreams* (1900).

Part 1 also examines the Freud/Fliess theory that menstruation is a sexual period in which the dammed-up libido, or sexual energy, is released. I suggest that libido is essentially a metaphor that imitates the menstrual process and that relates, as does menstruation, to the death instinct, to the Three Fates, and to the Great Goddess, who in her fertile phase represents menstruation. I propose that if menstrual blood, so long culturally tabooed, is recognized in its nurturing capacity, it can be perceived as *good* blood instead of as a contamination.

A discussion of menstrual taboo concludes Part 1. Freud, in *Totem and Taboo* (1913), presented menstruating women as "unclean," a concept that is related to Judaic law—to menstruating women as *niddah* (in a state of pollution). Although he generally neglected the menstrual taboo in his investigation, his analysis of menstruation and defloration as they relate to "The Taboo of Virginity" (1910) is particularly open to a menstrual/feminist reading.

Part 2, "Male Analysts," examines the works of a number of Freudian theorists who incorporated menstruation into their considerations of castration anxiety, circumcision, the Oedipus complex, and other concepts central to the foundations of psychoanalysis. Of the Freudians, it was Claude Dagmar Daly who most strongly insisted that a recognition of menstruation must be incorporated into the larger and much ignored theory of female sexuality. In his quest to define what he called the menstruation complex, Daly searched the fields of literature and anthropology for images of a bleeding mother, finding in the blood-thirsty Hindu goddess Kali his psychoanalytic symbol for menstruating women. Daly, in the course of his investigation, took issue with Freud on a number of matters: for Freud's having ignored female sexuality, for his neglect of the mother goddesses, and for his one-sided view of the primal horde and of the origins of the Oedipus complex.

Bleeding mothers are not the major subject in the writings on menstruation, though. Many of the studies in psychoanalysis and anthropology focus on male menstruation and on the male desire to participate in the menstrual process—to be purified or feminized or somehow altered through identification with bleeding women. In the Australian ritual of subincision, the male splits his penis to resemble a bleeding vagina, in imitation of the menstrual process. The male desire to menstruate (*saignade*), laid bare in this bizarre ritual, has been recapitulated among individuals in therapy, through masochistic fantasies, or through such symptoms as bleeding vicariously from the nose or rectum. Thus, on rare occasions, men actually envy women's difference, appropriating menstruation through vicarious bleeding or self-inflicted surgery or, in Freud's case, through identification with his menstruating daughter, Mathilde. "Male Analysts" also includes a discussion of a recent paper by Christopher Bollas, "CUTTING," in which the analyst identifies with his aggressive, bleeding female patient.

Part 3, "Women Analysts" examines menstruation as it was analytically perceived by women, for whom menstruation was a cultural and biological reality. It focuses on the prevalent assumptions about menstruation during the period that falls roughly between World War I and World War II, with emphasis on the writings of Mary Chadwick, Helene Deutsch, Marie Bonaparte, Karen Horney, Melanie Klein, Clara Thompson, and Therese Benedek. "Women Analysts" looks at certain themes common to much of their writings: menstruating mothers, menstruation and the witch, menstruation and masochism. It also reviews certain theories of menstruation formulated by women analysts between the wars, including the premenstrual syndrome and the effects of hormonal fluctuation.

Although both Karen Horney and Clara Thompson argued that the symptoms and restrictions surrounding menstruating women must be viewed within a cultural context in conjunction with any therapy, many of the psychoanalytic judgments examined in this chapter are resoundingly negative. Chadwick and Bonaparte saw menstruating women as hysterical, perverse, masochistic; several analysts agreed with Helene Deutsch that menstrual blood invokes "the idea of being torn or dismembered internally." [25]

"Women Analysts" also includes a discussion of Marie Cardinal's contemporary text, *Les mots pour le dire* (The Words to Say It). Cardinal, the victim of excessive menstrual flooding, ambivalently portrays menstruation as both life and death, both fertility and abortion. In consulting a psychoanalyst her symptoms cease but her words begin, generated by her menstrual identification. *The Words to Say It* mirrors many of the psychoanalytic themes investigated in *Menstruation and Psychoanalysis:* mothers, menstrual pain, language, female masochism, sexual difference.

Not all analysts held a fatalistic view of the menstrual process; Otto Rank, for example, associated menstruation with the powers of feeding and nurturance, with the primal mother. Nonetheless, the pervasive psychoanalytic verdict of the past fifty years is not encouraging. Menstruation, the source of periodic trauma and of internal damage, is rarely conceived as a positive indication of sexual difference. And despite their renewed interest in Freud, very few psychoanalytic feminists have examined Freud's dismissal of menstruation or sought to scrutinize women's bleeding within the framework of phallocentric discourse. More often, menstruation remains buried, sunk deep in the vaginal cave. Hidden from sight, menstruation represents lack or concealment, the red wound at the core of female sexuality.

In 1935 Claude Dagmar Daly stated his desire to make menstruation a conscious part of psychoanalytic thought, to show that "when the psychoanalytic inhibitions in relation to the theory of the menstruation complex are overcome, it will be discovered everywhere in literature, art, mythology, etc., by those who are willing and able to see."[26] In fact, the menstruation complex has *not* been "discovered everywhere"; the psychoanalytic inhibitions toward women's blood have not been overcome. The purpose of *Menstruation and Psychoanalysis* is to implement a menstrual consciousness within psychoanalytic discourse and to examine the implications of that consciousness toward a feminist theory of sexuality.

### Notes

1. Janice Delaney, Mary Jane Lupton, and Emily Toth, *The Curse: A Cultural History of Menstruation*, rev. ed. (Urbana: University of Illinois Press, 1988). Because so much of *Menstruation and Psychoanalysis* relies on information presented in *The Curse*, future references will appear parenthetically in the text.

2. A version of this anecdote is recounted in *The Curse*, xiii.

3. Paula Weideger, *Menstruation and Menopause* (New York: Knopf, 1975).

4. Penelope Shuttle and Peter Redgrove, *The Wise Wound: Eve's Curse and Every-woman*, rev. ed. (New York: Grove Press, 1986).

5. Chris Knight, *Blood Relations: Menstruation and the Origins of Culture* (New Haven: Yale University Press, 1991); and Louise Lander, *Images of Bleeding: Menstruation as Ideology* (New York: Orlando Press, 1988). See also my review essay of *The Wise Wound* and *Images of Bleeding* in *NWSA Journal* 1 (1989): 749–52.

6. In Otto Rank's *Trauma of Birth*, for example, the reference to menstruation as "birth *en masse*" is cited (51), but not the statements about the menstrual significance of the moon (75n) and of Christ's blood (125); see Otto Rank, *The Trauma of Birth* (1924; New York: Robert Brunner, 1952). In *The (M)other Tongue*, menstruation is not indexed at all; yet the topic is mentioned in the preface and in two of the essays. See *The (M)other Tongue: Essays in Feminist Psychoanalytic Interpretation*, ed. Shirley Nelson Garner, Claire Kahane, and Madelon Sprengnether (Ithaca: Cornell University Press, 1985), 10, 246, 358, 371.

7. While Shuttle and Redgrove point out certain menstrual themes that run through his works, they admit that Jung was "apparently never conscious of this application of his studies." See Shuttle and Redgrove, *The Wise Wound*, 100–106.

8. For a review of Adler, Sullivan, Fromm, and other analysts who rejected or modified Freud's theory of the instincts, see Clara M. Thompson, *Psychoanalysis: Evolution and Development* (New York: Hermitage House, 1950). In a letter of 15 September 1989, Stuart Schneiderman, a leading American Lacanian, informed me: "Off hand I do not know of any discussion of menstruation in Lacan."

9. Herman Nunberg and Ernest Federn, eds., *Minutes of the Vienna Psychoanalytic Society*, trans. M. Nunberg (New York: International Universities Press, 1962–75), 1:351–53.

10. See Sigmund Freud, *The Standard Edition of the Complete Psychological Works of Sigmund Freud*, ed. and trans. James Strachey (1966; London: Hogarth Press, 1986), 2:226, 57. All subsequent references to *The Standard Edition* will henceforth appear in the text, abbreviated as *SE*. For Freud's theory of sexual organization, see in particular *Three Essays on the Theory of Sexuality* (*SE* 7:207–30); "The Infantile Genital Organization: An Interpolation into the Theory of Sexuality" (*SE* 19:141–48); and "The Dissolution of the Oedipus Complex" (*SE* 19:173–82).

11. Marie Bonaparte, for example, thought that female sexuality was determined during the oedipal stage: "The menstrual flow, passing later through the vagina, will only confirm an erotogenic mode already present." Marie Bonaparte, *Female Sexuality*, trans. John Rodker (New York: International Universities Press, 1953), 140.

12. Melanie Klein, "Review of *Woman's Periodicity* by Mary Chadwick," in *Envy and Gratitude and Other Works 1946–1963* (1936; New York: Delacourte, 1975), 318.

13. Karen Horney, "The Dread of Women," in *Feminine Psychology*, ed. Harold Kelman (1932; New York: Norton, 1973), 133–46.

14. The word *menstrous* is from Sir James George Frazer, "The Seclusion of Girls at Puberty," *The Golden Bough* (London: Macmillan, 1913), 1:76. I use it in *Menstruation and Psychoanalysis* to indicate menstruating women as tabooed or threatening or monstrous. At times *menstrous* is used to connote the negative psychoanalytic attitude toward menstruation, as in the writings of Mary Chadwick.

15. Jacques Lacan, the influential French psychoanalyst, remarked: "Contrary to what is said, concerning phallic bliss [*jouissance*], Woman, if I may so speak, since she does not exist, is not deprived of it." Jacques Lacan, *A Challenge to the Psychoanalytic Establishment*, in *Television*, ed. Joan Copec, trans. Jeffrey Mehlman (1980; New York: Norton, 1990), 134. In an analysis of Lacan's remark, Jane Gallop explains: "Discursivity, the reigning system, cannot include women, because it demands the solid, the identical, to the exclusion of the fluid." Jane Gallop, *The Daughter's Seduction* (Ithaca: Cornell University Press, 1982), 39. If Woman as fluid does not exist, then it follows, if I may so speak, that Menstrual Fluid would not exist.

16. Julia Kristeva, "Women's Time," in *The Kristeva Reader*, ed. Toril Moi (New York: Columbia University Press, 1986), 191.

17. Luce Irigaray, *This Sex which Is Not One*, trans. Catherine Porter (1977; Ithaca: Cornell University Press, 1985), 113, ellipses hers. In her later texts, Irigaray moves from the blood/fluid signification of sexual difference toward a degendered philosophical/ethical analysis. See, for example, the essay "Sexual Difference," in *The Irigaray Reader*, ed. Margaret Whitford (Cambridge: Basil Blackwell, 1991), 165–77. For a study of the evolution of Irigaray's thought, see Margaret Whitford, *Luce Irigaray: Philosophy in the Feminine* (London: Routledge, 1991).

18. Irigaray, *Amante Marine* (1980), quoted in Whitford, *Luce Irigaray*, 118. Whitford reads this reference as a pun, subduing any biological reading. Jane Gallop writes, in her commentary on Irigaray: "Menstrual blood is not a wound in the closure of the body: the menstrual flow ignores the distinction virgin/deflowered." See Gallop, *Seduction*, 83. Among the critics I have read on French feminism, I have not observed fluid references being discussed as signs of women's menstrual difference. See, for example, *Revaluing French Feminism: Critical Essays on Difference, Agency, and Culture*, ed. Nancy Fraser and Sandra Lee Bartky (Bloomington: Indiana University Press, 1992).

19. Irigaray, "When Our Lips Speak Together," in *This Sex*, 206, 208–9. For further references to blood and writing see Hélène Cixous, "The Laugh of the Medusa," trans. Keith Cohen and Paula Cohen, in *New French Feminisms*, ed. Elaine Marks and Isabelle de Courtivron (New York: Schocken Books, 1981), 245; and Marie Cardinal and Annie Leclerc, *Autrement dit* (Paris: Bernard Grasset, 1977), 83. In a brilliant attempt to connect menstruation, defloration, and writing, the American feminist Susan Gubar claims that "one of the primary and most resonant metaphors provided by the female body is blood, and cultural forms of creativity are often experienced

as a painful wounding." Susan Gubar, " 'The Blank Page' and Female Creativity," in *The New Feminist Criticism*, ed. Elaine Showalter (New York: Pantheon, 1985), 296.

20. Simone de Beauvoir, "From an Interview," in *New French Feminisms*, 153.

21. Clara M. Thompson, *Interpersonal Psychoanalysis: The Selected Papers of Clara M. Thompson*, ed. Maurice R. Green (New York: Basic Books, 1964), 244–45.

22. Jane Gallop and Carolyn G. Burke, "Psychoanalysis and Feminism in France," in *The Future of Difference*, ed. Hester Eisenstein and Alice Jardine (New Brunswick: Rutgers University Press, 1985), 107. *The Future of Difference* is not concerned with menstruation as difference; there is only one (secondary) reference to menstruation, in which Carolyn Heilbrun quotes Sandra Bem's inclusion of menstruation as one of several indications that the world "consist[s] of two sexes." See Carolyn G. Heilbrun, "Androgyny and the Psychology of Sex Differences," 261.

23. Janet Sayers combines the "essentialist" and "biologist" charges in her critique of Irigaray, whose philosophy is "essentially constituted by female biology, by the 'two lips' of the female sex." See Janet Sayers, *Biological Politics* (London: Tavistock, 1982), 131. Another British feminist finds fault with Irigaray's "ahistoricality" but suggests that if "read metaphorically rather than literally," Irigaray offers "an alternative set of values based on maternal as opposed to paternal sensuality." Ann Ferguson, *Blood at the Root* (London: Pandora, 1989), 46. Despite its tantalizing title, there is no reference to menstruation in *Blood at the Root*.

24. Sayers, *Biological Politics*, 120.

25. Helene Deutsch, *The Psychology of Women* (New York: Grune and Stratton: 1944), 1:150.

26. Claude Dagmar Daly, "The Menstruation Complex in Literature," *Psychoanalytic Quarterly* 4 (1935): 340n.

# Part 1
# Freud

# 1

# *Menstrual Collaborations: The Case of Emma Eckstein*

In February 1895, Freud's friend and colleague Wilhelm Fliess performed nose surgery on one of Freud's patients, Emma Eckstein.[1] The unsuccessful surgery provoked in Freud confused responses of love, denial, and accusation that affected many of his later views—on female sexuality, on the theory of libido, on the methodology of dream interpretation, on menstruation. Before we can uncover his reactions to Emma Eckstein's bleeding, however, we must examine the basis of his relationship to Fliess, in which menstruation played a crucial role. I will mention only once the peculiar fact that Fliess's name derives from the German verb *fliessen*, which means *to flow*.

Freud, in his collected writings, exhibited only a slight interest in the menstrual cycle as an event in a patient's life or as a factor in psychic development; his colleague Wilhelm Fliess, on the other hand, was committed to a concept of "periodicity," a system of inescapable rhythms in both men and women that Fliess tabulated on the basis of a twenty-eight-day menstrual cycle. Fliess, a nose, ears, and throat specialist from Berlin, was the author of at least seventeen publications, all of them scarce and none of them available in English translation.[2] When *The Nose and the Female Sex Organs* was published in 1897, Fliess and Freud had been corresponding for ten years, offering mutual support for theories

## A Menstrual Calendar

**1894**

May 6 — The first allusion to menstruation in Freud's letters to Fliess

**1895**

mid-February — Fliess operated on Emma Eckstein

4 March — Freud informed Fliess about Emma Eckstein's hemorrhaging

23–24 July — The "Specimen Dream" (the Dream of Irma's Injection)

**1896**

1 March — Freud began his notations on his wife's periods

4 May — Freud claimed that Emma "bled out of *longing*" and "has always been a bleeder"

**1897**

Fliess published *The Nose and the Female Sex Organs*

17 January — Emma's fantasy in which the devil sticks pins in her finger

24 January — Emma's fantasy about female circumcision and sucking blood

31 May — The Staircase Dream (The Dirty Red Carpet)

4 October — The Dream of the Red Bath

15 October — Freud recorded his own menstruation

12 December — The last reference to Emma in the correspondence; she is an analyst

mid-December — The Dream of the Red-Nosed Nun

**1899**

27 June — Last notation of the Freud family's menstrual cycle (Mathilde's menarche)

**1900**

Freud published *The Interpretation of Dreams*

August — Freud and Fliess terminated their relationship

that were equally unacceptable by current medical standards: Freud for his belief in the sexual origin of the neuroses, Fliess for his belief in the sexual importance of the nose. It has also been suggested that their intense relationship, highlighted by a number of private meetings, or "congresses," showed strong signs of repressed homosexual desire between the two men.[3] This unacknowledged bonding created an emotional tension during the Eckstein operation and its aftermath.

In the preface to *The Nose and the Female Sex Organs*, Fliess stressed the complex relationship between the nose, the female sex organs, and the menstrual process: "The pathology of menstruation finds its reflection in birth: the same mechanisms and the same conditions that hold true for nasal dysmenorrhea also control the pains of contraction [*Wehenschmerz*]." The nose, he argued, was so closely connected to the female genitals that it would swell or bleed during menstruation; an abortion could be "provoked through the nose." Nasal therapy could relieve certain ailments such as dysmenorrhea (painful menstruation) or stomach pains or migraines; these could be treated either by cauterizing the mucous membranes or by applying cocaine to the "genital spots" of the nose or by operating on the turbinate bone. It was Fliess who operated on Freud's nose, removing a piece of the turbinate bone.[4] This surgical method of treatment was, in the case of Emma Eckstein, to cause insurmountable conflicts between them.

Freud was introduced to Fliess by Josef Breuer, with whom he wrote *Studies on Hysteria* (1893–95), a work that experiments with the use of hypnosis in the treatment of menstrual disorders. One of Breuer's patients, a young married woman, had a period that lasted two weeks; after hypnosis her cycle became more regular. Freud's patient Frau Emmy von N. also suffered from menstrual irregularity. Freud promised "to regulate this by hypnotic suggestion and, under hypnosis, set the interval at 28 days." Below appeared the sparest of footnotes: "A suggestion which was carried out" (*SE* 2:57, 57n). The first allusion to menstruation in the correspondence with Fliess was disguised as "stomachaches."[5] The word *menstruation* did not appear until three months later, in a similar context ("the stomach-menstruation business") but with marked praise for Fliess's discoveries: "The profession is waiting for this kind of thing" (*Letters*, 96). In a letter of 1896 he asked Fliess quickly to dispel his doubts "about male and female menstruation in the same individual" (*Letters*, 193).

Freud shared with Fliess an interest in the concept of "periodicity"— although he did not, like Fliess, commit himself to periodicity as a major factor in the development of his psychoanalytic theory. Fliess contended that women *and* men were affected by a periodic pattern, with the female interval being twenty-eight days and the male interval twenty-three days.

There are numerous references to male and female periodicity in the letters to Fliess, several of which found their way into *The Standard Edition*.[6] What might have developed into a theory about the relationship between menstruation and anxiety is generalized instead into both male and female periodic situations—an idea that seems to derive from Fliess's theory of bisexuality.

In his discussions with Fliess on the menstrual migraine (*Letters*, 142–44), Freud observed that menstrual migraines are rare in males and are related to periodicity; these can be caused by "human toxic emanations" and by certain smells. These shared concepts of periodicity, bisexuality, dysmenorrhea, menstrual migraines, and the nose are indications of the cross-fertilization of ideas that pervaded the correspondence. Both men were open to the possibility of treating Emma Eckstein's menstruation by way of the nose.

### The Bleeding of Emma Eckstein

Emma Eckstein was a patient who had been troubled by menstrual difficulties; according to Masson, "It appears that she suffered from stomach ailments and menstrual problems"; her menstrual pain "would have been attributed to masturbation."[7] Freud invited Fliess to do surgery, in accordance with the theory that operating on the nose would favorably affect the genitals. The surgery, which at first glance seemed successful, created a bond between the two men through the agency of the female patient, giving them the opportunity to execute the nasal/genital theory and apparently stimulating a latent homosexual relationship. Shirley Nelson Garner contends that the operation on Emma Eckstein had "some of the aura around it that frequently accompanies male bonding that substitutes for more intense love." It had the "feel of adventure, of a dangerous undertaking"; it was an aspect of the "erotic attachment" between Freud and Fliess.[8]

After Fliess returned to Berlin, Freud was responsible for postoperative care and subsequent psychoanalytic treatment. Regrettably, Fliess had failed to remove a piece of gauze during the surgery; two weeks later Emma began to hemorrhage.

Freud initially wrote to Fliess about Emma's bleeding in a letter of 4 March 1895, not getting to Emma's case until he had first, mentioned a photograph of the two men; second, expressed concern for Fliess's reputation; and third, expressed concern for Fliess's health. The fourth paragraph of this numerically organized letter referred to the operation Fliess had performed, in mid-February, on Emma Eckstein: "Fourth, Eckstein's condition is still unsatisfactory: persistent swelling, going up and down 'like an avalanche'; pain, so that morphine cannot be dispensed with; bad nights. The purulent secretion has been decreasing since yesterday; the day before yesterday (Saturday) she had a massive hemorrhage, probably as a result of expelling a bone chip the size of a heller [a coin]; there were two bowls full of pus" (*Letters*, 113). The account of Emma done with, Freud proceeded to item five: "Fifth, quickly something more pleasant after all this." These more pleasant items consisted of reassurances— Breuer has praised Fliess's work on nasal headaches; Breuer has been "won over" by Freud's account of his analysis of Emma Eckstein; another case has been considered "a feat of diagnostic acumen" (*Letters*, 114). The closing reads: "All of us and I wish you a speedy recovery."

One finds in this letter of 4 March 1895 a curious combination of emotions—a concern for Fliess's health at beginning and end; a delay in telling Fliess of Emma Eckstein's postoperative bleeding; a detachment toward that condition; and an insistent need to affirm, in writing, the validity of both Freud's work and his colleague's. Enclosed in the same letter was an astonishing document, called "Case History," in which Freud described the "thick, old pus in large clots" that appeared in both nostrils: "Since then the nose has again been flooded; only today has the purulent secretion become somewhat less dense" (*Letters*, 115–16). The patient with these symptoms was Emma Eckstein; however, in the "Case History" (singular case), Emma became fused with Freud, who, without a break in structure, began writing to Dr. Fliess about his own nasally related problems—difficult respiration, heart pain, and a "focal pus accumulation" in the nose. Such references are frequent in the correspondence, as in the letter of 25 May 1895: "I discharged exceedingly ample amounts of pus and all the while felt splendid; now the secretion has nearly dried up and I am still feeling very well" (*Letters*, 130). In the "Case History" Freud presented his symptoms through use of simile: the accumulations of pus produce "eruptions like a private Etna, as it were" (*Letters*, 116). He offered this information to Fliess as evidence "that the condition of the heart depends on the condition of the nose." Four days later, on 8 March, the condition (Eckstein's, not Freud's) worsened. In language that emphasizes his identity with his colleague, he wrote: "Fortunately I am finally seeing my way clear and am reassured about Miss Eckstein and can give you a report which will probably upset *you* as much as it did *me*, but I hope *you* will get over it as quickly as *I* did" (*Letters*, 116, emphasis mine). He explained to the absent surgeon: "I was awakened in the morning—profuse bleeding had started again, pain, and so on." There was "profuse bleeding" coming from Emma's nose, accompanied by a "fetid odor" (*Letters*, 116). Then appeared an astonishing passage:

> Rosanes [Ignaz Rosanes, a Viennese doctor] cleaned the area surrounding the opening, removed some sticky blood clots, and suddenly pulled at something like a thread, kept on pulling. Before either of us had time to think, at least half a meter of gauze had been removed from the cavity. The next moment came a flood of blood. . . . At the moment the foreign body came out and everything became clear to me—and I immediately afterward was confronted by the sight of the patient—I felt sick. . . .
>
> I do not believe it was the blood that overwhelmed me—at that moment strong emotions were welling up in me. So we had done her an injustice. . . . That this mishap should have happened to you . . . (*Letters*, 116–17)

One month later (11 April) he informed his colleague of yet another series of bleedings: "As soon as the packing was partly removed, there was a new, life-threatening hemorrhage which I witnessed. It did not spurt, it surged. Something like a [fluid] level rising extraordinarily rapidly, and then overflowing everything" (*Letters*, 124). This letter also ends with hopes for Fliess's good health.

Looking at the correspondence of early March and April 1895 one notes a discourse of blood, primarily nose-bleeding but also, by Fliessian analogy, the blood of excessive menstruation, the very symptom for which Emma was being treated: "purulent secretion," "hemorrhage," "clots," "flooded," "profuse bleeding," "sticky blood clots," "flood of blood," "spurt," "overflowing." Using metaphor, Freud compared Emma's nasal swelling to the up/down motion of an avalanche, whereas his own nose erupted "like a private Etna." Thus Freud's flowing Etna imitated Emma Eckstein's "avalanche," or overflowing nose. If the nose is, as Fliess had argued, a *sexual* organ related to the female genitals, then Freud is likely to have associated his and her nasal eruptions with menstrual flow, as a number of critics have suggested.[9]

His witnessing of Emma's bleeding occurred simultaneously with the realization that Fliess, whose theories he had affirmed, may in fact be guilty, the evidence being the half a meter of gauze that Fliess left in

Emma's nose. The once virginal packing may have been, as Lawrence Frank speculates, a "curious deposit signaling the ways in which he and Freud achieved intimacy through their patient's mediating presence." [10] Now fetid, it would no longer be an instrument of intimacy but an object of repulsion, a "foreign object." The gauze, a nasal tamp to stop the bleeding, perhaps recalled Freud's childhood interest in wounds and bandages; it would also resemble, both in function and substance, the homemade bandages European women used until the 1940s or later to collect their menstrual blood.[11] What was hidden or disguised by civilized women is now appearing in clots before his eyes. He denies that the blood made him sick ("I do not believe it was the blood that overwhelmed me").[12] The denial is paralleled by an admission of guilt ("So we had done her an injustice"), which he immediately counters with a double accusation: against Rosanes for not having taken Emma elsewhere; against himself for not having "immediately reproached" Rosanes (*Letters*, 116–17).

As in the letter of 4 March, Freud's concern is less for Emma's suffering than for its damaging effects on Fliess: "at the end it [the gauze] tore off and provoked the bleeding. That this mishap should have happened to *you* . . ." (my italics). The "mishap," however, had happened to Emma Eckstein; the man (Freud/Fliess) might feel sick, but the woman does the bleeding. Quite aware of this paradox, Emma Eckstein, who "never lost consciousness during the massive hemorrhage," responded to Freud's queasiness by proudly evoking her gender: "when I returned to the room somewhat shaky, she greeted me with the condescending remark, 'So this is the strong sex'" (*Letters*, 117). Emma's sarcastic rebuttal of gender stereotyping seems to have been based on an association between nasal and menstrual bleeding; Freud is "shaky" from the blood, whereas women, so accustomed to their menstrual difference, are periodically testing their capacity to bleed and endure. Woman is therefore the stronger sex.

In the immediacy of the Eckstein incident, Freud revealed an ambivalence toward Fliess, set into action by the sight of blood. One year later, however, he absolved Fliess of any responsibility for Emma's hemorrhage. Emma became the guilty one, the one who desired to bleed. In April 1896 he wrote: "Her hemorrhages were hysterical, brought on by *longing*, probably at the 'sexual period' (out of sheer resistance that *Frauenzimmer* has not yet given me the dates)." [13] According to Max Schur, Freud disguised the sexual references in this letter, using the Fliessian word "*Sexualtermine*" (sexual period) to substitute for menstruation, and the word *Frauenzimmer,* or "woman's apartment," to substitute for the vagina.[14] Furthermore, Freud called the hemorrhages "hysterical," a term of primary interest in his clinical work on women and one that originates in the womb (from the Greek *hysteria,* or uterus).[15] Emma, whose "hysterical" bleeding occurred at the womb's "sexual [or menstrual] period," obstinately resisted giving Freud the exact dates of her cycle, to which he responded by using the derogatory term *Frauenzimmer.* A letter written in early May 1896 was more specific about the menstrual aspects of Emma's disorder:

> As for Eckstein—I am taking notes on her history so that I can send it to you—so far I know only that she bled out of *longing.* She has always been a bleeder, when cutting herself and in similar circumstances; as a child she suffered from severe nosebleeds; during the years when she was not yet menstruating, she had headaches which were interpreted to her as malingering and which in truth had been generated by suggestion; for this reason she joyously welcomed her severe menstrual bleeding as proof that her illness was genuine. (*Letters,* 186)

Here the symbolic interchangeability between nasal and menstrual blood is more consciously recognized than it had been during the aftermath of the second hemorrhage. Emma's overwhelming "flood of blood," which Freud realized was the result of the forgotten gauze, had been ghastly enough to make him sick; now he claims that Emma's nose-bleeding has no particular medical origin. It is, like her menstrual bleeding, a symptom of desire: "so far I know only that she bled out of *longing.*" Emma's menstrual history reinforced the pathology of her nose-bleeding, proving that her "illness was genuine."

Freud had witnessed a similar manipulation of blood in Emma's behavior at the sanitorium: "Since I did not come during the night, she renewed the bleedings, as an unfailing means of rearousing my affection. She bled spontaneously three times and each bleeding lasted four days, which must have some significance" (4 May 1896, *Letters,* 186). Of course a four-day interval had "some significance," as he well knew; either he was joking with Fliess, as he often did in the letters, or he was repressing the periodic performance of the menstrual cycle. The nose/menses association suggests that he had come to link the word *blood,* representing the sexuality of menstruation (as in Emma's *joy*), with the Fliessian sexuality of the nose, an organ indelibly associated with the "putrid odor" of Emma Eckstein.

Blood was also a factor in a curious letter dated 17 January 1897: "Emma has a scene [in mind] where the *Diabolus* sticks pins into her finger and puts a piece of candy on each drop of blood. As far as the blood is concerned, you are altogether innocent!"[16] In Emma's fantasy the devil erotically penetrates her finger, then tamps the wound with candy; Freud glides by this reference, although two years earlier he had shared with Fliess the story of how the child, Emma, was on two occasions "grabbed at her genitals" by a shopkeeper when she was buying some "sweets" ("Project for a Scientific Psychology," *SE* 1:353). Emma's finger-bleeding in the above "scene" is both initiated and stopped by the *Diabolus*, the one who pricks and the one who tamps. Without transition, Freud denies that the devil is Fliess: "As far as the blood is concerned, you are altogether innocent!" But in fact Fliess *had* caused the bleeding, begun in surgery and tamped by Freud and Rosanes after the hemorrhaging. The lack of transition—the dramatic leap from devil to Fliess, from guilt to innocence—is one of the strongest expressions of ambivalence in Freud's letters to his colleague, an ambivalence that helps to explain why he did not distinguish between nasal and menstrual blood, why he did not fully interpret Emma's "scenes" for Fliess, and why he did not articulate the very obvious meaning of a four-day period. The finger is a nose is a vagina.

A week later he described another of Emma's "scenes," this one involving circumcision, blood-sucking, cannibalism, and mutilation: "Think of it; I have been given a scene about the circumcision of a girl, involving the cutting off of a piece of one of the labia minora (which is shorter even now) and the sucking off of the blood, after which the child got to eat a piece of the skin. This child at the age of thirteen once claimed that she could swallow a piece of an earthworm, which she actually did. And an operation once performed by you had to come to grief from a hemophilia based on all this."[17] Devils, bleeding fingers, sticky candy, cut labia: during her analysis, Emma had given Freud sufficient material from dreams and fantasy that she was suffering from menstrual maladjustment as well as from sexual trauma. What he sarcastically called her "hemophilia" (a hereditary condition in which the blood fails to clot normally, causing excessive bleeding) was most likely the condition of menorrhagia or excessive discharge, augmented in Emma's situation by unresolved sexual conflicts at puberty.[18] Freud's inability to deal with the complications of Emma Eckstein's act of menstruation and with his ambivalence toward Fliess resulted in his transference of her profuse bleeding from a physical to a psychological origin: she *wanted* to bleed. While there is ample evidence to support this judgment, there is also a coincident biological fact: Emma, as a woman, *had* to bleed. Thus, in his first major case involving menstruation, he initially minimalized and later repressed this most basic of "female problems." Emma Eckstein, one of his early patients, provided him with a wealth of data related to the menstrual cycle; but he was too involved with her role in the Fliess episode to formulate this data into an objective case study. As I will show in the next two chapters, Freud's omission created an irreparable gap in the development of a sexual theory about women and significantly limited his analysis of female patients.

### Menstrual Notations

Freud recorded the "scenes" for the purpose of sharing them with Fliess: "As for Eckstein—I am taking notes on her history so that I can send it to you." Although under ordinary circumstances he would be sending these reports as a matter of postoperative formality, other motives present themselves. The letters, which dwell on the aftermath of Emma's doomed operation, perpetuate, prolong, and reiterate the "genital" surgery that both doctors mutually shared and performed. In dispatching his notes about Emma, Freud somehow swerves from scientific objectivity to medical voyeurism, as he continues to share the symptoms of a woman who, as their mutual patient, was also their victim. Freud's note-taking, while it prolonged their vicarious interest in Emma's bleeding, was at the same time intent on diminishing his and Fliess's responsibility for it: Emma was to blame for her nasal uproars.

Paradoxically, Freud's note-taking of Emma Eckstein's bleeding was paralleled by his notations of his wife's periods, begun exactly one year after the operation and exactly two months before his exoneration of Fliess in the Eckstein affair.[19] The one-year interval between the nasal hemorrhage and the menstrual notations had a magical quality to it, particularly given Fliess's fascination with numbers and Freud's own superstitions concerning anniversaries and projected dates of death.[20] Over a three-year period (1886–89) Freud systematized his wife's and daughter's menstruation—took notes on the lengths of their cycles, on his daughter's first period, on irregular rhythms, and so forth—and sent the information to Berlin as substantiation for Fliess's menstrual calculations, much as he had sent Fliess the data concerning Emma.[21] Wayne Koestenbaum suggests, and I agree, that the notations were part of a series of dates through which the men erotically sought "links between their physical experiences." [22] The notations were a kind of anniversary gift, reassurances to Fliess that his concept of menstrual periodicity was valid and that the intellectual/emotional positions of the two men were in harmony, for better or worse, in sickness or in health. The repressed sexual patterns that dominated the Freud-Fliess congress tend to find release in areas such as recording the sexual experiences of a shared female patient or in together handling female sexual disorders.

Perhaps the most unusual incident of this nature was the simultaneous "fatherhoods" of both men. Frau Freud became pregnant "immediately before the Emma episode," followed a few weeks later by Frau Fliess. [23] So remarkable a coincidence may have seemed apocalyptic, although perhaps less so given Fliess's astute awareness of Martha Freud's menstrual patterns and of their implications. Freud's notes regarding menstruation, pregnancy, and other aspects of his wife's and daughter's sexuality were, in any blessed event, related to his repressed sexual feelings for Fliess and to Fliess's anticipated response.

The first note on Martha Freud's menstruation was appended to the letter of 1 March 1896—a letter that had a great deal to say about menstruation. Freud's primary purpose in writing was to comment on a manuscript Fliess had sent involving his "nasal findings" on menstrual fluctuation; he also confided that some of Fliess's "random remarks" on periodicity had helped him understand anxiety neurosis (*Letters*, 174). This crucial letter ended with an "aside" that maintained its scientific tone but was in actuality an intimate revelation:

> Perhaps it will interest you, as an aside, that Martha felt the first movements, with Annerl, on July 10. The birth occurred on December 3. The menstrual period occurred again on February 29. Since puberty Martha has always been regular. The interval between menstrual periods is a little over 29 days, let's say 29½. Now, from December 3 to February 29, there are 88 [days] = $3 \times 29\frac{1}{3}$:
>
> 28
> 31
> 29
> ———
> $88 \div 3 = 29\frac{1}{2}$ days
> −28
>
> (*Letters*, 175).

Then followed another, more elaborate diagram covering 10 July to 3 December 1896. The information evidently gratified Fliess, who was at the same time constructing far more complicated versions of the menstrual chart: double-columned illustrations of periodic intervals with corresponding symptoms (blood in the nose; aqueous secretions from the vagina; earache; stomach cramps; and many other ailments affected by periodicity). In fact, Fliess incorporated Freud's precise reference to Martha's periodicity into *The Nose and the Female Sex Organs*.[24]

Two months later Freud noted his wife's "paramenstrual discomfort" and her unhappiness with a twenty-nine-day cycle (*Letters*, 185). Although he offered this information as data for Fliess's research on periodicity, it is important to remember that he was simultaneously studying menstrual irregularity in an investigation of anxiety neurosis and recording his ambivalent nasal/menstrual thoughts regarding Emma Eckstein.

Freud also wrote to Fliess about the prepubescent rhythms of his daughter Mathilde, noting that the child had gotten a throat infection on "day 28" and connecting this observation to Martha's menstruation: "Her mother, incidentally, did exactly the same thing before the onset of her menstrual periods" (*Letters*, 342). Here Freud was suggesting a physiological/psychological link between mother and daughter regarding the menstrual process, an idea that Fliess was to emphasize in *The Nose and the Female Sex Organs:* "As the menstruation of the mother is related to the day of her birth and as that depends on the menstrual cycle of the grandmother, we recognize that three generations are combined among themselves through the same periodic process."[25]

When Mathilde did experience her menarche, Freud recorded the event in a brief paragraph: "On June 25 [1899] Mathilde made her entry into womanhood, somewhat prematurely. At the same time I received a poem about the journey from Martin—at least, it arrived at the same time—but certainly at the same time I had a migraine from which I thought I would die. It is the third of this kind and is absolutely awful" (*Letters*, 357). According to Masson, the reference to Martin's poem indicates the realization that "the date of composition is the critical date, and this could not be related to Mathilde's period, hence the lame substitution of his own migraine" (*Letters*, 357n). Admittedly, Freud was concerned about the flow of his writing in this and surrounding letters; but Masson's note to this key paragraph coasts too quickly over other significant details. I read the passage as a competition between male and female functions: Mathilde menstruates; Freud and his son write, with Martin's poem arriving "at the same time" as Mathilde's menarche and "at the same time" as Freud's migraine. The tone here is slightly comic, another joke with Fliess that triples the periodicity (the same-time-ness) and minimizes his daughter's "entry into womanhood." He recorded none of Mathilde's possible pain or discomfort as she experienced the event that officially acknowledged her gender. Instead, he recorded *his* pain, his symptom, an "absolutely awful" migraine that was both repetitive and periodic ("the third of this kind")—like Emma's having bled "spontaneously three times" (*Letters,* 186). If Freud's migraine was, as Masson argues, "a lame substitution," it is most likely a substitution for Mathilde's menarche—a fantasy of male menstruation.[26] In this detached account of his daughter's menarche, Freud seems to have assimilated her physical symptoms for himself, vicariously experiencing Mathilde's coming of age through his own (menstrual) migraine—much as earlier he had shifted from Emma's nasal "avalanche" to his own "eruptions" (*Letters,* 116). In each case there is an identification with the female, a sign of his homosexual desire or perhaps, as Madelon Sprengnether argues, of his castration: "When Freud looked at Eckstein what he saw was castration, a condition that he might have originally attributed to her position as victim, but that he theorized as a sign of femininity itself." [27]

In these richly associative notations, Freud was conducting for his colleague's benefit a peculiar form of scientific inquiry, and one that perhaps violated the privacy of the women in the household. For thousands of years, Jewish law had required silence, secrecy, and isolation from its menstruating women.[28] Freud's apparent openness toward menstruation indicated an unexpected divergence from this law. Although the attitude toward menstruation in the Freud family is impossible to ascertain, one can assume, from the biographical information, that Martha Bernays maintained certain Jewish beliefs after her marriage.[29] She may have been influenced by her grandmother Emmeline, an orthodox Jew who, in keeping with regulations, wore the *scheitel*—a hairstyle associated with the *mikvah,* or menstrual bath, of Judaism.[30]

As a Jewish woman, the menstruating mother of a menstruating daughter, Martha must have felt a need for privacy during her periods, although the topic itself is far too confidential a matter to have been documented. Given the traditional Judaic attitudes surrounding menstruation, it is hard to believe that Martha was so divorced from her heritage as to have willingly unlocked the secrets of her menstrual calendar, either to assist her husband in his definition of the anxiety neuroses or to verify Fliess's

concept of menstrual periodicity. I doubt that she was aware of his sending the information to Fliess—who was also Jewish and surely acquainted
with the private nature of menstrual practices in his culture. Freud's reluctance to see either side of the correspondence published may possibly
have involved, among other matters, the invasion of Martha's menstrual
privacy and misgivings about her conceivable displeasure.

On Freud's part, his gift-notes to Fliess on Martha's and Mathilde's
menstruations confirm his affection for the surgeon from Berlin, to whom
he had written: "I hope it will go so far that we can jointly build something definitive on it, and thereby blend our contributions to the point
where our individual property is no longer recognizable" (17 December,
1896, *Letters*, 215). His desire to surrender his individuality and blend
into Fliess intimates an identification with the feminine and thus with
menstruation, the sign of the female; in fact, the menstrual notations, in
their emphasis on an exclusively female function, place Freud in a female
role—as one who "gives birth" to intimate documents concerning the
bleeding, female body.[31]

Two final letters deserve attention in this discussion. On 15 October
1897 Freud recorded the phenomenon of his *own* menstruation, which he
claimed was interfering with the self-analysis:

> My self-analysis is in fact the most essential thing I have at present and
> promises to become of the greatest value to me if it reaches its end. In
> the middle of it, it suddenly ceased for three days, during which I had the
> feeling of being tied up inside (which patients complain of so much), and
> I was really disconsolate until I found that these same three days (twenty-
> eight days ago) were the bearers of identical somatic phenomena. Actually
> only two bad days with a remission in between. From this one should draw
> the conclusion that *the female period is not conducive to work*. Punctually on
> the fourth day, it started again. (*Letters*, 270, emphasis mine)

A three-day period of being "tied up inside," an interruption in the
"work," an identical experience that occurred twenty-eight days earlier:
the standard attributes of the menstrual cycle are resonant in the above
passage, indexed in the Masson edition under "Menstruation, male"
(*Letters*, 500). Then, he continued, "punctually on the fourth day, it
started again." *Punctually* (regularly, periodically): this word is applicable to the menstrual cycle; as in Martha's twenty-nine-and-a-half-day
period, which was nonpunctual; as in Mathilde's menarche, which arrived "somewhat prematurely"; as in Emma Eckstein's curious, four-day

bleeding; as in Fliess's elaborate measurements of male and female periodicity. That Freud in the above letter identified negatively with menstruation is apparent from his judgment that "the female period is not conducive to work." Menstruation is to women what work is to men, a gender division that we observed in the notation on Mathilde and that he maintained in his later writings.[32] But if one views this passage as another revelation of his ambivalence toward Fliess, then his potential identification with women's bleeding (Mathilde's but above all Emma's) is a threatening situation from which he must retreat in his efforts to absolve himself and his collaborator.

At this point in the revelation Freud abandoned the menstrual identification and switched to the thought that the break in his analysis had "another determinant—the resistance to something surprisingly new. Since then I have been once again intensely preoccupied [with it], mentally fresh, though afflicted with all sorts of minor disturbances that come from the content of the analysis" (*Letters*, 270). Looking at the cycle of the passage itself, one sees that his associations take him from an analysis of his own menstruation to thoughts about the female period not being conducive to work to *resistance* then back to the *work* of self-analysis (to "it")—much as the letter about Mathilde's menarche took him from menstruating daughter to poet/son to migraine, migraine being a symptom equivalent, in the above letter, to "all sorts of minor disturbances."[33] A year and a half earlier he had resisted the idea of Fliess's malpractice in the Emma Eckstein affair, claiming that Emma wanted to bleed. The "resistance" in this passage could signify his resistance to menstruation itself, a topic that had become too painful, too connected to the failed operation, to Fliess's menstrual preoccupations, and to an emerging homosexual desire, all of which he would be better off ignoring.[34]

In a letter written two months later, Freud is extremely negative toward menstruation: "I can scarcely detail for you all the things that resolve themselves into—excrement for me (a new Midas!). It fits in completely with the theory of internal stinking. Above all, money itself. I believe this proceeds via the word 'dirty' for 'miserly.' In the same way, everything related to birth, miscarriage, [menstrual] period goes back to the toilet via the word *Abort* [toilet] *Abortus* [abortion]" (*Letters*, 288).[35] In this exploration of his anality, Freud equated menstruation with abortion and with miscarriage, all three of which involve the flow of blood from the genitals. As studies have revealed, the "toilet" in male fantasies of menstruation is the site of both blood and defecation—of both the vagina and the anus. Koestenbaum, referring specifically to the Midas entry, observes that "Freud traces back to the toilet all language relating to female bleeding and female reproduction," while Poul M. Faergeman claims that "the chief organ of expression of the [male] fantasy of menstruation is usually the rectum." [36]

Freud's excremental vision was directly followed by an incident, not printed in *The Origins of Psychoanalysis*, in which a female patient verified for him "the intrinsic authenticity of infantile trauma" (*Letters*, 288). Blood is a major motif: the woman had lost blood when her father raped her at the age of two; the mother had bled "nearly to death from an injury inflicted by the father"; the mother had bled again from uterine cancer when the patient was sixteen. The blood of this account reiterates the internal stink of the menstrual blood that preceded it, while the strength of the language echoes the Eckstein narrative: Emma with her "fetid odor" and her "flood of blood."

### Dis/solutions

It is possible that the images of female "filth" in Freud's anal reverie surfaced as a result of his effort to protect Fliess's innocence in the Eckstein affair. In any case, his last reference to Emma in the correspondence appeared in the letter of 12 December 1897; it had to do with her successful treatment of a patient (*Letters*, 286). Emma Eckstein was now an analyst, assimilated into the professional world, eliciting other peoples' "scenes"; her bleedings were no longer a threat, except to herself. Ironically, Emma Eckstein died in her late fifties of a cerebral hemorrhage.[37]

As for Fliess, his break with Freud occurred in August of 1900, during a meeting in which "the two men quarreled violently." [38] There were earlier premonitions, however, one of them being that Freud had stopped sending his colleague the menstrual notations that began the year after the Emma Eckstein affair. By the summer of 1899 he "appears somewhat tired of the whole exercise" of supporting Fliess's theories on the numerical significance of menstruation (Masson, *Letters*, 357n). The letter about Mathilde's menarche (27 June 1899) was the last menstrual evidence from personal observation he sent to his friend, although as late as 1901 he continued to encourage Fliess's work on menstrual periodicity (see *Letters*, 428, 433).

The estrangement with Fliess is a complicated matter for which there are divergent explanations: jealousy, disillusionment, a confused sexual orientation, the lack of compatible ideas.[39] My own argument, based on the specific focus of this book, is that Freud deserted the bleeding Emma, and therefore women's bleeding, in his attempt to protect Fliess (and also himself) from personal anxiety and public disapproval. As he gradually retreated from Fliess and from the concept of the nose and its effect on the genital organs, so he retreated from menstruation, eliminating it as a possible major consideration in the study of female psychosexual development—as the marker of sexual difference. Had the collaboration with Fliess continued, Freud would surely have taken a different direction and menstruation would have played a more significant role in psychoanalytic treatment and in the issue of gender. It is no minor matter that as Freud was disassociating himself from Fliess in the process of his own analysis, he was simultaneously discovering the male-centered Oedipus complex.

Nor was menstruation to become an informing concept in his analytic treatment of female patients. In the noted case of Dora conducted in 1901, shortly after the estrangement with Fliess, there is one slight reference to periodicity ("Fragment of an Analysis of a Case of Hysteria," *SE* 7:53). Of the two references to Dora's menstruation, one has to do with irregularity and the other with fantasies of childbirth (*SE* 7:101, 103). Freud made no analytic use of Dora's menstruation, despite the fact that her neurotic symptoms—coughing, poor breathing, and "unilateral headaches in the nature of a migraine" (*SE* 7:22)—had intensified when Dora was twelve, a usual age for the onset of menstrual flow. Nor did he consider menstrual blood as an aspect of *wetness* in his interpretation of Dora's discharges, although many years later, an analyst who was treating her noted her "premenstrual pains and a vaginal discharge after menstruation."[40]

While there were important references to menstruation in Freud's later works, menstruation rarely became part of the analytic consideration. Not until the 1920s and 1930s, with the challenging of the Freudian view of female sexuality, was it recognized as having a significant effect on human behavior. Freud himself remained committed to the phallic nature of psychosexual development, forming other stressful relationships with men less open to female periodicity than was Wilhelm Fliess.

Fliess, after his separation from Freud and the psychoanalytic movement, had additional cause to become embittered. He suspected that

Freud had revealed his ideas on bisexuality to a patient, Hermann Swoboda; these ideas appeared in a book by Otto Weininger, without sufficient acknowledgment to Fliess.[41] Fliess was endorsed, in the Swoboda debate and in his continued defense of periodicity, by a number of prominent scientists. In 1913 the Medical Society for Sexual Science was organized in support of Fliess; this group of loyal defenders bore a strange similarity to Freud's Vienna Psychoanalytic Society. Most historians of psychoanalysis remember Fliess as the object of Freud's correspondence; they pay little attention to Fliess's work in its own right, other than to dismiss it. Ignored today by the European and American psychoanalytic institutions, Fliess nonetheless still enjoys a reputation, especially in Japan, where his biorhythmic science is used in industry, sportscasting, and other behavioral situations where the predictability of body cycles helps to reduce accidents and increase productivity.[42]

Presumably, Fliess had never anticipated so mundane a use of his theory of periodicity, originally connected to the psyche and to "psychopathic phenomena."[43] As Fliess's system, based on the twenty-eight-day menstrual cycle and on related forms of periodicity, has suffered from being severed from psychoanalysis, so Freudian theory has suffered from having substantially ignored the periodic aspects of female sexuality. Nonetheless, Fliess was to have a continuing impact on Freud; for the crucial exchange of letters, written from 1887 to 1904, served as the sounding board for Freud's psychoanalytic explorations of the dream work and affected his concept of libidinal energy. To investigate the interchange of ideas and emotions between Fliess and Freud is to recognize how close psychoanalysis came, during the shared experience with Emma Eckstein, to incorporating a concept of menstrual periodicity into its formulative theories.

*Notes*

1. The account of the surgery was omitted from *The Origins of Psychoanalysis: Letters to Wilhelm Fliess,* ed. Marie Bonaparte, Anna Freud, and Ernst Kris, trans. Eric Mosbacher and James Strachey (New York: Basic Books, 1954). It was first made public by the analyst Max Schur in "Some Additional 'Day Residues' of the Specimen Dream of Psychoanalysis," in *Psychoanalysis: A General Psychology—Essays in Honor of Heinz Hartmann,* ed. R. M. Lowenstein, Lottie M. Newman, Max Schur, and A. J. Solnit (New York: International Universities Press, 1966), 45–85. For other ac-

counts see in particular Jeffrey Moussaieff Masson, *Freud: The Assault on Truth* (New York: Farrar, Straus, and Giroux, 1984); Janet Malcolm, *In the Freud Archives* (New York: Alfred A. Knopf, 1984); and Madelon Sprengnether, *The Spectral Mother: Freud, Feminism, and Psychoanalysis* (Ithaca: Cornell University Press, 1990).

2. The most authoritative bibliography of Fliess's works appears in Frank J. Sulloway, *Freud, Biologist of the Mind: Beyond the Psychoanalytic Legend* (New York: Basic Books, 1979), 535. The book quoted in this chapter is *Die Beziehungen zwischen Nase und weiblichen Geschlectsorganen* (Leipzig/Vienna: Deuticke, 1897), referred to hereafter as *The Nose and the Female Sex Organs*. The translation is mine, with the assistance of Julia Reinhard Lupton. *The Nose and the Female Sex Organs* has been translated into French by Patrick Ach and Jean Guir, *Les relations entre le nez et les organes genitauz de la femme* (Paris: Editions du Seuil, 1977). Fliess's other books appeared after 1900, the year in which the friendship with Freud is thought to have ended.

3. See in particular Wayne Koestenbaum's impressive reading of the relationship, in "Privileging the Anus: Anna O. and the Collaborative Origin of Psychoanalysis," *Genders* 3 (1988): 57–90.

4. See the case histories in *The Nose and the Female Sex Organs*, 7–9. See Max Schur, *Freud: Living and Dying* (New York: International Universities Press, 1972), 77–90, for a discussion of Fliess's operation on Freud.

5. Sigmund Freud, *The Complete Letters of Sigmund Freud to Wilhelm Fliess*, ed. and trans. Jeffrey Moussaieff Masson (Cambridge: Harvard University Press, 1985), 6 May 1894, 70, 71n. Unless otherwise indicated, all citations from Freud's letters to Fliess are from the Masson edition and will be indicated in the text as *Letters*.

6. In an 1895 paper Freud contended that there may be a "periodicity in the emergence of the states of anxiety," *SE* 3:133. He discovered the presence of an "excitatory sexual process" that appeared at a periodic interval; this excitation in "abstinent women" is "menstrual," ibid. See also *The Interpretation of Dreams*, where Freud finds Fliess's twenty-eight-day/twenty-three-day cycles inconclusive in dream interpretation, *SE* 4:167–68. Freud extended the idea of periodicity to include not only nocturnal emissions but also "sexual intercourse itself (harmful from its being incomplete)," *SE* 3:133.

7. Masson, *Assault on Truth*, 57, 59. On the subject of masturbation, Helene Deutsch's opinion is unequivocal: "There is no young girl in whom menstruation does not arouse genital tension and a need to masturbate." Helene Deutsch, *The Psychology of Women* (New York: Grune and Stratton, 1944), 1:57.

8. Shirley Nelson Garner, "Freud and Fliess: Homophobia and Seduction," in *Seduction and Theory*, ed. Dianne Hunter (Urbana: University of Illinois Press, 1989), 103–4. Garner, who refers to Freud's comment on Eckstein's "hysterical bleeding," does not situate periodicity or menstruation within her argument.

9. Max Schur argues for a nose/menstrual pattern, stating that Freud had probably connected Emma's nasal bleeding with vicarious menstruation: that is, with a

periodic bleeding from somewhere other than the vagina, "Day Residues," 82. Peter Gay writes: "A psychoanalyst might well be expected to take a wry interest in the nose, so reminiscent of the male genitalia in its shape and of the female sexual apparatus in its tendency to bleed," in *Freud: A Life of Our Time* (New York: Norton, 1988), 57. See also Hannah Lerman, *A Mote in Freud's Eye: From Psychoanalysis to the Psychology of Women* (New York: Springer, 1986), 87.

10. Lawrence Frank, "Freud and Dora," in *Seduction and Theory*, ed. Dianne Hunter (Urbana: University of Illinois Press, 1989), 115.

11. At the age of ten, Freud was involved with making "Charpies," or bandages, for wounded soldiers. See Ernest Jones, *The Life and Work of Sigmund Freud* (New York: Basic Books, 1953), 1:21. In discussing the Eckstein surgery, Anzieu uses the French word *tampon* (in French, plug or swab) for *gauze;* see Didier Anzieu, *L'autoanalyse de Freud* (Paris: Presses Universitaires de France, 1975), 1:202. For a historical review of menstrual products, see *The Curse*, 138–40.

12. Ernest Jones reports that Freud's father thought a medical career might be a problem because of Sigmund's "considerable horror of blood," in *Life and Work* 1:24. This anecdote might have some bearing on the Eckstein incident.

13. Quoted by Schur, "Day Residues," 80.

14. Schur, "Day Residues," 80. Strachey claims that *Frauenzimmer* is often "a slightly derogatory synonym" for *woman;* see his note, *SE* 15:162n.

15. See Ilza Veith, *Hysteria: The History of a Disease* (Chicago: University of Chicago Press, 1965), for an history of medical attitudes toward hysteria, a disease doctors frequently related to menstrual disorders.

16. This passage was first published by Max Schur in 1966, in "Day Residues," 83; it appears in a slightly different translation in *Letters*, 224–25.

17. This is Schur's translation in "Day Residues," 83–84.

18. *Menorrhagia* is "excessive bleeding, either heavier than usual or of longer duration." See *Women's Studies Encyclopedia*, ed. Helen Tierney (Westport, Conn.: Greenwood Press, 1989), 1:234.

19. The French historian Jules Michelet made comparable charts of his wife's menstruation, noting when her period was late, when it was early, even, at times, its color. In *The Curse* we view his calculations as an attempt to control and master women; see 243–44, 265–66.

20. Freud had a number of mathematical superstitions, including the fear that he would die at the age of fifty-one. See Schur, *Freud*, 184–87. Still another significant interval involves the Oedipus complex, which was first articulated on 15 October 1897, one year after the death of Freud's father. See Octave Mannoni, *Freud*, trans. Renaud Bruce (New York: Pantheon, 1971), 46.

21. Both Sulloway, *Biologist*, 181, and Lerman, *Mote in Freud's Eye*, 87, refer to Freud's notation of his wife's periods, but without analyzing the significance of that situation. The editors of *The Origins of Psychoanalysis* did not publish Freud's nota-

tions about the menstrual periods of Martha and Mathilde Freud. They had the policy of "omitting or abbreviating everything publication of which would have been inconsistent with professional or personal confidence," xi.

22. Koestenbaum, "Privileging the Anus," 75.

23. See Schur, *Freud*, 85–86.

24. Fliess, *The Nose and the Female Sex Organs*, 133–56, 181.

25. Ibid., 159.

26. See chapter 9 for a discussion of male menstruation.

27. Sprengnether, *The Spectral Mother*, 182. At no time does Sprengnether associate Emma's bleeding with menstruation.

28. For an outlined discussion of menstrual regulations in Judaism, see Leonard Swidler, *Women in Judaism* (Metuchen, N.J.: Scarecrow Press, 1976). See also the section on taboos of Judaism in chapter 5.

29. See Jones, *Life and Work* 1:19, 100, 130, 152, 3:350; and Peter Gay, *A Godless Jew: Freud, Atheism, and the Making of Psychoanalysis* (New Haven: Yale University Press, 1987), 38. Two recent studies of Freud and Judaism indicate that the Freuds were far more orthodox than has been generally assumed. See Emmanuel Rice, *Freud and Moses: The Long Journey Home* (Albany: State University of New York Press, 1991); and Yosef Hayim Yerushalmi, *Freud's Moses: Judaism Terminable and Interminable* (New Haven: Yale University Press, 1991).

30. According to Martin Freud, Emmeline "had sacrificed her own hair, her head being crowned with two close-fitting artificial plaits," in *Sigmund Freud: Man and Father* (New York: Vanguard Press, 1958), 14. Epstein associates the *scheitel* with menstruation: "The law requires that every part of the woman's body, including her hair, be immersed in the water of the ritual bath, and in order that the water may reach every part the hair may not be tied up." This custom of cutting the hair was prevalent at the beginning of the nineteenth century; see Louis M. Epstein, *Sex Laws and Customs under Judaism* (New York: Ktav, 1948), 59–60.

31. As Stanley J. Coen observes, "the written work is often linked in these letters with pregnancy and childbirth," in "Freud and Fliess: Supportive Literary Relationship," *American Imago* 42 (1985): 398.

32. See Judith Van Herik, *Freud on Femininity and Faith* (Berkeley: University of California Press, 1982). Van Herik believes that Freud saw women as seeking fulfillment and lacking intellect (as in Christianity), whereas he saw men as capable of renunciation and having intellectual powers (as in Judaism). She in no way attributes this difference to menstruation.

33. Freud used the term *resistance* to describe the mechanism that prevents a person's memories from "becoming conscious and compel[s] them to remain unconscious" (*SE* 11:23).

34. Didier Anzieu connects homosexuality and menstruation, suggesting that Freud may have initially welcomed Fliess's concept of male/female menstruation

because it denied sexual difference while at the same time satisfying his latent homosexuality, in *L'autoanalyse de Freud* 1:229.

35. The brackets "[menstrual]" are Masson's. This reference to menstruation does not appear in the index to Masson's edition of *Letters*. In *The Origins of Psychoanalysis* it is indexed under *menstruation*, under the subheading *equated with filth*.

36. See Koestenbaum, "Privileging the Anus," 73; and Poul M. Faergeman, "Fantasies of Menstruation in Men," *Psychoanalytic Quarterly* 24 (1955): 16.

37. Frank R. Hartman, "A Reappraisal of the Emma Episode and the Specimen Dream," *Journal of the American Psychoanalytic Association* 31 (1983): 557.

38. Gay, *Freud*, 101. The date for the estrangement is controversial; Henri F. Ellenberger, for example, makes a case for 1902 in *The Discovery of the Unconscious* (New York: Basic Books, 1970), 447.

39. Ernst Kris says that Fliess was hindering Freud's self-analysis, "Introduction," *The Origins of Psychoanalysis*, 45–46; whereas Max Schur claims that Freud was becoming disillusioned by Fliess's "fanciful hypotheses," *Freud*, 96. William Beatty Warner theorizes that Fliess, as a representative of nineteenth-century neurophysiology, was no longer an asset in Freud's analytic investigations; see *Chance and the Text of Experience: Freud, Neitzche, and Shakespeare's "Hamlet"* (Ithaca: Cornell University Press, 1986), 88. Sulloway, however, refutes all such reasoning, claiming that it was Fliess, not Freud, who dissolved the relationship because of Freud's jealousy and his psychosomatic illness, in *Biologist*, 217.

40. Felix Deutsch, "A Footnote to Freud's 'Fragment of an Analysis of a Case of Hysteria,'" in *In Dora's Case: Freud—Hysteria—Feminism*, ed. Charles Bernheimer and Claire Kahane (1957; New York: Columbia University Press, 1985), 39.

41. Sulloway, *Biologist*, 226–32.

42. Ibid., 233n. See also *The Curse*, 268–71.

43. Fliess, quoted in *The Origins of Psychoanalysis*, 324n.

# 2

# Nocturnal Omissions: Dreaming (Away) Menstruation

There are several straightforward references to menstruation in Freud's writing. In the *Introductory Lectures on Psycho-analysis* he equated clocks with menstrual regularity (*SE* 16:266); in *Psychopathology of Everyday Life* he recorded a conversation with a young man who had forgotten the word *aliquis*, which he traced to menstruation through his companion's associations with fluid and saint's blood (*SE* 6:8–11).[1] Writing about a man whose wife had dreamed that she was having her period, Freud explained that the wife had been announcing her pregnancy and that her dream of menstruation fulfilled her wish *not* to be pregnant (*SE* 5:646). But most of his references to menstruation are oblique or veiled; the Freud-Fliess-Eckstein triangle, with its various complications of blood, the nose, and sexuality, colored his interpretation of dreams.

Freud first articulated his theory of dreams in his correspondence with Fliess in a self-analysis conducted by himself on himself. In such an exceptional analytic situation—Freud analyzing Freud—certain buried materials must inevitably have gone unexplored. On the premise that he could not have known his own most deeply repressed thoughts, recent theorists have been radically rereading his texts, looking, as Marie Balmary puts it, "not at what psychoanalysis wishes to show but at what it has perhaps covered up."[2] My reading of the letters to Fliess has shown his tendency to identify with the menstrual process and then to "cover it up." Similar but more dramatic mechanisms are at work in his analysis of several dreams of special importance to this study: the Dream of Irma's Injection, the Dream of the Red Bath, the Dream of the Red-Nosed Nun, and the Staircase Dream.

### The Dream of Irma's Injection

During the night of 23–24 July 1895—five months after Fliess's operation on Emma Eckstein—Freud dreamed the Dream of Irma's Injection (*SE* 4:107–21). It was so important to him that he called it the "specimen dream," the dream that was to serve as the primary example of his methodology throughout *The Interpretation of Dreams*. It is set in a large hall filled with guests, one of whom is Irma, a former patient. Irma complains to the dream-Freud of pains in her throat, her stomach, and her abdomen—pains he perceives to be his patient's fault for not following his solution to her problems: "*I said to her: 'If you still get pains it's really only your fault.'*"[3] But he suggests that it is also his fault: "*I thought to myself that after all I must be missing some organic trouble*" (*SE* 4:107). Examining Irma's mouth, he observes a "*big white patch*" but also certain scabs or "*curly structures which were evidently modelled on the turbinal bones of the nose*" (*SE* 4:107). He calls in a "Dr. M." to confirm the examination; later, two other doctors (Otto and Leopold) arrive to examine the patient.[4] Dr. M. diagnoses Irma's disorder as an infection, which Freud attributes to Otto's malpractice: "*Injections of that sort ought not to be made so thoughtlessly. . . . And probably the syringe had not been clean*" (*SE* 4:107). The dream ends with the "organic trouble" still undiscovered, hidden—like the scabs in Irma's mouth.

There are numerous parallels between the Irma of the specimen dream and Emma Eckstein.[5] In both cases, the medical problem is situated in what Fliess had designated the center of sexual activity, the turbinate bone of the nose. In both cases Freud solicits the aid of (an) outside consultant(s)—Drs. M., Otto, and Leopold in the dream; Dr. Fliess in the Eckstein case. And we learn, in the subsequent analysis, that he had in fact called in Fliess as a consultant to determine if Irma's gastric problems might have a "nasal origin" (*SE* 4:117). In both situations there is the insinuation of malpractice: Otto "*thoughtlessly*" injects Irma with "propyl," "propianic acid" and "trimethylamin" (*SE* 4:115–16), probably using a dirty syringe, whereas Fliess had thoughtlessly failed to remove the nasal packing following Emma's surgery, causing a hemorrhage. In both the case history and the dream there is a shift of blame, from doctor to patient and back again. Irma's unidentified abdominal pains are dreamed to be "really only [her] fault"; in the ensuing analysis, however, he reverses the blame, placing it on Otto's injection (SE 4:118–19). In Emma's case he had initially blamed the attendant physician, Rosanes, but, in a displacement from victimizer to victim, was later to claim that Emma's painful bleeding was really *her* fault (*Letters*, 186).[6] The vacillation in the Dream of Irma's Injection over the question of blame thus replicates his uncertainty concerning the blame for Emma's hemorrhaging.

In the self-analysis that follows the dream, the figure of Fliess appears prominently, although Fliess himself did not know about the dream.[7] First is the reference to trimethlamin, the drug Otto injects. Fliess (identified in the analysis not by name but as "a friend") had demonstrated to Freud the belief that trimethylamin, a good drug, was related to sexual metabolism and thus had helped him identify the cause for nervous disorders. In the analysis he praises Fliess: the drug was a reference "to a person whose agreement I recalled with satisfaction whenever I felt isolated in my opinions" (*SE* 4:117). In the dream, however, trimethylamin is represented negatively; it is the source of infection and the agent of malpractice. He recalls still another drug in his discussion of the text, cocaine, which had been used by both men in their treatment of nasal ailments. Freud, who had admittedly misused cocaine in an effort to cure his colleague Ernst Fleischl of morphine addiction, examines his feelings of guilt about cocaine in the analytic section of the dream of Irma's injection (*SE* 4:111); the identification with Fliess is implicit. These contradictory remarks on "good" or "bad" medicine reflect the ambivalence toward Fliess and himself that was a constant in their relationship.

He then praises his friend for his knowledge of the nasal cavities, referring directly to the dream text but failing to mention Fliess's work on periodicity, a theory inseparable from the nose: Fliess "had drawn scientific attention to some very remarkable connections between the turbinal bones and the female organs of sex. (Cf. the three curly structures in Irma's throat)" (*SE* 4:117). He further remarks that Fliess is suffering from rhinitis, a nasal disorder, and expresses his "anxiety" concerning that condition (*SE* 4:117, 120). His distress about Fliess's health, so persistent in the letters, has now become part of the analytic material of *The*

*Interpretation of Dreams;* it is also a source of his guilt, the underlying theme in the Dream of Irma's Injection.

Another specific projection of Fliess involves the split figures of "Otto," who was "too hasty," and Dr. M., who was an "ignoramus"; rejecting them both, Freud turns to "someone else with greater knowledge" (*SE* 4: 119). These projections reveal Freud's efforts to suppress his ambivalence toward his erudite but bumbling colleague, an ambivalence that recalls the patterns of blame and guilt surrounding Emma Eckstein's operation. Like Otto in the dream, Fliess had acted "thoughtlessly." Yet Fliess is at the same time the person whose "*agreement*" he remembers "with satisfaction" (*SE* 4:117). The desire for agreement struggles against the desire to condemn, disclosing "Freud's anxiety to conceal his doubts about Fliess not just from Fliess but from himself." [8]

Emma Eckstein is also concealed, both in the dream-text and in the analysis, where Freud consciously associated the dream figure not with Emma but with numerous other women: with his wife Martha, with his eldest daughter Mathilde, with two female patients who had been "recalcitrant to treatment," with a former patient in whom he had once "produced a severe toxic state" by prescribing what he had regarded as a "harmless remedy (sulphonal)," and with an old woman to whom he gave injections of morphine twice a day (*SE* 4:110, 111). Faulty medical treatment disturbs his sleep again and again.

Although few of the details of the specimen dream can be tangibly identified with the person Emma Eckstein, nonetheless "Irma," whatever her historical relevance to Freud's biography, functions in the injection dream as an object of desire, acted upon by male doctors. She is a figure of pain, guilt, and mistreatment—characteristics that play strongly into his associations of Emma Eckstein. Freud, who excluded any consideration of Emma Eckstein from his analysis, made no attempt to justify his exclusions, admitting that there are gaps in the interpretation: "But considerations which arise in the case of every dream of my own restrain me from pursuing my interpretative work" (*SE* 4:121). These gaps may have derived from the strength of the repression or from a disinterest in the organic aspects of female illness or from a reluctance to damage Fliess or from any number of causes. The answer is missing from the text. Emma herself becomes a missing person. [9]

If Emma Eckstein is missing from the dream interpretation, the nature of the patient's medical disorder is also missing: "*I must be missing some organic trouble.*" In his reading of the Irma dream, Jacques Lacan focuses on the missing or "undiscovered" quality of the illness, lodged in her mouth, which he describes as "the flesh one never sees . . . the flesh from which everything exudes, at the very heart of the mystery, the flesh in as much as it is suffering, is formless, in as much as its form in itself is something which provokes anxiety."[10] But the same mouth veils the "three curly structures in Irma's throat" (*SE* 4:117), structures that pertain to the turbinate bone and the sex organs. It is the mouth of the womb, rather than the mouth of the face, from which "everything exudes." Menstruation is at the heart of the mystery. Freud had recognized, from his investigation of Emma Eckstein's bleeding, that menstruation was both an organic and a psychic phenomenon, capable of provoking anxiety in both patient and doctor. Irma's aches and pains, however, are "undiscovered" in the dream, despite his elaborate use of medical terminology in the accompanying text.[11]

Menstruation is repressed, missing from Freud's (and Lacan's) analysis, its mysterious absence highlighted by an anecdote that concludes the medical examination. The Otto of the dream had observed that the skin of Irma's shoulder was "infiltrated"; Freud explains that the word *infiltrated* refers to his own shoulder and to his rheumatism, a meaning he "saw at once" (113). In its medical sense, *infiltration* is "the act of passing into or interpenetrating a substance, cell or tissue; said of gases, fluids, or matters held in solution."[12] The word has little relevance either to his shoulder or to Irma's, though, unless one considers its connotation of aggressive penetration: "the gradual or surreptitious penetration of enemy lines by small numbers of troops" (*Oxford English Dictionary*). Freud comments: "*(I noticed this* [the infiltration] *just as he did* [Otto], *in spite of her dress)*" (*SE* 4:107). The pronoun references are clouded, unclear—as is Irma's body, covered and protected from the gaze of the small troop of examining physicians. Irma is fully clothed, a then-standard hospital procedure in the treatment of adult women; Freud recalls a well-known doctor who never examined any patients "except through their clothes" (*SE* 4:113). And then he stops, retreats: "Further than this I could not see. Frankly, I had no desire to penetrate more deeply at this point" (*SE* 4:113). The sexual language—"desire," "penetrate," "infiltrate"— suggests first a penetration but then a premature withdrawal from the female "body" of the dream, which remains safely clothed or covered up, as do Emma, female troubles, the genitalia.[13] Freud's lack of desire as dreamer/doctor to "undress" Irma could serve as metaphor for his attitude toward female sexuality, whose most abject indicator is menstrual blood. Don't look under the dress; don't penetrate further. The problem, the menstrous female body, remains hidden or taboo.[14]

In placing the primary emphasis of his interpretation on the attending male physicians, Freud in effect marginalizes the role of the passive female patient; the dream would have been more appropriately titled the Dream of Otto's Injection—since Irma, as victim, merely receives the needle. Her actual presence, emblematized by her illness, has been repressed or clothed. And yet the turbinate bones of Irma's nose, more convenient for examination than was her lower region, should have led Freud, however circuitously, to a discussion of periodicity and to Fliess, who had actually examined Irma's nose. Although he is enthusiastic, during the analysis of the dream, about Fliess's "remarkable connections between the turbinate bones and the female organs of sex" (*SE* 4:117), Freud does not follow the clues that would join the turbinate bones to menstruation, the abdominal pains to dysmenorrhea, *Irma* to *Emma*.

Emma Eckstein's prolific bleeding and its psychoanalytic connections to the menstrual cycle—"She has always been a bleeder"—are missing from the dream, like a missing wad of gauze, like a missed period. As I argued in chapter 1, Freud's repression of Emma Eckstein's hemorrhaging was related to his turning away from menstruation as a viable consideration in the evaluation of female sexuality and human psychology. A similar repression prevented him from considering menstruation as a possible source of Irma's abdominal pains and of his own "anxiety" about Fliess.

### The Dream of the Red Bath

What I call the Dream of the Red Bath (4 October 1897) continues a number of the motifs found in the Dream of Irma's Injection: medical irresponsibility, guilt, anxiety, references to Fliess's work on the nose, missing persons. Because it was recorded not in the *Interpretation of Dreams* but in his private letters to Fliess, the Dream of the Red Bath is particularly rich; one reads not only the text but also the day residues—elements in dreams "derived from the waking activity of the previous day."[15] Thus it is possible to place this pivotal dream within the context of Freud's menstrual associations.

At the time of the dream Freud was on the brink of articulating the

Oedipus complex, bringing to consciousness certain threatening recollections about male relationships—the death of his father in the preceding October, the death of his younger brother, the continued torment
over Fliess, the recollections of a cruel nephew, the tortured irresolution
of Hamlet (*Letters*, 268–72). The Dream of the Red Bath is thus crucial
to an understanding of his shift, in 1897, away from menstruation and
Fliess and toward an analytic theory that would move the centrality of
experience toward the phallus/father and the analytic process toward the
male patient. By 1898 he informed Fliess that he had increased the ratio
of male patients: "Half my patients are now men." [16]

Among the male entourage, however, there hovers a menstruating
dream-woman whose nightmarish quality disturbs the self-analysis. In
the letter of 3 October 1897, the day preceding the dream, he introduces
his nanny, his *Kinderfrau*, describing her as "the prime originator," an
"elderly" woman who has been identified as Monica Sajik, Theresa Wittek, and other women from Freiberg, the small town in Moravia where
Freud spent his formative years. He describes her as "an ugly, elderly, but
clever woman, who told me a great deal about God Almighty and hell and
who instilled in me a high opinion of my own capacities" and contrasts
her to his seductive mother (*matrem*), whom he had seen nude (*nudam*).
He then addresses Fliess: "(you inferred the consequences of this [seeing
his mother naked] for your son long ago, as a remark revealed to me)"
(*Letters*, 268).[17]

The ambiguous separation of nurse and mother (as Jim Swan, Mary
Jacobus, and others have observed) is emphasized by Freud's placing
*mother* and *naked* in Latin—thus purifying her, removing her from the
common language.[18] Freud, who earlier in the passage had claimed that
his deceased father ("the old man") had played "no active part in my
case," parenthetically confers the father's role onto Fliess: "(you inferred
the consequences of this for your son long ago)." It is the evocation of
the nurse, coupled with the memory of having (like Fliess's son) seen his
mother naked (*nudam*)—unlike Irma's being "dressed"—that appears to
trigger the Dream of the Red Bath.

Another piece of day residue in the October 3 letter to Fliess has gone
unnoticed by Freud's explicators: the formula

$$A \times 28 \text{ plus } B \times 23$$

which is the subject of the opening paragraph and which directly precedes the description of the nurse/mother.[19] Having recently returned

from Berlin after a visit with Fliess and his wife, he begins the letter with a reference to Fliess's discoveries; he has had the opportunity, during the visit, of becoming acquainted with Fliess's "current work in its entirety"—work that, he confesses, "is strange to me and my judgment weak" (*Letters*, 267). "Nevertheless," he humbly adds, "I am grateful to you for every little item that you unselfishly let come my way." Freud then explores the connection between "infection and conception in mother and daughter," a theory that, as we learn from *The Nose and the Female Sex Organs* (also 1897) was intrinsic to Fliess's concept of periodicity. He suggests that the connection may perhaps relate to the Fliessian formula "A × 28 plus B × 23," although "whether this is nonsense I cannot tell" (*Letters*, 268). After requesting Fliess's "timely disposition" on the matter, he moves immediately into his self-analysis and his recollection of the "ugly, elderly, but clever woman" who was his nanny.

The paragraph on periodicity, which was excluded from the excerpted letters to Fliess in *The Standard Edition* and from *The Origins of Psychoanalysis*, is far more significant than has been recognized. First, it shows a clear connection between Freud's thoughts on infection and the scientific application of Fliess's concept, based on the twenty-eight-day/twenty-three-day fluctuation of menstrual rhythms. Second, it shows his peculiar subservience to Fliess—"your work is strange to me and my judgment weak"—at a time when he was repressing both his homosexual feelings and the guilt he felt in response to Fliess's negligence in the case of Emma Eckstein. Third, the concern over the relationship between disease and conception is expressed at a time when he has been marking the menstrual periods of both his wife and his daughter, sending the information to Fliess. Finally, the scientific reference to periodicity seems to activate his memory of his nanny. For at this confused moment in his life, during the initial stages of self-analysis and during the period of doubting his ability to cure hysteria, she invades his dreamworld, causing him to question the seduction theory—the theory that hysteria can invariably be traced to an experience of sexual abuse that occurred in childhood.

"Today's dream," he begins, "has, under the strangest disguises, produced the following: she was my teacher in sexual matters and complained because I was clumsy and unable to do anything" (*Letters*, 269).[20] He recalls that he last saw her when he was two and a half, when she was caught stealing from the family, dismissed, and sent to jail. In recounting the Dream of the Red Bath, he records a number of associations, among them "the skull of a small animal," which he relates to his "impotence as a therapist" and the nurse's forcing him to steal money, which evokes the fear that he is being paid for bad treatment. The latter concern, also at the heart of the Dream of Irma's Injection, reiterates his emotions concerning the bad treatment of Emma Eckstein following the operation of 1895.

Then suddenly appears, in the midst of the associations, a reference to menstruation, to being bathed in "reddish water." The reference springs from the text, its physical specificity contrasting sharply with Freud's musings about his medical career: "The whole dream was full of the most mortifying allusions to my present impotence as a therapist. Perhaps this is where the inclination to believe in the incurability of hysteria begins. *Moreover, she washed me in reddish water in which she had previously washed herself.* (The interpretation is not so difficult; I find nothing like this in the chain of my memories, so I regard it as a genuine ancient discovery)" (*Letters*, 269, emphasis mine). After presenting the dream image of the red bath, he assures Fliess that the "interpretation is not so difficult." We learn no more. The apparent unwillingness to disturb the surface of the bath is itself a resistance to interpretation; as Balmary comments on this very passage, "We have learned from Freud himself that something apparently easy portends nothing other than a resistance against any further interpretation." [21]

Many readers mention the dream but slight the bath or, at best, duplicate Freud's vagueness, demonstrating yet further resistance to the menstrual interpretation.[22] A few critics, however, have shattered this resistance, identifying the reddish water of the above dream with the nurse's menstruation. Didier Anzieu quite literally reads the menstrual bath as his nanny's "bad treatment"; she washed him in the reddish water where she herself had bathed at the time of her "règles" (period).[23] Jim Swan suggests that Freud "imagined that the water was red" from the nurse's menstrual blood; through his association with her, he had become passive, or "feminized." [24] Marie Balmary, who places the nurse within the Catholic tradition of Freiberg, describes her as the woman who took young Freud to church and suggests that the bath is a form of purification, as in the dipping into holy water. In a series of questions she raises blood issues: "Is it menstrual blood?" Or is it "Christ's blood, the blood spilled on the cross, that mankind is cleansed of its faults?" [25] In light of Freud's Judaism and his pronounced criticism of Christian doctrine, the question about Christ's blood seems misdirected; while Balmary recognizes his nanny's Catholic influence on Freud, she never approaches the red bath from his own religious tradition of the *mikvah*, the bath in which Jewish women are immersed for purification following their menstrual periods.[26] Although he at no point in his writings refers to the *mikvah*, Freud was certainly aware of its function for the community of Jewish women; this community would have included almost all of the women he knew intimately—his wife, his daughter Mathilde, the *matrem* so noticeably missing in the letters to Fliess and *The Interpretation of Dreams*, his patient Emma Eckstein.

In her crucial discussion of the reddish water, Mary Jacobus stresses the maternal emphasis of the symbol, contending that by "defiling his nurse with menstrual blood," he purifies his mother, thus preventing himself from "sinking irretrievably into the maternal body." [27] Her argument weakens, though, when she contends that menstruation is not attributable to the Catholic nurse, whom Freud had described as "elderly" and therefore too old to menstruate. Jacobus takes too literally Freud's recollection, by way of his mother, that the nurse was "elderly"; there is consensus that she was around forty years old when she tended him—young enough to still be menstruating.[28]

The question, I think, is not so much *who* is menstruating—since virtually all women menstruate—but rather the image itself: the menstrual blood that, in the guise of a reddish bath, has surfaced from its tabooed site in the unconscious to the center of the dream, disguised yet "not so difficult" to interpret. Why did he hide the easy solution from Fliess? To attempt an answer is to turn again to Emma Eckstein—to her prolific bleeding but also to her impact on Freud's rejection of the seduction theory.

### Seduction at the Bath

Jeffrey Masson, in his controversial book *Freud: The Assault on Truth*, suggests that Freud's analysis of Emma Eckstein represents the transformation in theory from a female to a male focus, from a theory of hysteria to a theory of incest. Masson is emphatic about the Eckstein connection, arguing that Freud's theory of "hysterical lying" was constructed to protect Fliess: "If Emma Eckstein's problems (her bleeding) had nothing to do with the real world (Fliess's operation), then her earlier account of seduction could well be fantasies too." [29]

At the time he recorded the Dream of the Red Bath, Eckstein was Freud's patient. According to Max Schur, she was one of the first to help Freud realize that "what his patients had described to him as actual seduction episodes were fantasies," a perception that "opened the way to the discovery of early infantile sexuality and its manifestations in infancy." [30] Schur is referring to Emma's analytic "scenes," such as the fantasy in which the devil stuck pins into her fingers and tamped the blood with candy. We know that Emma Eckstein was confiding such fantasies of bleeding to Freud during the period preceding the Dream of the Red Bath; we suspect that he did not trust their reality, certainly not enough to have made the connection between her menstrual anxiety and her memory of having been sexually accosted by a shopkeeper ("Project for a Scientific Psychology," *SE* 1:353).

It terms of theory itself, Emma Eckstein and the female patients that followed her have been accosted in another sense: offended, replaced. In Freud's shift from the seduction theory to the Oedipus complex, Martha Noel Evans has observed a significant substitution: "at the center of the seduction theory is a young girl seduced by the father; at the center of the oedipus complex, there is a young boy constructing erotic fantasies about his mother. In the new, substitute theoretical formulation, then, the little boy takes the place of the victimized girl." [31]

Freud's "discovery" that the seduction theory was of little assistance in treating hysteria was confirmed by the Dream of the Red Bath: "I find nothing like this in the chain of my memories, so I regard it as a genuine ancient discovery." Apparently he has realized that the red bath was a repressed fantasy and that its relationship to any *real* experience of seduction was no longer the central issue. The "genuine ancient discovery" thus authenticated the "great secret" confided to Fliess on 21 September 1897, two weeks before the Dream of the Red Bath: "The certain insight that there are no indications of reality in the unconscious, so that one cannot distinguish between truth and fiction" (*Letters,* 264).

The red bath, with its implications of menstrual blood, enters the dream *immediately* after Freud laments his inability to cure hysteria: "Perhaps this [his confessed medical 'impotence'] is where the inclination to believe in the incurability of hysteria begins." Then follows, without transition, the leap to the bath: "Moreover, she washed me in reddish water in which she had previously washed herself" (*Letters*, 269). The bath, while it might well reflect a childhood memory of the nurse's menstruation, can also be read as Freud's projection of Emma Eckstein's victimization, recollected in the story about the shopkeeper and reenacted in nasal surgery. His conscious and unconscious feelings of guilt regarding her treatment are eruptions of the same medical matters that had contributed to his anxiety from the spring of 1885 throughout the fall of 1887—Emma's bleeding and his complicity in proclaiming Fliess innocent. Freud's ambivalence concerning Fliess would have made the metaphor of the bloody bath *extremely* difficult to analyze for his colleague. The nurse, like the bath itself, appears "under the strangest disguises," indicating a projection, a disguise within a disguise: a condensation of the "elderly" nurse, Martha Bernays, the undefiled *mater*, the defiled and violated Emma Eckstein.

Looking at the dream as a childhood memory, it is quite possible that the young Freud had *in truth* experienced an immersion in water previously discolored by his nurse's menstrual blood; people during the nineteenth century commonly shared the same water for two or three separate baths.[32] Or perhaps he had *in truth* observed his nurse or his mother periodically washing menstrual rags and had felt defiled by them.[33] Or perhaps there is some relevance to the old Jewish rule that prohibited a man from washing "in the same water previously used by a woman, lest it might contain a trace of menstrual blood."[34] Or perhaps, moving closer to the factual, the bath is a substituted form for *basin*, some device used in surgery. What seems most vital is that Freud, prompted by his new understanding of the mechanism of dreams, has recalled the incident of the red bath as *fiction*, as fantasy. He evidently theorized that the imagined immersion was equally as valid in the unconscious as an actual one, thus discovering substantiation for the momentous reversal articulated to Fliess two weeks earlier—the theory that a sexual experience during childhood does not have to be real for it to be recalled as having happened.[35]

The red bath may or may not have happened: what mattered to Freud psychoanalytically was the fantasy itself and where its associations might lead, perhaps to his bisexuality and to his identification with women, to his seduction by the "clever" nurse. Unfortunately, he could not fully share this specific discovery with Fliess; for given the patterns of denial and guilt following Emma Eckstein's surgery, he was in no position to explore with his colleague the possibility, even had he recognized it, that the reddish water was related to Emma's bleeding and victimization. The vagueness surrounding the Dream of the Red Bath is problematic; either he was deceiving himself or he was deceiving Fliess or both.

### The Nurse in Veils

The disguised nurse reappeared in several other dreams from May through December 1897. In what I call the Dream of the Red-Nosed Nun, dated two months after the Dream of the Red Bath and later published in *The Interpretation of Dreams,* there are certain nasal/fluid images that suggest menstrual periodicity. In the dream Freud sits at the gateway of the city of Siena, alone; because of "*certain events*" in Rome, he had been forced to "*remove the children to safety.*" As he sits by a fountain, "*greatly depressed and almost in tears,*" he notices a "*female figure—an attendant or nun,*" accompanied by two boys, one of them his eldest son. "*She was noticeable for having a red nose*" (*SE* 5:441). The son, refusing to kiss the red-nosed woman, turns to his father in farewell, uttering the words "AUF GESERES" and "AUF UNGESERES" (*SE* 5:441–42).[36]

In the interpretation that follows, Freud investigated these words of farewell, tracing the curious phrases through Hebrew and German until, at the end of the analysis, he and his "Berlin friend" have arrived at the office door of one Dr. Herodes, or King Herod, an allusion that again suggests mistreatment or malpractice.[37] The analysis concludes with a discussion of the term *Myops,* which dispels Freud's fears of "one-sidedness of intellectual development" (*SE* 5:444). Ken Frieden interprets this "one-sidedness" as a "denial of Judaic traditions," whereas I would use the term, as Claude Dagmar Daly was to do in 1943, to indicate Freud's "one-sided" view of sexuality.[38] In either case, the argument is similar; the dream represents a denial, a repression of some element that disturbs him—Jewish tradition, the bleeding female.

The Dream of the Red-Nosed Nun closely conforms to the one-sided pattern found in the Dream of Irma's Injection. There is a woman at the periphery of the dream whose physical presence is alluded to but passed by, through the process of free association, in favor of a linguistic investigation. In both instances his thoughts lead him from the female body to his male colleagues—to Josef Breuer, Oskar Rie, and Ludwig Rosenberg in the Dream of Irma's Injection; to "Herodes," Professor M., and Fliess in the Dream of the Red-Nosed Nun. Fliess's presence, while less prominent here than in the Dream of Irma's Injection, is similarly connected with poor practice; Freud recalls that a year earlier, as he and his friend were walking through the streets of Berlin, a "little girl" had asked for directions. "It is to be hoped," he told Fliess, "that when she grows up that little girl will show more discrimination in her choice of the people whom she gets to direct her" (*SE* 5:443). This recollection parallels other self-doubts about his skills as doctor and therapist; it also implicates Fliess, his street companion in the dream but, in the cases of Irma and Emma, his consulting physician.

A woman-centered reading of the dream would yield an entirely different set of associations, for the images of the nun, the tears, and the fountain create a distinct, female pattern within the architecture of the dream. As Freud himself emphasized, the dream takes place in front of a fountain, associated with the fountain from Psalm 137—"By the waters of Babylon we sat down and wept"—and with the persecution of Jews in Egypt and in the Europe of his own time (*SE* 5:442). Fluid and flow, however, can also be read as representations of menstruation in dream symbolism, emblematized by such symbols as fountains, rivers, and floods.[39] The fountain of Siena is the fluid setting for a curious reference to menstruation, veiled in this text as it was in the Dream of Irma's Injection and the Dream of the Red Bath: the red-nosed nun.[40]

Like the "reddish water," so the nun's red nose calls attention to itself. If in the earlier instance Freud had resisted analysis by claiming that the "interpretation is not so difficult" (*Letters*, 269), so in the Dream of the Red-Nosed Nun he ignored the association, even though the red nose is "noticeable": "*she was noticeable for having a red nose*" (*SE* 5:441). If his exploration of the male references in the dream—eldest son, "Berlin friend," Professor M.—provide important clues in the interpretation, then surely the red-nosed attendant would have provided them as well. But in the analysis she is dismissed in one sentence: "This tallied with the fact that another member of my household, our excellent nurse, was recognizably portrayed in the female attendant or nun in the dream" (*SE* 5:442–43). Although the nurse should have recalled the recent discovery of the "ugly, elderly, but clever woman," he adamantly denied that the attendant could be anyone other than the "recognizably portrayed" nurse of his sons. By proclaiming that she was *recognizably* his sons' nurse, he disclaimed that she could have been the same nurse described to Fliess two months earlier—as others believe her to be.[41] The profound clarity with which Freud explained away the nurse is an indication of the strength of his repugnance toward her.[42] To avoid the "unrecognizable," he distorted or repressed the disguised subject; the denial of the nurse seems to replicate the denial of Emma Eckstein, whose *red nose* was the source of pain and anxiety during the extent of his analytic relationship with her.

One final nanny dream, briefly described to Fliess in the letter of 31 May 1897 and later published in 1900 in *The Interpretation of Dreams*, includes in its later version certain critical details omitted in the letter to Fliess—the identification of the "woman" as his childhood nurse and the menstrually suggestive symbol of the dirty red carpet (compare *Letters*, 249). Freud dreamed that on a staircase in a house where he used to go twice a day to give injections to an old woman, he meets a servant who chastises him for spitting on the floor; another servant scolds him for making the red carpet dirty with his boots (*SE* 4:238). There are specific associations between the Staircase Dream and the Dream of Irma's Injection: he is climbing the staircase to administer an injection; he feels ashamed at being "very incompletely dressed" (*SE* 4:238)—unlike Irma, who was fully clothed. Like other dream figures, the servants taunt him for his bad behavior, accusing him of dirtying the staircase with his spit and berating him for soiling the red carpet. The day before the dream, one servant said: "You've made the red carpet all dirty again with your feet" (*SE* 4:239). The *dirty red carpet* can be read as one further allusion to menstruation—to vaginal filth and defilement. The term *carpet*, neither indexed in *The Standard Edition* nor interpreted in Freud's analysis, would assumedly represent the female genitals, as do fur and velvet, for example, in the 1927 essay "Fetishism" (*SE* 21:155).

A menstrual reading would connect the carpet with women's bleeding; "Another common ancient symbol of the blood-river of life [menstruation] was the red carpet, traditionally trod by sacred kings, heroes, and brides."[43] The guilty doctor is violating the patient's "carpet," as Fliess had violated Emma with the dirty wad of gauze. The spit on the staircase recalls Freud's identification with female bleeding; in its vileness of discharge, it recollects the "focal pus accumulation" of his own "Etna" (*Letters*, 115–16), but also of Emma's avalanche, his nanny's bath, and other effluvia that permeate the letters and dreams.

By 1900, although the fluid images persist, he had dismantled his cloak of secrecy regarding "the prime originator," announcing that the Staircase Dream is one of a series of dreams "based on a recollection of a nurse in whose charge I had been from some date during my earliest infancy till I was two and a half. I even retain an obscure conscious memory of her" (*SE* 4:247). Through his gradual refinement of psychoanalytic technique, he had expanded his comprehension of the unconscious and of the specter who lay forgotten there. Two other factors, however, seem to have simultaneously contributed to the resurfacing of childhood memories. First, Emma Eckstein's analysis had been terminated; second, the friendship with Fliess had ended—Fliess, whose "innocence" Freud so badly needed to protect during the painful work of self-analysis. Having passed through the Eckstein/Fliess crisis, Freud was released to pursue the Oedipus complex, the foundational theory of psychoanalysis. In a letter to Masson written in September 1981, Anna Freud stressed just how important the shift actually was: "Keeping up the seduction theory would mean to abandon the Oedipus complex, and with it the whole importance of phantasy life, conscious or unconscious phantasy. In fact, I think there would have been no psychoanalysis afterwards."[44] I truly doubt that there would have been "no psychoanalysis." But it would have been psychoanalysis of a radically different sort, with an emphasis on women and women's desires. Instead, the phallus was to replace the womb and the father to replace the seduced female victim.[45]

Freud's continuous resistance to menstruation during this period of discovery almost certainly contributed to the new course of psychoanalytic inquiry, in that the censorship of Emma Eckstein and her bloody "scenes" facilitated Freud's movement away from female patients and toward a phallocentric construction of sexuality. His disavowal of women's menstrual reality was mirrored in the minimalization of female sexuality in his later anthropological and psychoanalytic works.

Menstruation must, in light of Freud's resistance, be perceived as *absence* in his dream analysis. In the Dream of Irma's Injection, menstruation is buried within the latent content of the dream; in the Dream of the Red Bath its presence is too obvious to be worthy of discussion; in the Dream of the Red-Nosed Nun it is dreamed away; in the Staircase Dream it is swept under the carpet. Had he consciously articulated the menstruating mother as he had the oedipal father, then the course of dream interpretation would have been quite different. In the seminal case

of Emma Eckstein, however, Freud retreated from her menstrual difference, attributing her bleeding to "hemophilia" or to "hysteria" or to her
insatiable desire to bleed. In his published works, menstruation appears
not as an extensive, psychological theory but as an occasional symbol.
And yet its periodic rhythms somehow continue to invade his other formulations: in other dreams; in his theories of libido and the death instinct;
in his metaphorical, mythological, and anthropological constructions.

### Notes

1. The Aliquis narrative is not indexed under *menstruation* in the index to *The
Standard Edition*. I am indebted to Janet Malcolm's *In the Freud Archives* (New York:
Alfred A. Knopf, 1984), 122–23, for this reference to menstruation.

2. Marie Balmary, *Psychoanalyzing Psychoanalysis*, trans. Ned Lukacher (1979;
Baltimore: Johns Hopkins University Press, 1982), 5.

3. *SE* 4:107. In *The Standard Edition* the dream is set in italics. Unless otherwise
indicated, any emphases within the dreams quoted in this book are Freud's.

4. Grinstein identifies these three figures as follows: Dr. M. was Josef Breuer,
with whom Freud collaborated on *Studies in Hysteria;* Otto was Oskar Rie, another
collaborator and the family pediatrician; Leopold, the least important of the dream
figures, was Ludwig Rosenberg, a pediatrician and the husband of Rie's sister. See
Alexander Grinstein, *Sigmund Freud's Dreams* (New York: International Universities
Press, 1968), 23–33.

5. Of the many critics who connect Irma to Emma, see the following: Max Schur,
in "Some Additional 'Day Residues' of the Specimen Dream of Psychoanalysis,"
*Psychoanalysis: A General Psychology—Essays in Honor of Heinz Hartmann*, ed. R. M.
Lowenstein, Lottie M. Newman, Max Schur, and A. J. Solnit (New York: International Universities Press, 1966), 67; Ken Frieden, *Freud's Dream of Interpretation*
(Albany: State University of New York Press, 1990), 13; Henri F. Ellenberger, *The
Discovery of the Unconscious* (New York: Basic Books, 1970), 445; Grinstein, *Dreams*,
26–29; and Madelon Sprengnether, *The Spectral Mother: Freud, Feminism, and Psychoanalysis* (Ithaca: Cornell University Press, 1990), 171–74. Masson takes the opposite
position, insisting that Irma is not Emma Eckstein at all, but rather Anna Freud's
godmother, Anna Hammerschlag—a fact Anna Freud has "confirmed"; see Jeffrey
Moussaieff Masson, *Freud: The Assault on Truth* (New York: Farrar, Straus, and
Giroux, 1984), 205n.

6. Because it continues to be frequently cited in this chapter, *The Complete Letters of Sigmund Freud to Wilhelm Fliess*, ed. Jeffrey Moussaieff Masson (Cambridge:
Harvard University Press, 1985), is referred to parenthetically in the text as *Letters*.

7. Peter Gay, *Freud: A Life of Our Time* (New York: Norton, 1988), 86.

8. Ibid., 86.

9. Compare Stanley Fish's use of the term *missing* in his study of Freud's Wolf-Man as a case in rhetorical argument, in "Withholding the Missing Portion: Psycho-analysis and Rhetoric," in *Doing What Comes Naturally* (Durham: Duke University Press, 1989), 525–54.

10. Jacques Lacan, *The Seminar of Jacques Lacan, Book 2: The Ego In Freud's Theory and in the Technique of Psychoanalysis 1954–1955*, trans. Sylvana Tomaselli, ed. Jacques-Alain Miller (1978; New York: Norton, 1988), 154.

11. Irma's symptoms, even the site of the dream, are strikingly reiterated in a 1955 case study. A woman dreams, on "the night her period began," of being at a party. On the way home "the skin and flesh of her mouth began to grow," which represents menstruation that was "confined to her mouth." See Emilio M. Rodrigue, "Notes on Menstruation," *International Journal of Psycho-analysis* 36 (1955): 329–31.

12. *Stedman's Medical Dictionary*, 24th ed. (Baltimore: Williams and Wilkins, 1982).

13. In one perhaps excessively sexual reading of the dream, Eric Erikson calls the needle a "dirty squirter" or "spritz"; it represents Freud's having made Martha pregnant and is also a recollection of childhood urination. See Eric Erikson, "The Dream Specimen of Psychoanalysis," *Journal of the American Psychoanalytic Association* 2 (1954): 26, 42, 54. An *injection* has obvious associations with entering or "infiltrating" the female body.

14. Psychoanalytic critics are often reluctant to ad/dress the *clothed* aspect of the examination. Grinstein, as a prime example, notices that Freud omits the words "percussing her through her bodice" in a later edition of *The Interpretation of Dreams*, an omission that "may be significant in the light of subsequent material," *Dreams*, 32. But Grinstein himself fails to follow through on that potential significance—the veiling of the female body and of its hidden illness.

15. J. Laplanche and J.-B. Pontalis, *The Language of Psycho-analysis*, trans. Donald Nicholson-Smith (New York: Norton, 1973), 96.

16. Quoted by Stanley Edgar Hyman in *The Tangled Bank* (New York: Grosset and Dunlap, 1966), 305.

17. According to Jones, the Catholic nurse had a "terrifying influence" that may have affected Freud's later dislike for Christian ritual; see Ernest Jones, *The Life and Work of Sigmund Freud* (New York: Basic Books, 1953), 1:19. For key discussions of the identity of the Catholic nurse, see Josef Sajner (1968), "The Freiberg Period of the Freud Family," trans. Renée Gickhorn, *Journal of the History of Medicine* 24 (1969): 37–43; Marianne Krüll, *Freud and His Father*, trans. Arnold J. Pomerans (1979; New York: Norton, 1986); Paul C. Vitz, *Sigmund Freud's Christian Unconscious* (New York: Guilford Press, 1988); and Harry T. Hardin, "On the Vicissitudes of Freud's Early Mothering," *Psychoanalytic Quarterly* 56 (1987): 628–44; 57 (1988): 72–76, 209–23.

18. See Jim Swan, "*Mater* and Nannie: Freud's Two Mothers and the Discovery of

the Oedipus Complex," *American Imago* 31 (1974): 1–64; and Mary Jacobus, *Reading Women: Essays in Feminist Criticism* (New York: Columbia University Press, 1986).

19. Max Schur, in *Freud: Living and Dying* (New York: International Universities Press, 1972), quotes this passage but trivializes it by commenting that Freud "was certainly going Fliess one better here in the 'numbers game,' " 116.

20. A number of critics believe that the "sexual matters" to which Freud refers are masturbatory. See, for example, Krüll, *Freud and His Father,* 121; and Peter Rudnytsky, *Freud and Oedipus* (New York: Columbia University Press, 1987), 58.

21. Balmary, *Psychoanalysis,* 139.

22. Critics who ignore the reddish water include Kenneth A. Grigg, in "All Roads Lead to Rome: The Role of the Nursemaid in Freud's Dreams," *Journal of the American Psychoanalytic Association* 21 (1973): 115; and Harry T. Hardin, in "Freud's Early Mothering," 629. Sprengnether, in *The Spectral Mother,* reads the red bath as a representation of castration, 37. Jones merely restates Freud's position, finding the red water to be "a particularly convincing detail," in *Life and Work* 1:326. Similarly, Grinstein finds the red bath "especially interesting from the standpoint of her [the nurse's] insistence upon his cleanliness," in *Dreams,* 208. The words *interesting* and *convincing* are evasions of interpretation.

23. Didier Anzieu, *L'autoanalyse de Freud* (Paris: Presses Universitaires de France, 1975), 1:231.

24. Swan, "*Mater* and Nannie," 39. Ultimately, Swan subordinates (rather than connects) the blood of menstruation to the blood of childbirth, relating Freud's anxiety to his "engulfment in the bloody womb of his birth."

25. Balmary, *Psychoanalysis,* 139.

26. See chapter 5 for further discussion of the *mikvah.* For a deplorably one-sided Christian interpretation of the red bath and the Blood of the Lamb, see Vitz, *Christian Unconscious,* 20–22.

27. Jacobus, *Reading Women,* 191. The Jacobus interpretation is in part based on Julia Kristeva's conception of abjection. See Julia Kristeva, *Powers of Horror: An Essay on Abjection,* trans. Leon S. Roudiez (1980; New York: Columbia University Press, 1982).

28. The average age of menopause for European women in the midnineteenth century is difficult to ascertain, not only because of secrecy but because of lower life expectancy and inconsistent medical records. Sajner puts the age of Monika Zajic at forty, whereas Anzieu estimates that she was "in her forties"; see Sajner, "Freiberg Period," 37–43; and Anzieu, *L'autoanalyse de Freud* 1:38. Vitz, who identifies the nurse as Theresa Wittek, claims that she "may have been only in her late 30's or early 40's" when she was Freud's nurse; see *Christian Unconscious,* 20–21. Freud's daughter, Anna, told Jeffrey Masson that "she thinks she may have been in her forties," in *Assault on Truth,* 215n.

29. Masson, *Assault on Truth,* 99. Menstruation is not in the index.

30. Schur, "Day Residues," 83n.

31. Martha Noel Evans, "Hysteria and the Seduction of Theory," in *Seduction and Theory*, ed. Dianne Hunter (Urbana: University of Illinois Press, 1989), 80.

32. See, for example, the account of bathing standards of the Drinker family, in Richard L. Bushman and Claudia L. Bushman, "The Early History of Cleanliness in America," *Journal of American History* 74 (1988): 1215–38. Similar bathing patterns, in which "two or three people in succession often used the same water" (1215), are likely to have applied to conditions in Freiberg, Moravia. I thank J. Abbott Miller for this information.

33. Max Schur suggests that the young Freud must have observed "signs of menstrual bleeding in his environment," *Freud*, 126–27. Vitz, in *Christian Unconscious*, describes the washing of menstrual rags during Freud's day, 21–23.

34. Barbara G. Walker, *The Woman's Encyclopedia of Myths and Secrets* (San Francisco: Harper and Row, 1983), 643.

35. See Masson, *Assault on Truth*, 99–103, for the immediate psychoanalytic response to that theory.

36. Frieden reads *auf geseres* and *auf ungeseres* as Yiddish-German coinages that recall the Jewish captivity in Egypt, in *Freud's Dream*, 121–24.

37. Grinstein, in *Dreams*, identifies Herodes as King Herod of the New Testament, the killer of Christ, 329–30. Vitz adds, however, that it was Herod who also murdered the first-born males of Judea, a story perhaps told to Freud by his nanny, 92. See also Frieden, *Freud's Dream*, 124.

38. Claude Dagmar Daly, "The Role of Menstruation in Human Phylogenesis and Ontogenesis," *International Journal of Psycho-analysis* 24 (1943): 164.

39. For a discussion of the menstrual connotations of oceans and rivers in dreams, see Mary Chadwick, *The Psychological Effects of Menstruation* (New York: Nervous and Mental Disease Publishing Company, 1932), 34–36, 44–45.

40. One might compare this dream to the dream of one of Freud's male patients, who runs in terror from a woman with "*red flesh*," not of her nose but of her lower eyelids. Freud connects the red eyes to the "gaping genitals" and to the physiological process of urination (not menstruation). In the patient's memory, the woman's exposed vagina reappears as "'*proud flesh*'—as a wound" (*SE* 4:201).

41. See Frieden, *Freud's Dream*, 124n. Vitz comments: "The nun or nurse was an obvious reference to the old nanny, and yet Freud never mentioned her," in *Christian Unconscious*, 91. In *Dreams*, Grinstein tentatively associates the red-nosed attendant with Freud's nanny, 323–24. Grinstein's reading of the dream is oedipal, focusing on the male figures and on Freud's mourning over the death of his father and of his fatherland.

42. The avoidance in the Dream of the Red-Nosed Nun demonstrates one of Freud's basic precepts: that the wish fulfillment in unpleasurable dreams is "disguised to the point of being unrecognizable precisely owing to the repugnance felt for the

topic of the dream or from the wish derived from it and to an intention to repress them" (*SE* 4:160).

43. Walker, *Woman's Encyclopedia*, 638.

44. Quoted by Masson, *Assault on Truth*, 113.

45. Freud's rejection of the seduction theory, initially tenuous, eventually became precept. Writing in 1924, he acknowledged that he had been "at last obliged to recognize that these scenes of seduction had never taken place, and that they were only phantasies which my patients had made up or which I myself had perhaps forced on them" (*SE* 20:34).

# 3

# *Menstrual Representations: Flowers and Floods*

As we demonstrated in *The Curse*, studies of menstrual imagery in folklore, film, and literature suggest that the bleeding vagina generates its own elaborate system of metaphors, many of them applicable to this discussion of dreams (186–99). Metaphor, as part of the psychoanalytic system of symbolization (dream images, slips of the tongue, and similar linguistic signs), articulates repressed bodily functions in a chronology that, according to Ella Sharpe, postdates the child's control of problems like wetting the bed and messing the underwear. Metaphorically, a male patient's saying he had "made a mess of things" would refer to having messed his trousers, while being "sodden with despair" would indicate lack of urethral control.[1] Sharpe's perspective, while it does not address the sodden or messy qualities of menstruation, does help us to position menstrual metaphor within a pattern of blocking/release that represents the rhythms of the menstrual process.[2] In this chapter I search *The Interpretation of Dreams,* and particularly the dream called the Language of Flowers, for menstrual metaphors—for veiled, blocked, often unconscious allusions to a bleeding woman.[3]

Because of their regularity and repetition, clocks, Freud claimed, were representative of the menstrual cycle (*The Introductory Lectures on Psycho-*

*analysis, SE* 16:226). The moon and its tides, which share this menstrual characteristic of measurement, are widely recognized images of menstruation in cultures throughout history.[4] Less evident metaphors include the witch, filth, flowers, volcanoes, the earth, deluges—often depicted as being the color *red*.[5] *Red*, coupled with flowers and fluid, is an occasional emblem for menstruation in Freud's writings.[6] Yet despite his meticulous attention to representations of the female genitalia (caskets, keyholes, boxes, baskets, and similar substitutions), it was Freud's tendency to disregard or even disavow menstrual signifiers.

As metaphor, menstruation is not a simple substitution of one word for another but rather a submerged signifier that is veiled or curtained. As veiled, menstruation necessitates oblique, covert, *metaphoric* representation; as the unspoken, menstruation appears in disguise, resisting interpretation, both within Freud's works and in his milieu. In its gendered "otherness," its exclusively female aspect, menstrual blood is the most monstrous example of Julia Kristeva's "abject": it "threatens the relationship between the sexes within a social aggregate and, through internalization, the identity of each sex in the face of sexual difference."[7] Whereas the phallus is, in current psychoanalytic theory, the signifier of desire, menstrual blood is the undesired; as the phallus protrudes dominantly into space, menstruation hides in a closet—unspoken, reticent, veiled, ashamed to declare its difference. Menstruation is the gap in the text, the gaping wound concealed in the dream interpretation—as Emma's wound was concealed in Freud's self-analysis; as the nurse's menstruation was concealed in the Dream of the Red Bath.

### The Garden of Paradox

The Language of Flowers is, like the Dream of Irma's Injection, open to a menstrual reading; it occupies a special place, however, in Freud's dream interpretation in that it is directly attentive to menstrual imagery: to "some unmistakable allusions to menstruation" at the center of the female patient's dream (*SE* 4:319).[8] The dream is presented in a fragmented twice-telling that echoes the split structure of the dream itself; it is first described in volume 4 of *The Standard Edition;* but the full text of the flower sequence—what he calls "the main dream"—does not appear until the fifth volume, where it is "appended" to other, unnamed material.[9] Similarly, the text of the Language of Flowers is divided into two unequal parts—a short "introductory dream," involving a flood, and the "main dream," involving flowers.

To read the dream, one must move back and forth, from volume 5 to volume 4, from introductory dream to main dream, from flooding kitchen to flowering branch. My own reading further complicates the interpretation by incorporating an additional element: the paragraph in volume 5 that immediately precedes the Language of Flowers and to which, claimed Freud, the dream was "appended" (*SE* 5:347). I call this paragraph the "text-residue," a term meant to parallel "day residues," what he identified as thoughts "dwelt upon cursorily" during the day preceding a dream (*SE* 2:69). This paragraph, a theoretical discussion of the use of disguise in dreams, anticipates a number of the menstrual associations in the recorded dream that follows it. A recognition of the intertwined, structural connections among these seemingly disjointed elements reveals the Language of Flowers to have a complex intratextuality in which the spoken/unspoken allusions to menstruation are intermittently acknowledged, resisted, and/or repressed.

The menstrual metaphor that persists both in the dream and in the interpretation is the *camellia*, the red flower the dreamer bears on a branch as she descends from a hill into a garden (*SE* 5:347–48). In the earlier discussion of the dream, Freud had noticed certain references to menstruation (*SE* 4:319), specifically to the menstrual periods of Camille, the suffering heroine of a novel by Alexandre Dumas fils. Freud alluded to the menstrual flowers without fully exploring their sexual implications; yet the menstrual signification of *flowers* is widespread—a familiar emblem in mythology, a symbol in dreams and poetry.[10] Menstrual flowers are of particular importance within Freud's own literary-cultural tradition, for in the Old Testament injunction against intercourse with a menstruating woman, flowers are synonymous with menstrual blood: "And if any man lie with her at all, and her flowers be upon him, he shall be unclean seven days" (Lev. 15:24).[11] The reading of *flowers* as menstruation was quite common among nineteenth-century biblical scholars; Rev. John Brown, in his 1829 dictionary of the Bible, gave as the first definition of *flowers* "a running of blood," whereas James Hastings, in a similar dictionary (1899), defined *flowers* as "menstrual discharge."[12] Freud, who probably would have known the biblical equation of flowers and menstrual blood, is unresponsive to this association in his patient's analysis.

The absence of a reference to Leviticus is accentuated by the proximity of the Language of Flowers to the text-residue, where he foreshadowed many of the motifs that appear in the dream and where he twice referred to the most erotic book from the Old Testament, *The Song of Solomon,* first to the bodily associations between legs and gateways; second to the sexual images of "the Lord's vineyard, the seed, and the Maiden's garden" (*SE* 5:346–47). Freud did not, in the text-residue, refer to menstruation, although there are a number of images in the *Song of Solomon* that suggest the sexuality of women's bleeding. The bride, for example, is compared to "a spring enclosed, a sealed fountain," to "a garden fountain/a well of flowing water/streaming down from Lebanon."[13] She is associated with spicy odors, fragrant garments, and other olfactory enticements that Freud, in *Civilization and Its Discontents,* was to link to the cultural repression of menstruation (*SE* 21:99–100, 105–6). In one striking metaphor from *Song of Solomon,* the lover compares his bride's navel to "a rounded goblet that never lacks blended wine," a metaphor that reproduces the fullness and continuity of the menstrual process.[14] Freud's apparent resistance to the menstrual reverberations from *Song of Solomon* generates an overflow of associations to the Language of Flowers—the dream in which he most fully admitted that menstrual images were significant elements in the unconscious.

The text-residue that precedes the Language of Flowers amplifies the material repressed in the interpretation. The word *kitchen,* which governs the introductory dream, appears twice in the text-residue. Freud associates that domestic space with a presumed innocence: "The ugliest as well as the most intimate details of sexual life may be thought and dreamt of in seemingly innocent allusions to activities in the kitchen" (*SE* 5:346). Freud is elusive here. What is the "ugliest" aspect of sexuality, which is at the same time the "most intimate"? What "seemingly innocent" thoughts relate to activities in the kitchen? What are the displacements—architectural, physiological, and symbolic—that connect the kitchen and the garden, the profane and the edenic? If he was, as I believe, repressing menstruation, then the linguistic veiling guards the secret of menstrual blood—the secret that menstruation is the "ugliest" sexual phenomenon. The very food in the kitchen is contaminated by it, an idea reinforced in the numerous cultural prohibitions against women preparing food or touching dishes during their periods.[15]

In the text-residue Freud offers the clinical example of a "neurotic child" who demonstrated an "intolerance of *blood* or raw meat" and who became sick "at the sight of eggs or macaroni" (*SE* 5:346, my emphasis). The raw meat and the eggs would point ominously to the bloody uterus of our first home, the mother's "kitchen," whereas macaroni, a form of pasta or *Knödel*, figures prominently in his childhood discovery of death, discussed in the next chapter. The word *blood* stands out, like something very familiar that has been forgotten, something "commonplace" and therefore conspicuous: the abject, the "uncanny." [16]

Following the description of the neurotic child, Freud appends, with no logical connective, the "flowery dream," which begins in a kitchen that is threatened by an approaching flood: "*She went into the kitchen, where her two maidservants were, and found fault with them for not having got her 'bite of food' ready. At the same time she saw quite a quantity of crockery standing upside down to drain, common crockery piled up in heaps.* Later addition: *The two maidservants went to fetch some water and had to step into a kind of river which came right up to the house into the yard*" ("Introductory Dream," *SE* 5: 347).[17] The images of fluid and flooding link the un/named matters of the Old Testament with the menstrual naming of the dream that follows. As the "introductory dream" begins, the patient, like the "neurotic child" of the text-residue, is in a kitchen looking for food. When the two servants go for water, they have to "step into a kind of river" that comes up to the house (*SE* 5:347). Referring to the patient's case history, Freud explained that the crockery is from a hardware shop located in the building, while the flood relates to her father, "who used always to run after the maids and who eventually contracted a fatal illness during a flood" (*SE* 4:315).[18]

The kitchen pots are upside down, draining their residue—a structure that parallels menstruation. The river is coming up to the house. If *house* and *crockery* are common Freudian symbols for the genitalia, if the *flooding yard* has a sexual meaning comparable to the garden of the main dream, then the encroaching flood may have less to do with the father's fatal "illness" than with the patient's periodic one. The pots, the flood, and the river invite a menstrual reading—which Freud initiated in the flowery text but avoids in the introductory dream.[19]

The initial images of flow, which I find so relevant to the menstrual anxiety of the entire text, are neither acknowledged nor in any way related to the patient's sexual experiences. Nonetheless, the metaphor of fluid, in its downward movement and in its ability to overflow, similarly projects "unmistakable allusions to menstruation," allusions that spill from the introductory dream into the main dream—where Freud capitalized the words that "are to be given a sexual interpretation" (*SE* 5:347). Thus we find the dreamer holding a "BIG BRANCH" covered with "RED BLOSSOMS" that look like double "CAMELLIAS." As she descends a hill she sees a worker with similar branches and asks if they might be "TRANSPLANTED INTO HER OWN GARDEN." [20] The worker embraces her and reveals his desire to follow her into the "OTHER GARDEN" to show her how to plant. Paradoxically, Freud's discussion of the main dream (the camellias) is but a continuation of the repression of menstruation. He had earlier insisted that the allusions to menstruation are "unmistakable"; yet he neither elaborates on those references nor calls upon his extensive reading or his case histories to do so. [21]

For Freud's interpretation of the red blossoms, one must therefore turn back to the earlier discussion, in volume 4, where he drew contrasts between white and red, between innocence and menstruation: "the same branch which was carried like a lily and as though by an innocent girl was at the same time an allusion to the *Dame aux camélias* who, as we know, usually wore a white camellia, except during her periods, when she wore a red one" (*SE* 4:319). [22] If the white flower of the dreamer represents "innocence," then the red one, representing menstruation, must surely connote the *unclean*, the abject—an analogy that he hinted at when he noted the divergence between the patient's supposedly "immaculate" life and her having been, in childhood, "guilty of various sins against sexual purity" (*SE* 4:319). [23]

In alluding to *La dame aux camélias*, Freud was constructing a psychoanalytic interpretation by way of literary precedent—as he had more extensively done in his studies of Hamlet and Oedipus. The camellia is a flower in the 1848 novel by Dumas, the tragic story of the love affair between Armand Duval and Marguerite Gautier, a courtesan who habitually wore camellias. The narrator of the story, an acquaintance of Duval's, observes that when Marguerite attends the theater, she always carries a curious bouquet of camellias: "For twenty-five days of the month the camellias were white, and for five they were red; no one ever knew the reason for this change of colour, which I mention though I cannot explain it [on n'a jamais su la raison de cette variété de coleurs, que je signale sans pouvoir l'expliquer]; it was noticed both by her friends and by the *habitués* of the theatres to which she most often went. She was never seen with any flowers but camellias." [24] The naive narrator, unable to "explain" (*expliquer*) Camille's red flowers, proclaims his ignorance in such matters. Had he considered their menstrual significance, he might have "explained" them to be a deliberate sign of menstruation, a flaunting of female periodicity before an audience of sexual admirers. The red camellias would brazenly signify her desire, her accessibility, her defiance of the five-day taboo—not hidden but made public, made spectacle.[25] The paradox inherent in the Dumas novel equally reflects the attitude toward menstruation in Freud's psychoanalytic case study; the narrator (or in Freud's case, the narrator/analyst) is aware of the woman's flowers but cannot "explain" them—as he cannot explain female sexuality, whose distinguishing physical emblem is the red flower, or menstruation. The phenomenon of menstruation is thus observed but unexplicated, much as Freud, in the analysis of the Language of Flowers, observed the Dumas allusion to menstruation but failed to "explicate" its relevance to his patient's dream—although she, in her act of telling the dream, is also acting her menstruation, making it public.

Linked to menstruation is Camille's other bleeding, a bloody discharge from her lungs onto a napkin: "The poor girl turned crimson, closed her eyes upon the pain, and put her napkin to her lips. It was stained with a drop of blood."[26] She is suffering from consumption, an illness that, although accompanied by weight loss, coughing, and loss of appetite, has as its primary symptom the spitting of blood.[27] Camille's blood-spitting progresses throughout the novel, subverting its erotic texture; the red camellias would thus suggest not only menstrual bleeding (when Camille was "well" enough to attend the theater) but also blood-spitting (the mark of her disease).[28] Neither of Camille's bleedings is addressed in the novel; her doctor's final treatment is to bleed *her*, a medical practice called venesection, or bloodletting. Venesection thus imitates the symptoms of Camille's disease; but when applied, as it in fact was, in the treatment of menstruating women, it also imitates the menstrual process—the "letting" of blood.[29]

Freud's patient's dream and Dumas's heroine's melancholia may well have had their roots in the traumatic potential of the menstrual cycle. During the nineteenth and early twentieth centuries, women were both secretive and anxious about menstruation, swayed by a medical profession that tended to associate menstruation with pathology and to relate it to such disturbances as hysteria and madness.[30]

The Language of Flowers Dream might be read as a secret diary in which Freud's patient both masks and reveals her menstrual anxiety, offering her symbolic camellias for him to interpret. One wonders what medical consolation Freud, in the privacy of his office, extended to this patient who had shed her flowers. Perhaps he asked her questions about her cycle, as he had once asked Emma Eckstein (without receiving her co-operation).[31] Perhaps she confided a trauma from puberty, as had Emma Eckstein: sexual seduction or rape. It is possible that her menstruation had been accidentally witnessed by her brother or her father or that she had seen her mother's blood or that she was suffering from painful menstruation or that she associated menstruation with urine and bedwetting or that she viewed menstruation as a mark of shame, a sign of disease.[32] Perhaps, keeping her menstruation to herself, she told him nothing, although he told the reader that she "lost her liking for this pretty little dream after it had been interpreted" (*SE* 5:347).

It is possible that Freud, in his disavowal of women's bleeding, was ill equipped to handle the patient's menstrually related disorders. Like Irma's undiagnosed "organic trouble," the patient's menstrual anxiety went unexplored. Whatever his private response, he analyzed this "pretty little dream" in only the vaguest of ways; in the published texts of the Language of Flowers, the language of menstruation is un/spoken. Like his thoughts about the reddish water, his thoughts about the red camellias remain undisclosed.

### The Wedding Bouquet

Closely following the Language of Flowers is another flower dream—the dream of a "normal" young woman about to be married. Each flower in the dream—the pink, the violet, the lily of the valley, the carnation—has a specific symbolic meaning that would include "virginal femininity, masculinity and an allusion to defloration by violence" (*SE* 5:376). In this interpretation Freud does not associate violent defloration with menstruation, although in a later essay, "The Taboo of Virginity," he was to recognize defloration as a sadistic component during rites surrounding the first menstruation (*SE* 11:197). In the above dream the patient associates the flower *violet* with the verb *violate*, which Freud reads as the fear of violent defloration by her fiance.

In an addendum to the dream the woman says: "*I decorate the flowers with green crinkled paper . . . to hide untidy things, whatever was to be seen, which was not pretty to the eye; there is a gap, a little space in the flowers. The paper looks like velvet or moss"* (*SE* 5:376). She associates the green color with the desire for pregnancy, the untidy things with physical shame, and the moss with pubic hair, overlooking, however, the possibility that she may also be anticipating her period, which she "hides" from her future bridegroom by "decorating" with paper "whatever was to be seen, which was not pretty to the eye" (i.e., the "ugliest as well as the most intimate details of sexual life," *SE* 5:346). Many women, having been trained to see marriage as the achievement of womanhood, approach their wedding night fearful of the sexual act but even more fearful that they might prevent it by getting their periods. For a surprising number of brides, the undesired bleeding occurs: "It happens with astonishing frequency that menstruation starts precisely on the wedding day, often at the very moment when the bride and groom are for the first time together." [33] The "untidy" matter of menstrual blood might be the gap in the above text. The young woman facing marriage is also perhaps facing the humiliation of bleeding on her wedding night; she covers up her "gap," her "little space," with flowers, as she has covered up from herself the anxiety surrounding bleeding and defloration. [34]

Further references to flowers in *The Standard Edition* reveal a disinterest in menstruation. In the *Introductory Lectures on Psycho-analysis,* for example, Freud was explicit as to the sexual meaning of flowers. "*Blossoms* and *flowers,*" he said, "indicate women's genitals, or, in particular, virginity. Do not forget that blossoms are actually the genitals of plants" (*SE* 15:158). In "Jensen's 'Gravida' " he claimed that "the red rose had become the symbol of a love-relation" (*SE* 9:75), while in "Screen Memories," a dialogue focusing on flowers, the snatching of dandelions from a young girl's hands represented defloration, as Freud's acquaintance had come to realize: "Now I understand for the first time. Think for a moment! Taking flowers away from a girl means to deflower her." (*SE* 3:316). These and other references to flowers in his writings convey a recognition of the link between flowers and female sexuality but omit any consideration of their menstrual signification.

Freud's general resistance to menstrual metaphor was no small matter. Through the interpretation of symbols he was able to explore his patients' childhood memories in an effort to treat neurosis; in marginalizing those symbols that refer to the menstrual process, he was curtailing access to the female psyche, so often fragmented during puberty (a word he used frequently, but rarely to connote the initial appearance of menstrual blood).[35] Such material was available during the initial stages of psychoanalysis, at the time of his disquieting analysis of Emma Eckstein, whose fantastic eruptions of fluid might well have provided him with a verifying case history of menstrual trauma. His inattention to menstrual metaphor—to the symbolic language of fluid, flowers, and redness—parallels, as we shall see in the next chapter, his inattention to the bleeding mother of mythology, the Goddess of Death and Life, and to the question of female sexuality as difference.

## Notes

1. Ella Sharpe, "An Examination of Metaphor: Psycho-physical Problems Revealed in Language," in *The Psychoanalytic Reader: An Anthology of Essential Papers with Critical Introductions,* ed. Robert Fliess (New York: International Universities Press, 1973), 313–14.

2. In her final example Sharpe refers to menstruation. A male patient, in describing his mother's dirty nightgown, expresses a number of infantile emotions evoked by "the sight of the female genitals, the sight of menstrual blood." Ibid., 318–19.

3. Freud's use of metaphor as a *conscious* element in his writing has been discussed by Stanley Edgar Hyman, in *The Tangled Bank* (New York: Grosset and Dunlap, 1966), and by Jonathan T. Edelson, in "Freud's Use of Metaphor," *Psychoanalytic Study of the Child* 38 (1983): 17–59. Edelson concludes that Freud "knew the difference between the manifest and latent content in dreams as well as the difference between metaphor and reality," 57–58. My own investigation suggests rather that Freud did *not know* about menstruation as metaphorical representation in dreams.

4. For extensive discussions of the moon and menstruation, see Penelope Shuttle and Peter Redgrove, *The Wise Wound: Eve's Curse and Everywoman,* rev. ed. (1978; New York: Grove Press, 1986); and *The Curse.* Jung occasionally notes the relationship between the moon and menstrual blood in *The Collected Works of C. G. Jung,* ed. Herbert Read, Michael Fordham, and Gerhard Adler, trans. R. F. C. Hull, Bollingen Series, no. 20 (Princeton: Princeton University Press, 1979), 8:437, 16:173–75. When I quote from Jung's *Collected Works* I am indicating page numbers and not the paragraph indices used in the general index to his works.

5. In his work with "genitally masochistic women," Rado related their preference for *red* clothes during their periods to an unconscious seduction; Sándor Rado, "Fear of Castration in Women," *Psychoanalytic Quarterly* 2 (1933): 450. In his study of male fascism, Klaus Theweleit links redness and menstrual flooding; see *Male Fantasies: Women, Floods, Bodies, History,* trans. Stephen Conway, with Erica Carter and Chris Turner (Minneapolis: University of Minnesota Press, 1987), 1:414. Bettelheim ob-

served that in numerous initiation ceremonies, red mud, which represents menstrual blood, is smeared on the participant's body; see Bruno Bettelheim, *Symbolic Wounds: Puberty Rites and the Envious Male* (New York: Collier, 1962), 98. In one imaginative journal entry, a woman in a British remand center compares menstruation to a red river: " 'It is J. [her twin sister] who put this curse on me, the curse of the red, running river,' she complained. 'It was as though through the rivers, was my own child, like inky dye.' " See Marjorie Wallace, *The Silent Twins* (New York: Prentice Hall, 1986), 150.

6. In tracing menstrual metaphors throughout Freud's works, I have relied on *The Concordance to the Standard Edition of the Complete Psychological Works of Sigmund Freud*, ed. Samuel A. Guttman, Randall L. Jones, and Stephen M. Parrish (Boston: G. K. Hall, 1980). The index contains nineteen references to menstruation.

 7. Julia Kristeva, *Powers of Horror: An Essay on Abjection*, trans. Leon S. Roudiez (1980; New York: Columbia University Press, 1982), 71.

8. In discussing the dream, Freud tended to use the Fliessian term *Periode* rather than the more common term, *menstruation*. See *Die Traumdeutung: Studienausgabe Band 2* (Frankfurt am Main: S. Fischer Verlag, 1972), 317.

9. Compare *SE* 4:315, 319, 325 and *SE* 5:347–49.

10. In India menstrual blood is identified with the Kula flower, whereas according to Welsh mythology the goddess Blodeuwedd had a body formed from the blood flower. See Barbara G. Walker, *The Woman's Encyclopedia of Myths and Secrets* (San Francisco: Harper and Row, 1983), 638. Ramprasad, a Bengali poet, associated women's blood with flowers: "Like the spring adorned with red flowers, her limbs bear stains of bright blood"; cited by C. Mackenzie Brown, "Kali, the Mad Mother," in *The Book of the Goddess: Past and Present*, ed. Carl Olson (New York: Crossroad, 1989), 118–19. See also *The Curse* for a discussion of the menstrual flower in the poetry of Ovid, Baudelaire, Ann Sexton, and Sylvia Plath, 190–92; and the essay by Catherine Thompson, "Dawn Poems in Blood: Sylvia Plath and PMS," *Tri-Quarterly* 80 (1990–91): 221–49.

11. *The Holy Bible*, Authorized (King James) Version (Philadelphia: National Bible Press, n.d.), Lev. 15:24, 114. The *New English Bible*, with its less metaphorical approach, deletes the reference to flowers. See *The New English Bible*, ed. Samuel Sandmel (New York: Oxford University Press, 1972). In a nineteenth-century German edition, the word for *flowers* is *Monatliches*, or *monthly*. See *Die Bible: Ober die Schriften des Alten und Neuen Bandes* (Leipzig: F. A. Brodhaus, 1858).

12. John Brown, *A Dictionary of the Holy Bible* (New York: J. and J. Harper, 1829), 266; James Hastings, *A Dictionary of the Bible* (New York: Scribners, 1899), 2:24. The word *flowers* is translated as *discharge* in the *New English Bible*, ibid., whereas in the *Oxford NIV Scofield Study Bible: New International Version*, edited by C. I. Scofield, *flowers* becomes *monthly flow* (New York: Oxford University Press, 1984), 130.

13. "Song of Songs," *Oxford Study Bible*, 668–69.

14. According to Shuttle and Redgrove, the goblet represents the vagina and the wine, menstrual blood; see *The Wise Wound*, 20–21.

15. See, for example, Leonard Swidler, *Women in Judaism* (Metuchen, N.J.: Scarecrow Press, 1976); Narendra Nath Bhattacharyya, *Indian Puberty Rites* (1968; Calcutta, India: Munshiram Manoharlal, 1980); and Alfred Ernest Crawley, *The Mystic Rose: A Study of Primitive Marriage* (New York: n.p., 1902). Crawley, one of Freud's sources for *Totem and Taboo*, claimed that through separating the sexes, the food taboo helped to strengthen sexual identity, 149.

16. Blood exhibits a quality that in 1919 Freud would call "the uncanny," or "*unheimlich*": "that class of the frightening which leads back to what is known of old and long familiar" ("The Uncanny," *SE* 17:220). For "neurotic men," the uncanny, or *unheimlich*, place is situated in the female genital organs. Claude Dagmar Daly related Freud's uncanny to menstruation, in "Der Kern des Oedipuskomplexes," *Internationale Zeitschrift für Pschoanalyse* 21 (1935): 175.

17. In recording the dreams, Freud frequently *italicized* the dream text to distinguish the dream from the interpretation. Unless otherwise indicated, all emphases are Freud's. The above passage is the full text of the Introductory Dream, as it appears in volume 5 of *The Standard Edition*. The earlier version of the introductory dream is the same, with the exception of the word *or* added to the last sentence: "*or* into the yard" (*SE* 4:315).

18. The information about the patient's father appears only in the earlier version of the dream. In the version that appears in volume 5, Freud refers in a footnote to the woman's brother and her uncle, but not to her father (*SE* 5:347).

19. For Freud, the connectedness or "causality" between the introductory dream (the flood) and the main dream (the flower) stems not from the sexual imagery but from the patient's movement from low to high descent—from the modest circumstances of her childhood to the "height" with which the main dream begins (*SE* 4:315).

20. Freud interpreted the branch to be a representation of the penis (*SE* 5:348n). Neumann, however, traces the symbol of the branch to the Goddess of Summer and other goddesses, seeing it as an image of female fertility. Erich Neumann, *The Great Mother*, trans. Ralph Manheim, Bollingen Series, vol. 47 (1955; Princeton: Princeton University Press, 1972), 262.

21. The phrase "some unmistakable allusions to menstruation" is from volume 4 only (319); the only reference to menstruation in the "appended" version is in a footnote: "For the explanation of this composite image see p. 319: innocence, menstruation, *La dame au camélias*" (*SE* 5:347n7).

22. The blossoms also indicate gifts of cherries and camellias that had been given to "win her favor" (*SE* 4:325).

23. Freud probably was referring to masturbation, an act that confounded him in many instances, as for example in the Dora case. See Lawrence Frank's discussion,

"Freud and Dora," in *Seduction and Theory*, ed. Dianne Hunter (Urbana: University of Illinois Press, 1989), 120–22. Chadwick contended that the menstrual flow of adolescence is often connected with the guilt of childhood masturbation; see Mary Chadwick, *Difficulties in Child Development* (New York: John Day, 1928), 263.

24. Alexandre Dumas fils, *La dame aux camélias* (1848; Paris: Calmann-Lévy, 1951), 41.; *Camille*, trans. Edmond Gosse (New York: New American Library, 1984), 15.

25. The theatrical version of *La dame aux camélias* was published in 1849 as *Camille*. Of the many changes that Dumas made in the adaptation, the most alarming was the suppression of the camellia. For a discussion of Camille as spectacle, see Judith Pike, "Exquisite Cadavers: Spectacle into Fetish: Or, the Heroine as Still Life in Dumas and Verdi," University of California, Irvine, 1990.

26. Dumas, *Camille*, 82.

27. For a brief history of this ailment see Lester S. King, *Growth of Medical Thought* (Chicago: University of Chicago Press, 1969), 301–3.

28. Marie Bonaparte saw these two forms of bleeding, menstrual and consumptive, as related, in *The Life and Works of Edgar Allan Poe: A Psycho-analytic Interpretation*, trans. John Rodker (1933; New York: Humanities Press, 1971).

29. Showalter notes that during the Victorian era, the wrong amount of menstrual blood was thought to affect the brain; "thus psychiatric physicians attempted to control the blood by diet and venesection." See Elaine Showalter, *The Female Malady: Women, Madness, and English Culture, 1830–1980* (New York: Pantheon, 1985), 50. For a survey of the ancient practice of bloodletting see James Lewton Brain, "Male Menstruation in History and Anthropology," *Journal of Psychohistory* 15 (1988): 311–23.

30. For a compendium of information on turn-of-the-century menstrual pathology see Richard Krafft-Ebing, *Psychosis Menstrualis* (Erlangen: Verlag von Ferdinand Enke in Stuttgart, 1902). Daly argued that a woman's tendency toward constant illness (hypochondria) has menstrual origins, deriving from "repressed libidinal desire connected with the hereditarily ingrained belief that menstruation is a disease"; see "The Psychology of Man's Attitude Towards Woman," *Imago* 10 (1930): 237. See also Otto Rank, *The Trauma of Birth* (1924; New York: Robert Brunner, 1952), 51n, where Rank states that the repression of menstruation has resulted in "the most various neurotic disturbances." Many of the (male) medical assumptions about female illness are examined in an insightful essay by Ann-Louise Shapiro, "Disordered Bodies, Disorderly Acts: Medical Discourse and the Female Criminal in Nineteenth Century Paris," *Genders* 4 (1989): 68–86.

31. See Max Schur, "Some Additional 'Day Residues' of the Specimen Dream of Psychoanalysis," in *Psychoanalysis: A General Psychology—Essays in Honor of Heinz Hartmann*, ed. R. M. Lowenstein, Lottie M. Newman, Max Schur, and A. J. Solnit (New York: International Universities Press, 1966), 80.

32. The association between menstruation and urine is common in psychoana-

lytic literature. Most of Freud's discussions of urine appear in *The Interpretation of Dreams;* see, for example, *SE* 4:209–18, 227, 5:402–3. Mary Chadwick observed that menstrual staining repeats the shame of bed-wetting; see *The Psychological Effects of Menstruation* (New York: Nervous and Mental Disease Publishing Company, 1932), 45. Sándor Ferenczi described the pubescent girl's inability to control her bleeding: "Menstrual bleeding takes her back to the time when she was not yet able to control her stool and urine." *The Clinical Diary of Sándor Ferenczi,* ed. Judith Dupont, trans. Michael Bálint and Nicola Zarday Jackson (Cambridge: Harvard University Press, 1988), 165.

33. Michael Bálint, "A Contribution to the Psychology of Menstruation," *Psychoanalytic Quarterly* 6 (1937): 346. Menninger claims that the "sudden and irregular appearance" of menstrual blood on the wedding day is "protective," in that it delays a feared event. See Karl A. Menninger, "Psychogenic Influences on the Appearance of the Menstrual Period," *International Journal of Psycho-analysis* 22 (1941): 60–64.

34. Julia Reinhard Lupton relates the "gap" in the above dream to fetishism and to the "perceived absence of the maternal phallus," in "Sphinx with Bouquet," paper delivered at the conference "Freud/Art/History," University of California, Irvine, Nov. 1990, 15.

35. In his first reference to *puberty* in *The Standard Edition,* Freud used the term to identify a stage of sexual development that applies to both sexes: "In boys and girls of intense hysterical disposition, the period before and after puberty brings about a first outbreak of the neurosis" (*SE* 1:32). Similar concepts appear throughout his work, for example, puberty is the stage that give the "genitals primacy," both for boys and for girls (*SE* 9:133–34). On rare occasions the girl's pubescence involves the recognition of her menstrual blood—as in the case of a fourteen-year-old girl who assaults a menstruating friend (*SE* 9:223).

# 4

# *Libido, Menstruation, and Death*

The fluid metaphor, foreshadowed in the letters to Fliess and observable in the Language of Flowers Dream, intensified during Freud's articulation of the theory of libidinal energy. In the correspondence, Freud had associated the menstrual migraine with periodicity, toxic emanations, and olfactory stimuli; a further characteristic of the menstrual migraine was its inability to "discharge": the toxic effects were "produced by the sexual stimulating substance when this cannot find sufficient discharge."[1]

There are numerous references to a menstrual economics of buildup and discharge in his early remarks about menstruation; in an 1896 letter to Fliess he argued that "during menstruation and other sexual processes the body produces an increased Q of these substances and therefore of the stimuli."[2] The increased Q, or excitation, generated a language of buildup and discharge, of damming and facilitation. These scientific abstractions—substance, Q, increase, discharge, libido—formulated and refined during the 1890s, have Fliessian reverberations; it seems fairly certain that during the height of his association with Fliess, Freud had assimilated a good deal of Fliess's theory of periodicity and that menstruation became a hidden metaphor in many of his later theories and in his dreams. The scientific language used to express his theory of menstrual migraine and menstrual increase in the above passages is also the language used by Fliess in the theory of periodicity. This mutual way of thinking became, in the conceptualization of the sexual instincts, intertwined with Freud's writings on the menstrual stages in women's lives; it simultaneously affected his theory of libido.

The term *libido* is one of the most difficult in Freud's vocabulary; although many psychoanalytic critics use the word to imply something like "sex drive," in Freud's writings *libido* is surrounded by an aura of indeterminacy.[3] In a letter to Fliess dated 17 December 1896, he called it a "28-day anxiety substance," a definition that reiterated Fliess's concept of menstrual periodicity. "Anxiety," Freud wrote, "would arise through the somatic deployment of the female 28-D substance if the sexual discharge is denied to it."[4] His exploration of menstrual discharge climaxes in this letter—the same letter in which he hoped to blend his contributions with Fliess "to the point where our individual property is no longer recognizable."[5] But he finally abandoned Fliess's periodic concept of libido for a more generalized instinctual force, writing that in the course of sexual development certain transformations occurred, "such as the abolition of the periodicity of the libido and the exploitation of the part played by menstruation in the relation between the sexes" ("An Outline of Psycho-analysis," *SE* 23:153n).

In their dictionary of psychoanalysis, Laplanche and Pontalis state that "the concept of libido itself has never been clearly defined" and that Freud admitted his theory of the libido—from the Latin meaning *wish* or *desire*—to be "frankly speculative."[6] By 1932 he had come to view the theory of libido as a "mythology": "Instincts are mythical entities, magnificent in their indefiniteness. In our work we cannot for a moment disregard them, yet we are never sure that we are seeing them clearly" (*SE* 22:95). Lacan, in his reconstruction of Freud, accentuated the mythic quality of libido: "In the end, at this existential level, we can only talk about the libido satisfactorily in a mythical way."[7] Given the uncertainty surrounding *libido*, it becomes quite plausible to view it as what Freud himself called a "mythology," an imaginative representation of the elusive sexual process whose roots, as Freud had determined, are grounded in the symbolism of dreams. We encountered this relationship earlier, in his discussion of the imagery in the *Song of Solomon*, where the poet conveyed his vision through intense sexual images: gateways, exotic odors, fountains, gardens (*SE* 5:346–47).

Of the first-generation analysts concerned with the interrelationships among image, dream, and myth, it was Carl Jung who, in his attention to myth as collective dream, most comprehensively argued for these connections: "Many dreams present images and associations that are analogous to primitive ideas, myths, and rites. These dream-images were called 'archaic remnants' by Freud. The term suggests that there are psychic elements left over from times long ago and still adhering to the modern mind. . . . All the creative power that modern man pours into science and techics the man of antiquity devoted to his myths."[8] If, in mythology, the dream metaphor is incorporated into a universalized narrative, then in a mythology of menstruation, a red flower would, in the movement from symbol to dream to myth, become part of a symbolic, vaginal garden—the caretaker's garden in the Language of Flowers Dream but also the garden of Solomon or the Garden of Eden—with Eve's "curse" or menstrual flower the punishment for her disobedience. The menstrual metaphor of fluid or flooding, so relevant to a number of the world's mythologies, would take a similar psychic turn.[9] These structural crosscurrents—image, dream, mythology—have bearing on Freud's conception of libidinal flow.

Like the metaphoric representations of menstruation in dreams and mythology, so the "myth" of libido is veiled or masked, its meaning not easily accessible. Like menstruation, libido signifies buildup, breakthrough, energy, discharge, flow, overflow, a "28-day anxiety substance," language employed by Freud and his colleagues to describe both menstruation and libido. Wilhelm Reich called the comparison between libido and flow a "hydraulic metaphor": "If you can imagine a current, a natural current, you have to let it flow. If you obstruct it with a dam, it overflows, that's all."[10] Jung referred to the "Freudian comparison of the libido with a stream, which is divisible, which can be dammed up, which overflows into branches, and so on," whereas in a similar vein Otto Fenichel argued that if in a neurotic condition a discharge is blocked, even a slight influx may amplify the trauma, "creating a flooding."[11] Marie Bonaparte parted the metaphoric waters into male versus female, claiming that for women the libidinal "stream" is "deflected" from the clitoris to the "definitive adult organ, the vagina."[12] In its analogies to overflow, deflection, streams, discharge, and flooding, the libido appears to imitate the dynamics of the menstrual process—much in the way that Emma Eckstein's "flood of blood," with its buildup, damming, and release, imitated the same process.[13]

Looking at the several remarks in *The Standard Edition* about the menstrual stages (puberty, menstruation, and menopause), one observes that Freud, in discussing the physiological and psychological complications surrounding menstrual anxiety, stressed the beginning and ending stages of that process—the menarche (what he tended to call "puberty") and the menopause (the end of menstruation).[14] He argued that both puberty and menopause are times of potential trauma in which the dammed-up libido can release disturbances ordinarily held in check, a connection he first made in the 1912 essay "Types of Onset of Neurosis." Here, in a discussion of increases of libido at puberty and menopause, Freud presented a metaphoric treatment of menstruation:

> In some people they [libidinal increases] may in addition be manifested in periodicities that are still unknown. Here the damming-up of libido is the primary factor; it becomes pathogenic as a consequence of a *relative* frustration on the part of the external world, which would still have granted satisfaction to a smaller claim by the libido. The unsatisfied and dammed-up libido can once again open up paths to regression and kindle the same conflicts which we have demonstrated in the case of absolute external frustration. ("Types of Onset of Neurosis," *SE* 12:236)

In this passage the Fliess-Freud conception of an increase and discharge of energy in the anxiety neuroses is extended to the theory of libido and explicitly maintained in his later analyses of the menstrual process. As in the famous Zuider Zee analogy, libido is likened to water that is dammed up, then drains or overflows.[15] Yet within the above passage there appears a contradiction: for in the first instance the dam overflows, releasing the libido, described in terms of flooding; but, conversely, the unleashed libido is equated with fire. The overflowing libido can kindle conflicts (*anfachen*, meaning to fan or inflame), in antithesis to flooding, which insinuates not a burning but a dampening or putting out.[16] The ambiguity of these oppositional metaphors suggests that in "Types of Onset of Neurosis" Freud was striving for a language by which to describe what happens to women emotionally at these two crucial points in their reproductive lives: puberty and menopause. And like Camille's narrator, he can't quite explain it.

What contemporary endocrinologists would call a decrease or increase in estrogen-progesterone levels during the menstrual cycle imitates in structure the theory of libido as a buildup then release of libidinal energy. In a sense Freud's concept of shifting levels of libido foreshadowed the current scientific theory of shifting hormone levels—much as Fliess's elaborate diagrams of menstrual periodicity predict current psychological studies on placental protein 14 or platelet 5-HT uptake during a given series of menstrual cycles.[17] Looking backward, though, Freud's scientific explanation of libidinal increase curiously resembled a belief that has persisted since the ancient Egyptians: bloodletting as a version of menstruation.[18] In 1857 a British gynecologist, Edward John Tilt, published his findings on the treatment of the menopause as a disease, ascertaining that menopausal women suffered from a damming-up—not of sexual energy but of menstrual blood itself. He reasoned that because the body was unable to dispose of the excess of blood accumulated during the menopause, woman were prone to severe headaches, indicating a buildup of menstrual blood in the head. Through venesection, or bleeding from the arm, the excess blood would be released and health restored.[19] Thus Tilt, in "bleeding" his menopausally anxious patients, appears to have appropriated the menstrual function, imitating in both theory and treatment what he imagined as a menstrual excess. Venesection mirrors menstruation.

While there is no index term for either John Tilt or venesection in *The Standard Edition*, Freud would certainly have known of the widespread use of venesection as a medical treatment. It is possible that he, in an analogous manner, metaphorically associated the so-called libidinal increase of menopause and puberty with the periodic accumulation and release of menstrual blood. His "unsatisfied and dammed-up libido" (*SE* 12: 236) would then also imitate menstruation—an analogy that is physically accurate in the sense that menstrual blood does build up in the walls of the uterus, flowing forth in the absence of a fertilized egg. Libidinal flow mirrors menstrual flow.

Nor is the passage from "Types of Onset of Neurosis" an isolated example of Freud's associations between menstrual stages and the libido. In *Introductory Lectures on Psycho-analysis* (1916–17), he again observed that in "certain phases of life," namely puberty and menopause, there is a relationship between libido and anxiety due to "a considerable increase in the production of libido" (*SE* 16:403). In this passage he forbore the metaphor. But a few years before his death he returned to it, in language reminiscent both of the 1912 essay on neurosis and of his December 1896 letter to Fliess on menstrual anxiety neurosis: "Twice in the course of individual development certain instincts are considerably reinforced: at puberty, and, in women, at the menopause. We are not in the least surprised if a person who was not neurotic before becomes so at these times. When his instincts were not so strong, he succeeded in taming them; but when they were reinforced he can no longer do so. The repressions behave like dams against the pressure of water" ("Analysis Terminable and Interminable," *SE* 23:226). Once again the fluid image is present, the repressions or inhibiting factors acting like dams against the "pressure of water." One gets the sense, as in the earlier passage, of some heinous liquid forcing itself against the fragile walls of the ego, waiting to crush it—like the pressure of Emma Eckstein's blood against the gauze.

In describing the "person" of this passage, Freud used the male pronoun—except in the specific instance of menopause. In this late essay he continued to suggest a bisexual theory of the instincts, a concept that dates back to the relationship with Fliess. At the same time he insisted, as he had done in *Three Essays on the Theory of Sexuality* (1905), that libido is always masculine: "Indeed, if we were able to give a more definite connotation to the concepts of 'masculine' and 'feminine', it would even be possible to maintain that libido is invariably and necessarily of a masculine nature, whether it occurs in men or in women and irrespectively of whether its object is a man or a woman" (*SE* 7:219).[20] The above passage is from "Transformations of Puberty," a section of *Three Essays* in which Freud enunciated his notion that to achieve sexual maturity the girl must abandon the clitoris. Nowhere in *Three Essays* did he include menstruation as a transformation of puberty; the sexual modifications at this time are, for boys, "the erection of the male organ" and for girls "the lubrication of the vagina," a "lubrication" that appears to have little affinity with menstrual discharge. As the male is the dominant gender, so libido is masculine. I read his insistence on *masculine* as a denial of *feminine,* as a wish to see female sexual energy as passive or inconsequential; men are active, women passive—in their personalities, their sexual responses, and their libidinal constructions.

These various fluid metaphors suggest a hidden parallel between menstrual discharge and libidinal flow; at the same time, the parallel, which is not consciously articulated, remains masked, disguised, unspoken: a metaphoric representation of a physiological/psychological process. The abstract equation between menstruation and dammed-up libido some-how protected Freud from a more direct, personal engagement with its unleashed forces. To talk about an "increased Q" or about "substance" or "stimuli" was a safer alternative than to endure Emma Eckstein's "flood of blood" or her menstruous "scenes." Yet ironically, the architecture of the libidinal drive mirrors that most female of processes, menstruation, whose issue of blood—like libido itself—actively and dynamically builds up and evacuates, in a discharge more steadfast than male ejaculation.

### The Place of Mourning

Laplanche and Pontalis define *discharge* as the "evacuation into the ex-ternal world of the energy brought into this apparatus by excitations of either internal or external origins."[21] *Menstrual* evacuation is a *discharge,* a word used in the late nineteenth century as a synonym for menstruation.[22] No longer vital to the process of reproduction, the unfertilized egg cell is discharged from the uterus. At the end of her flow a woman will often feel empty, like her uterus—both of them forced to return, in the aftermath of menstruation, to an earlier state of things, to a place of mourning.

"Each menstruation," wrote Eric Erikson, "is a crying to heaven in the mourning over a child."[23] Although one might object to Erikson's implication that all wombs want children, he is insightful in his grasp of the repetitious, regressive, and inescapable nature of menstruation. It is not a "child" that one mourns, however, but rather an egg and a uterine lining, engaged in a continuous performance of the womb's Rite-to-Death. Each menstruation is a going backward, a physiological acting out of the compulsion to repeat the uterine buildup and discharge, the movement toward life and the movement toward death.[24] Menstruation is both pre/conception and after/birth, an act performed again and again in the compulsion to welcome the new egg: "For in a profound way life and birth are always bound up with death and destruction."[25]

According to Max Schur, the death instinct and libido are theoretically related: "The metapsychological points of view are interrelated with the concepts of narcissism and the conflict between Thanatos and Eros—the death instinct and libido."[26] James Strachey compared the physiological weakening of the ego during the stages of puberty and menopause with the devastating force of the death instinct; in his view the death instinct is the "most powerful impeding factor of all and one totally beyond any possibility of control" (*SE* 23:212). Puberty, menopause, the death instinct: all of them, Strachey suggested, are impediments to the ego. The passage moves from one term to the next—from an ego weakened by the menopause to an ego weakened by the death instinct—acknowledging a union between them. It would appear that Freud's ideas about the conflict between the overflowing libido and the fragile ego during puberty and menopause are tenuously associated with "the most powerful impeding factor of all," with the death instinct.

Freud first delineated the death instinct in *Beyond the Pleasure Principle* (1920): "If we are to take it as a truth that knows no exception that everything living dies for *internal* reasons—becomes inorganic once again—then we shall be compelled to say that '*the aim of all life is death*' and, looking backwards, that '*inanimate things existed before living ones*'" (*SE* 18:38).[27] This is one of his major statements about the inevitability of death: all living things must die; all life must move toward death. His language here is more vitally conceived than in his scientific inquiries into libido, where his discourse, like libido itself, seems blocked or dammed up, bloodless. This stunning passage, with its Old Testament overtones, its apocalyptic vision, is nonetheless anticipated twenty years earlier in *The Interpretation of Dreams*.

When Freud was six years old his mother first told him about death, about the inescapable return to the earth, dispelling his skepticism with physical proof, the blackish yet rejuvenating scales of her skin: "My mother thereupon rubbed the palms of her hands together—just as she did in making dumplings, except that there was no dough between them—and showed me the blackish scales of *epidermis* produced by the friction as a proof that we were made of earth" (*SE* 4:205). As one has come to expect in Freud's writing, his childhood lesson is preceded by an attendant dream that begins: "*I went into a kitchen in search of some pudding. Three women were standing in it; one of them was the hostess of the inn and was twisting something about in her hand, as though she was making Knödel* [dumplings]" (*SE* 4:204). The women remind him of the three Fates, of whom Atropos was most feared, for she had the power to cut the thread of life.[28] In this reference to the Fates, he dwells on Atropos, the innkeeper: she is "the mother who gives life, and furthermore (as in my own case) gives the living creature its first nourishment. Love and hunger, I reflected, meet at a woman's breast" (*SE* 4:204).

Significantly, Freud's dream opens with a confession of his own hunger: "*I went into a kitchen in search of some pudding*" (*SE* 4:204). In the kitchen Atropos is "twisting something about in her hand," whereas in the commentary his mother "rubbed the palms of her hands together." His re/vision of the dream (from "twisting" to "rubbing") leads him to his mother, who, like Atropos, represents both nourishment (the dumpling) and death (the peeling skin). At this point, Freud's palm reading stops as he suddenly abandons the mother/Fate analysis and turns, by way of the word *Knödel,* from female to male, from breast to phallus, to a discussion of plagiarism among his male colleagues. He thus maintains the pattern observable in the analytic sections of the Dream of Irma's Injection, the Dream of the Red-Nosed Nun, and elsewhere: the encounter with the female ends abruptly, "because the personal sacrifice demanded would be too great" (*SE* 4:206).

The three Fates reappear, in a modified form, in the discussion of *King Lear* in "The Theme of the Three Caskets" (1913). From his reading of mythology and fairy tales Freud had observed a recurrent pattern: a man, forced to choose among three women, is left with death. According to Lacan, the repetitious *three* in Freud's writing generally represents death: "The three women, the three sisters, the three caskets, Freud has since shown us its meaning. The last term is death as simple as that."[29] For Freud, the myth of the three Fates illustrates humanity's impossible desire to displace death with love. The Fates, he concludes, are attributes of the mother: "The mother herself, the beloved one who is chosen after her pattern, and lastly the Mother Earth who receives him [Lear] once more" (*SE* 12:301). Mother Earth or Atropos thus replicates his mother's palm telling and anticipates his theory of the death instinct.[30]

### The Good Blood

Another threefold goddess pre/visions the Three Fates and the Three Caskets: the Great Goddess of ancient mythology, symbol of fertility and power. Critical to the concept of the Great Goddess is her menstruation, recognized and revered by early civilizations as a source of life and death.[31] Perceived as a triad—the Virgin, the Mother, and the Crone—the Great Goddess moves through cyclical phases that reflect such phenomena as the changes in the moon, in the seasons, in the trimesters of pregnancy, in the menstrual cycle. During puberty she represents virginity; her symbols are the color white and the new moon. In her reproductive years she embodies the fullness of female sexuality (the menstruating woman); her color is red, her emblem the full moon. The final phase, the menopause, is comparable to Freud's Atropos; represented by the color black, the menopausal Great Goddess is the witch, the old moon, the Mother Earth who prepares the grave.

The female triad of the mother, the beloved, and death—allegorized in the Greek myth of the Three Fates, in the Shakespearean theme of the Three Caskets, and in the universal concept of a primordial goddess— is of course prefigured in the "introductory dream" of the Language of Flowers (*SE* 5:347). One returns, full cycle, to the female patient, annoyed at the two servants for not having food ready, as they stand in a kitchen in the wake of an approaching flood. Freud's inattention to the menstrual importance of the three women in the introductory dream is analogous to his neglect of female mythology.

To restore menstruation to Freud's childhood story and to his allegorical framework would be to situate his mother within the menstrual structure of the Great Goddess: the white, the red, and the black. His mother (Atropos or the innkeeper) makes white, pure dumplings, or *Knödel*, a substance resembling the macaroni in the passage preceding the Language of Flowers Dream—bland, white, nonthreatening—a symbol that reflects the purified mother who "gives the living creature its first nourishment." Yet Freud, in stationing love and hunger at the breast, has somehow disregarded the primordial feeding ground, the raw and bloody lining of the uterus, emblematized in the text-residue of the Language of Flowers Dream as the raw and bloody meat that had so repelled the "neurotic child" (*SE* 5:346). A menstrual refocusing of Freud's material would identify women's blood (and only secondarily their milk) as the fount of the first nourishment. The breast, that sanctified symbol of female perfection in psychoanalysis and art, is in effect a displacement of oral gratification from the blood-red womb to the milk-white breast—as, in Freud's Dream of the Red Bath, Emma's blood was displaced onto the *matrem*'s purified flesh. A folk belief from the Middle Ages miraculously illustrates this displacement; St. Isodore of Seville allegedly wrote that "after the birth whatever blood has not yet been spent in the nourishing of the womb flows by a natural passage to the breasts, and whitening by their virtue, receives the quality of milk."[32] St. Isodore's fantasy of the good milk anticipates by about thirteen centuries Melanie Klein's observations on infantile gratification; the breast is "instinctively felt [by infants] to be not only the source of nourishment but of life itself."[33] The infant identifies with what Klein calls the "good object," the breast that gratifies; when the breast is taken away, the child experiences the "loss of the love object."[34]

In a challenge to the patriarchy, Clara Thompson imagined what would happen if it were the breast, not the penis, that were the empowered sexual organ: "The type of power would be somewhat different, the breast standing for life-giving capacity rather than force and energy."[35] But imagine if it were the "life-giving capacity" of menstrual blood that were envied—as it has been in individual and societal situations.[36] I would alternatively propose that the primal "good" object of nourishment and life is the womb, an endometrial paradise where all fetal desires are gratified and no one goes thirsty.

Through the menstrual feeding process the mother first prepares food for the unborn child and then discharges the leftovers. The womb is woman's kitchen pot, the basket/casket, symbolized in the Language of Flowers dream by the crockery *"standing upside down to drain"* (*SE* 5: 347)—the source of life when full, but empty, the embodiment of the death instinct.[37] In an eloquent reading of the menstrual process, Chris Knight explores the life-death paradox inherent in woman's "temporary" death: "Women resurrect themselves monthly, just as does the moon, and all animal life is thought to renew itself at the same time."[38]

When menstrual blood, defiled and tabooed since prehistory, is recognized for its primary functions of nurturance and renewal, it must be seen as *good* blood, what Jung alluded to as "creative mana."[39] To slight this good blood and overvalue the breast is both to marginalize the menstrual process within the maternal function and to forget, as many psychoanalytic feminists have, that uterine feeding precedes the acts of conception, pregnancy, parturition, and suckling. This continued omission of menstrual blood in psychoanalytic discourse is a denial of interiority, an abjection of woman's inner space; it is also a rejection of menstruation as significant difference.

My argument, while unorthodox, finds support in the writings of Marie Bonaparte, Otto Rank, and a few others. Bonaparte, in her study of Poe, equated the female body with the womb landscape and nourishment with blood: in the womb existence "it is blood not milk which nourishes the foetus."[40] One analyst tells of a patient who, during menstruation, associated her vagina with an "empty stomach," a metaphor that makes rather clear the veiled connection between bleeding uterus and failed nurturance.[41] Luce Irigaray positions the bond between mother and child in the "primal womb, our first nourishing earth, first waters, first envelopes, where the child was *whole*, the mother *whole* through the mediation of her blood."[42]

The fullest exploration of this theme, though, appears in Otto Rank's *The Trauma of Birth*, a book that was one of the first to privilege the uterus. Rank observed that in the land of fairy tales, there are plentiful wombs where no one is hungry; these wombs are represented in fantasies of "the edible house, or the cage where one is so richly fed that one has finally to escape."[43] Similar fantasies exist among hunters, who associate eating slain animals with uterine nourishment: "The warm blood of slain animals was drunk in direct continuance of the intrauterine nourishment, and the raw flesh was swallowed—lingering echoes of which still reach us in myths of swallowing, where the hero in the interior of the animal eats of its soft parts."[44] In several other, quite specific allusions to menstruation, Rank associated women's bleeding with the lunar phases and with the blood of Christ.[45] But his most spectacular comment on menstruation appeared in a footnote: "Also the typical menstrual difficulties can be understood in this sense, as birth is actually only a menstruation *en masse*. Menstruation, which also 'periodically' continues the womb existence, seems to have been drawn into the general repression of the birth trauma by our civilization."[46] "Birth is actually only a menstruation *en masse*." Although Rank does not flesh out this extraordinary metaphor, one might speculate on its meaning. Menstruation "continues the womb existence," refurbishes the home of the fertilized egg.

In that sense Rank's epigram echoes a curious idea of Havelock Ellis, who had explained menstruation as a "miniature childbirth," as an "abortion of a decidua" (a mucous membrane of the uterus that is discharged during childbirth).[47] It also recalls a belief of the nineteenth-century Mohave Indians, who thought that birth was a "super-menstruation, expelling all at once the accumulated menstrual blood of ten missed periods."[48] Menstruation is birth and massive after/birth; for the placenta, or storehouse of nourishment, is also evacuated from the womb, its function completed and appropriated by the breast. Given the primacy of the womb, then the infant must somehow have "lingering echoes" of the first home—the nurturing *Heim* that shifts from plenitude to loss during menstruation, whose perpetual cycle begins when "blood, glandular secretions, and dead tissue flow from the uterus into the vagina."[49] In menstruation the tissue of the womb, like libido, builds up and flows from the uterus, then builds again, in a continuing cycle of life and death.[50]

In *Life against Death*, Norman O. Brown described men's neurotic flight from death: "If death is a part of life, man represses his own death just as he represses his own life."[51] The repression of death, however, is inextricably connected to the repression of menstruation, of the bleeding mother. As men have feared death, they also have feared menstruation for its intimations of death and difference, a difference so threatening as to require control through injunctions, taboos, and punishment. I am convinced that the denial of the female throughout the centuries is reflected in the denial of the female within psychoanalytic theory; to entertain the power of menstrual blood is to unveil the unbearable and invite one's own annihilation.

## Notes

1. Sigmund Freud, *The Complete Letters of Sigmund Freud to Wilhelm Fliess*, ed. Jeffrey Moussaieff Masson (Cambridge: Harvard University Press, 1985), 142–44.

2. Ibid., 161. James Strachey discusses the relevance of the term $Q$ in the appendix to volume 1; Q appears in two forms, the first of which is "Q in flow" (*SE* 1:392). For an application of the dynamics of buildup and flow in Freud's early work, see "Project for a Scientific Psychology" (*SE* 1:283–343), written in 1895 in anticipation of collaboration with Fliess. In one representative sentence Freud writes that the excitation "which has left the *facilitation* behind is no doubt *discharged*—precisely as a result of the facilitation, which, indeed, *increases* permeability" (*SE* 1:301, emphasis mine).

3. Henri F. Ellenberger discusses the history of the term *libido* from 1905 until 1914 in *The Discovery of the Unconscious* (New York: Basic Books, 1970), 504–12, claiming that Freud took it from Herman's *Libido and Mania* (1903). J. Laplanche and J.-B. Pontalis, however, are less certain of its origins. Freud may have taken it from Moll, the author of *Untersuchen über die Libido Sexualis* (1898); see *The Language of Psycho-analysis*, trans. Donald Nicholson-Smith (New York: Norton, 1973), 239. Calvin Hall defines *libido* as "sexual energy," refined in Freud's later writings to mean "the form of energy which is used by the life instincts," in *A Primer of Freudian Psychology* (New York: New American Library, 1954), 58.

4. Masson, *Letters*, 216.

5. Ibid., 215.

6. Laplanche and Pontalis, *Language of Psycho-analysis*, 239–40.

7. Jacques Lacan, *The Seminar of Jacques Lacan, Book 2: The Ego In Freud's Theory and in the Technique of Psychoanalysis 1954–1955*, trans. Sylvana Tomaselli, ed. Jacques-

Alain Miller (1978; New York: Norton, 1988), 265. Shoshana Felman quotes and repeats Lacan's statement in *Jacques Lacan and the Adventure of Insight* (Cambridge: Harvard University Press, 1987), 144, 159. According to Michael Clark, Lacan interpreted Freud's libido not as the sexual instinct but as an energy; its sexual coloring is a color of emptiness (couleur-de-vide) suspended in the light of a wound (une béance). The "béance," or wound, has definite menstrual connections, as we have elsewhere observed. See Michael Clark, *Jacques Lacan: An Annotated Bibliography* (New York: Garland, 1988), 1:231.

8. Carl G. Jung, *The Collected Works of C. G. Jung*, ed. Herbert Read, Michael Fordham, and Gerhard Adler, trans. R. F. C. Hull, Bollingen Series, no. 20 (Princeton: Princeton University Press, 1979), 5:20–24. See also Jung's essay "The Language of Dreams," 18:461–94. Otto Rank understood myths to be "a mass dream of the people," while Karl Abraham defined myth as "a retained fragment from the infantile psychic life of the race" resembling the dream, or "the myth of the individual." See Otto Rank, *The Myth of the Birth of the Hero*, trans. F. Robbins and Smith Ely Jelliffe (1909; New York: Robert Brunner, 1952), 7; and Karl Abraham, *Dreams and Myths*, trans. William A. White (New York: Journal of Nervous and Mental Disease Publishing Company, 1913), 72.

9. In the Babylonian myth of creation, for example, Marduk cuts open his mother and makes her blood flow into secret places, while in the Greek myth of Persephone the water nymph Cyane is turned from living blood to clear water. See *The Curse*, 188–90. See also the relationship between water, menstruation, and the sacred snake, in Chris Knight, *Blood Relations: Menstruation and the Origins of Culture* (New Haven: Yale University Press, 1991), 486–93.

10. Wilhelm Reich, quoted in Janine Chasseguet-Smirgel and Béla Grunberger, *Freud or Reich?: Psychoanalysis and Illusion*, trans. Claire Pajaczkowska (London: Free Association Books, 1986), 141.

11. See Carl G. Jung, *Psychology of the Unconscious*, trans. Beatrice M. Hinkle (New York: Moffat, Yard, 1916), 139; and Otto Fenichel, *The Psychoanalytic Theory of Neurosis* (New York: Norton, 1945), 541.

12. Marie Bonaparte, *Female Sexuality*, trans. John Rodker (1949; New York: International Universities Press, 1953), 66.

13. See Emily Martin's insightful critique of menstrual metaphor as a negative image of "production gone awry, making products of no use, not to specification, unsalable, wasted, scrap," in *The Woman in the Body* (Boston: Beacon Press, 1987), 47.

14. For a feminist treatment of the menopause see *The Curse*, 213–39. See also Paula Weideger, *Menstruation and Menopause* (New York: Alfred A. Knopf, 1975); and Geri L. Dickson, "A Feminist Poststructuralist Analysis of the Knowledge of Menopause," *Advances in Nursing Science* 12 (1990): 15–31.

15. Freud used a similar buildup/draining configuration in his well-known description of the function of the ego: "Where id was, there ego shall be. It is a work

of culture—not unlike the draining of the Zuider Zee" (*New Introductory Lectures on Psycho-analysis, SE* 22:80).

16. "Die unbefriedigte und gestaute Libido kann wieder die Wege zur Regression eröffnen und dieselben Konflikte anfachen"; in Freud, "Über neurotische Erkrankungstypen," *Studienausgabe Band 6* (Frankfurt am Main: Fischer Taschenbuch Verlag, 1982), 223–24.

17. See M. Julkunen, J. Koistenen, J. Sjöberg, E. M. Rutanen, T. Wahlström, and M. Seppälä, "Secretory Endometrium Synthesizes Placental Protein 14," *Endocrinology* 118 (1986): 1782–86; and W. W. Tam, Mo-yin Chan, and P. H. Lee, "The Menstrual Cycle and Platelet 5-HT Uptake," *Psychosomatic Medicine* 47 (1985): 352–62.

18. See James Lewton Brain, "Male Menstruation in History and Anthropology," *Journal of Psychohistory* 15 (1988): 311–23. Brain traces the menstrual implications of venesection from Egypt and Rome into modern times, including references to the Wogeo, the Elizabethans, and others. There is one sentence on Freud, Fliess, and nasal bleeding, 318.

19. Edward John Tilt, *The Change of Life in Health and Disease*, 2d ed. (London: n.p., 1857), 28–29; see our discussion in *The Curse*, 179–81.

20. Certain women analysts were to revise the concept of libido as masculine. As early as 1925, Helene Deutsch affirmed the presence of a *feminine libido;* see Helene Deutsch, "The Psychology of Women in Relation to the Functions of Reproduction," in *The Psychoanalytic Reader: An Anthology of Essential Papers with Critical Introductions*, ed. Robert Fliess (1925; New York: International Universities Press, 1973), 194. Similarly, Ruth Mack Brunswick viewed the girl's passive libido as being "called forth at her menses"; at that phase of development the libido is aimed at the father "in an intensification of the oedipal libido position which we may now call feminine." Ruth Mack Brunswick, "The Preoedipal Phase of the Libido Development," *Psychoanalytic Quarterly* 9 (1940): 303.

21. Laplanche and Pontalis, *Language of Psycho-analysis*, 121.

22. James Hastings, *A Dictionary of the Bible* (New York: Scribners, 1899), 2:24.

23. Eric Erikson, "Womanhood and Inner Space," in *Identity: Youth and Crisis* (New York: Norton, 1968), 278.

24. The language of this sentence is a deliberate echoing of Freud's memorable defense of the death instinct in *Beyond the Pleasure Principle* (1920), *SE* 18:38–61. For a synopsis of the death instinct in Freud's work, see Laplanche and Pontalis, *Language of Psycho-analysis*, 97–103.

25. Erich Neumann, *The Great Mother*, trans. Ralph Manheim, Bollingen Series, vol. 47 (1955; Princeton: Princeton University Press, 1972), 153. One authority from the early 1940s took an unusual position, contending that the lining of the womb was a death force rather than a life force and that the function of menstruation was to rid the system of cancer-causing estrogen. B. Zondek, cited by Isodor Silbermann, "A Con-

tribution to the Psychology of Menstruation," *International Journal of Psycho-analysis* 31 (1950): 258.

26. Max Schur, *Freud: Living and Dying* (New York: International Universities Press, 1972), 369.

27. For an excellent discussion of *Beyond the Pleasure Principle* as it relates to Anne Sexton's "The Death Baby," see Diana Hume George, *Oedipus Anne: The Poetry of Anne Sexton* (Urbana: University of Illinois Press, 1987), 164–85.

28. See Karl Kerenyi's discussion of Atropos the "Inevitable," in *The Gods of the Greeks* (London: Thames and Hudson, 1951), 31–32; see also Edith Hamilton, *Mythology* (New York: Mentor, 1940), 43. Freud's death instinct has often been referred to as the "Thanatos theory," although the term does not appear in Freud's writings. Thanatos, the last brother in a triad signifying death, would provide a male analogue to Atropos. See Jacques Desautels, *Dieux et myths de la Grèce ancienne* (Quebec: Les Presses de l'Université Laval, 1988), 112; and Pierre Grimal, *Dictionnaire de la mythologie Grècque et Romaine* (Paris: Presses Universitaires de France, 1958), 447.

29. Lacan, *Seminar Book 2*, 157.

30. Madelon Sprengnether and I have independently recognized the interconnection among the Fates, the innkeeper, and the death instinct. In Sprengnether's reading these associations anticipate Freud's "extended and convoluted meditation on separation from the mother and the role of the death instinct in *Beyond the Pleasure Principle*," whereas in mine the Fates and the dumplings point to the menstrual aspect of uterine death. See Sprengnether, *The Spectral Mother: Freud, Feminism, and Psychoanalysis* (Ithaca: Cornell University Press, 1990), 124. For my discussion of Freud's "allegory of the feminine" in the casket theme, I am indebted to Kenneth Maurice Reinhard and Julia Reinhard Lupton, "Shapes of Grief: Freud, *Hamlet*, and Mourning," *Genders* 4 (1989): 61–64.

31. See *The Curse*, 162–69, 263. For further discussion of the *menstrual* aspects of the Great Goddess, see, among others: Elizabeth Gould Davis, *The First Sex* (New York: G. P. Putnam's Sons, 1971); Mary Daly, *Gyn/ecology: The Metaethics of Radical Feminism* (Boston: Beacon Press, 1978); M. Esther Harding, *Woman's Mysteries* (New York: Pantheon, 1955); Wolfgang Lederer, *The Fear of Women* (New York: Grune, 1968); Neumann, *The Great Mother;* Monica Sjöö and Barbara Mor, *The Great Cosmic Mother* (San Francisco: Harper and Row, 1987); and Barbara G. Walker, *The Woman's Encyclopedia of Myths and Secrets* (New York: Harper and Row, 1983). One particularly useful resource for information on the tripartite goddess is Anne Carson, *Feminine Spirituality and the Feminine Divine: An Annotated Bibliography* (Trumansburg, New York: Crossing Press, 1986).

32. Quoted by Charles T. Wood, "The Doctor's Dilemma: Sin, Salvation, and the Menstrual Cycle in Medieval Thought," *Speculum* 56 (1981): 719.

33. Melanie Klein, "A Study of Envy and Gratitude," in *The Selected Melanie Klein*, ed. Juliet Mitchell (1955; Harmondsworth, England: Penguin Books, 1986), 211.

34. Melanie Klein, "The Psychogenesis of Manic Depressive States," in *The Selected Melanie Klein,* 142.

35. Clara M. Thompson, *Interpersonal Psychoanalysis: The Selected Papers of Clara M. Thompson,* ed. Maurice R. Green (New York: Basic Books, 1964), 243.

36. Bettelheim speculates that "childbearing and menstruation were once viewed as so elevating women that men, out of envy, imposed unpleasant taboos." Bruno Bettelheim, *Symbolic Wounds: Puberty Rites and the Envious Male* (New York: Collier, 1962), 137. The male envy of menstruation is developed in chapter 9, "The Bleeding Body and Male Desire."

37. In some cultures, the life-giving attributes of the menstrual process are recognized. Among people in a Turkish village, for instance, menstruation "signals the possibility of life," although it also can represent "life's corruptibility"; see Carol Delaney, "Mortal Flow: Menstruation in Turkish Village Society," in *Blood Magic,* ed. Thomas Buckley and Alma Gottlieb (Berkeley: University of California Press, 1988), 88.

38. Knight, *Blood Relations,* 493.

39. Jung, *Collected Works* 16:157.

40. Marie Bonaparte, *The Life and Works of Edgar Allan Poe: A Psycho-analytic Interpretation,* trans. John Rodker (1933; New York: Humanities Press, 1971), 332.

41. Marcel Heiman, "Sleep Orgasm in Women," in *Female Psychology,* ed. Harold Blum (New York: International Universities Press, 1977), 290. The stomach-uterus metaphor is relevant to Freud's first notation to Fliess on periodicity: he referred to menstruation as "stomachaches." See Masson, *Letters,* 70, 71n.

 42. Luce Irigaray, *The Irigaray Reader,* ed. Margaret Whitford (Cambridge: Basil Blackwell, 1991), 38–39.

43. See Otto Rank, *The Trauma of Birth* (1924; New York: Robert Brunner, 1952), 96–97, 109–10.

44. Ibid., 211.

45. Ibid., 75, 125. Other psychoanalytic writings have pursued the Christ-menstruation analogy, as in Sarah Kofman's description of the Pieta, which "presents a Virgin holding on her lap a bloodied Christ who conceals the maternal wounds by inscribing them upon his own body." See Sarah Kofman, *The Enigma of Woman: Woman in Freud's Writings,* trans. Catherine Porter (Ithaca: Cornell University Press, 1985), 215. For other references see Marie Balmary, *Psychoanalyzing Psychoanalysis,* trans. Ned Lukacher (Baltimore: Johns Hopkins University Press, 1982), 215; and Havelock Ellis, *Studies in the Psychology of Sex* (1900; Philadelphia: F. A. Davis, 1931), 1:292.

46. Rank, *Trauma of Birth,* 51n.

47. Ellis, *Psychology of Sex* 1:95.

48. George Devereux, "The Psychology of Genital Bleeding: An Analysis of

Mohave Indian Puberty and Menstrual Rites," *International Journal of Psycho-analysis* 31 (1950): 252.

49. *Women's Studies Encyclopedia,* ed. Helen Tierney (Westport, Conn.: Greenwood Press, 1989), 1:120.

50. According to Helene Deutsch, there are close psychological associations between birth, death, and menstruation; many people believe that blood "constitutes the connecting link between death and birth." Helene Deutsch, *The Psychology of Women* (New York: Grune and Stratton, 1944), 1:179.

51. Norman O. Brown, *Life against Death* (New York: Vintage, 1959), 101.

# 5

# *The Blood Taboo*

The menstrual taboo has been called "*the most virulent of all the taboos*."[1] To be tabooed is to be set aside, to be designated as "different" within a cultural construction. For menstruating women, cultural differentiation is determined by the biological fact of their blood—blood that in its potency represents shame, difference, castration, filth, reproductive power, disease, and death to the Other. So rich in psychosexual associations, the menstrual taboo and its surrounding ceremonies would seem an evocative subject for analysis in *Totem and Taboo* (1913), Freud's text devoted to early prohibitions and desires. Instead, one finds there a colorless treatment of this "most virulent" of the taboos, a repression of both women and of menstruation within the text.[2] Although there are references to the menstrual taboo, they are minimal in contrast with other considerations, for example the taboo against rulers or against incest—each of which is informed by Freud's theory of the Oedipus complex.

When, in *Totem and Taboo*, Freud referred to the societal regulation of menstruation, he usually classified rather than explicated this phenomenon, using the models established by Wilhelm Wundt, a social psychologist with whom Freud felt an affinity of purpose even though Wundt's methodology was "*non*-analytic."[3] Thus menstruation is classified as a "temporary taboo" that may be "attached to certain particular states," along with childbirth, war, fishing, and hunting (*SE* 13:20–21). A page later there appears a different classification, involving unexplained prohibitions against persons "charged with a dangerous power, which can be transferred through contact with them, almost like an infection" (*SE* 13:21); this power applies to particular people (rulers, for example) as well as to "all *exceptional* states, such as the physical states of menstruation, puberty, or birth, and to all *uncanny* things, such as sickness and death and what is associated with them through their power of infection or contagion" (*SE* 13:22). Dangerous, infected, powerful—these traits have been associated with menstruating women since Pliny, who cataloged their ominous capacity to wither crops, to turn wine sour, to dull steel, and to drive dogs mad; who claimed that in their presence "a horrible smell fills the air."[4] Yet Freud, although he referred to Pliny's *Natural History* in *Totem and Taboo* (*SE* 13:82), did not allude to his well-known passage on menstruous women.

The catalog continues. Menstruation is also an "unusual situation" that is grouped with men being initiated, women after childbirth, infants at birth, the sick, and the dead (*SE* 13:23). The final type of menstrual taboo, still derived from Wundt, involves those who arouse desire in others: "Dead men, new-born babies and women menstruating or in labour stimulate desires by their special helplessness" (*SE* 13:33). Freud's remarks on menstruation in *Totem and Taboo* are evasive and inconsistent. In the above citations there are no analyses, no speculations, no dialogues with his source of information. On the basis of his readings and not of his psychoanalytic experience, he tediously reiterates Wundt's categories—without questioning the logic of the classifications, without investigating the dread/awe of blood at the core of the prohibition. The menstrual taboo was for Freud a list of words; nowhere in *Totem and Taboo* did he envision the ferocity of these regulations: confinement, flagellation, and painful tattooing are only a few of the rituals that have accompanied women's first blood in many cultures, practices he would have been aware of from his readings.[5] *Totem and Taboo*, so energetic and persuasive in delineating the incest taboo, is, on the subject of menstruation, a mere exercise; menstruation has been "tabooed" from the text.

## The Unclean versus the Hygienic

Only twice in *Totem and Taboo* did Freud specifically address the menstrual taboo. The first is a citation of a passage from *The Golden Bough*. He quotes Frazer: "Among the Monumbos of German New Guinea anyone who has slain a foe in war becomes thereby 'unclean'—the same term being applied to women who are menstruating or in child-bed" (Frazer, qtd. in Freud, *SE* 13:40). Later Freud expanded the concept of "woman unclean," offering an explanation for the menstrual taboo: "The countless taboo regulations to which the women in savage communities are subject during menstruation are said to be due to a superstitious horror of blood, and this is no doubt in fact one of their determinants. But it would be wrong to overlook the possibility that in this case the horror of blood also serves aesthetic and hygienic purposes, which are obliged in every case to cloak themselves behind magical motives" (*SE* 13:98). Understating the "superstitious horror of blood" from which taboos are often said to originate, he posited another justification: the restrictions serve "aesthetic and hygienic purposes" within the community. His postindustrial defense of early regulations suggests that he too may have regarded menstruating women as unclean—a view in keeping not only with the hygienic concerns of the twentieth century but also with the prohibitions of countless other traditions.[6] The Trobianders of British New Guinea, on the other hand, are exceptionally relaxed about menstruation; menstruating women reportedly cleanse themselves without ceremony in the same water hole that supplies the village water.[7]

The emphasis on cleanliness in *Totem and Taboo* acts as a sophisticated reinforcement of menstrual injunctions. Freud had argued that the hygienic aspects of taboo are cloaked behind magic; I would suggest the converse—that an excessive attention to hygiene often hides the arcane disgust for menstrual blood.[8] The argument from hygiene, common in anthropological accounts of early societies, in Judaism, in European literature, and in modern menstrual taboo—in the antiseptic nature of advertisements for "sanitary" napkins, for example—veils a fear of menstrual blood, of its reminder of castration and death.

Frazer, though, emphatically rejected cleanliness as the motive for menstrual restrictions in early cultures, contending that menstrual regulations originated instead from the "deeply engrained dread which primitive man usually entertains of menstruous blood": "He fears it at all times but especially on its first appearance; hence the restrictions under which women lie at their first menstruation are usually more stringent than those which they have to observe at any subsequent recurrence of the mysterious flow."[9] In "The Seclusion of Girls at Puberty" Frazer described, in exacting detail, the kinds of restrictions imposed on menarcheal girls in various cultures: confinement in the dark; impoundment in unbearably hot cages; separation from sunlight for seven years; long periods of fasting; being kept in one position, without moving, for days at a time; flagellation.[10] Freud, in *Totem and Taboo*, seemed unwilling either to contemplate the severity of these cultural taboos or to attribute them to men's fear of women's bleeding; yet Frazer's *Totemism and Exogamy* (1910) and *The Golden Bough* (1911–12) were the major sources for the ethnological data in *Totem and Taboo*.[11]

Nor did Freud pursue the taboos against women in Judeo-Christian tradition—the ageless prohibitions against intramenstrual intercourse and more general contact. Although in *Moses and Monotheism* (*SE* 23:3–137) he looked closely at other aspects of Hebrew ritual, he was altogether silent on the significance of the *mikvah*, the bath of purification required of orthodox Jewish women.[12] Under Jewish law menstruating women are *niddah* (in a state of pollution); "unclean" and thus unfit for sexual intercourse; "unclean" and therefore required to participate in the purification ritual called the *mikvah*.[13] According to Leonard Swidler, the word *niddah* means "banishment"; the *niddah*, or "menstruant," was associated with uncleanliness and "the most loathsome impurity." [14] Swidler summarizes the various injunctions against menstruating women under rabbinical law: restrictions against eating with others, against touching, against entering the synagogue, against lighting Sabbath candles, against sexual intercourse.[15]

## The Intercourse Taboo

Clearly, menstrual taboos, particularly the avoidance of sexual intercourse during a woman's cycle, are cross-cultural matters; they have been observed among the Hindus, among the peoples of New Guinea, among Southern Californians.[16] And, if no regulations existed at all, many people are still likely to abstain from intercourse during menstruation, influenced by the general belief that such behavior is messy or unhealthy. Given the prevailing cultural attitudes, given his antipathy for Emma Eckstein's menstrual "scenes," one could hardly expect Freud to have championed the universal eradication of the menstrual intercourse taboo. On the other hand, he was the inventor of psychoanalysis, the man whose therapy was envisioned to release women and men from their neuroses—from the psychic blockages that prevented them from achieving full sexuality. Mary Chadwick, in her observations on the intercourse taboo, presented the case quite clearly: "Thwarted sexual desire, even when not consciously admitted or recognized, constitutes a reason for a great deal of the physical and psychological restlessness of the menses, with the gathering momentum of tension and subsequent release." [17]

Any investigation of menstruation and psychoanalysis must finally confront Freud's silence concerning the menstrual intercourse taboo—which in Judaic tradition included the five-day period and also the seven days following it (Lev. 15:19–33). Swidler claims that the period of abstinence would sometimes be increased in the case of sporadic bleeding; if a spot "as large as a mustard seed" should appear, seven additional "clean" days were added. [18] A menstrually regular Jewish woman bound by cultural regulations against intercourse would thus be prohibited for at least twelve days, or 40 percent of the month, from discharging her libidinal energy. She would also have negative feelings about her sexuality, knowing that she was considered unclean, or *niddah*. [19]

Freud's response to the prevalent taboos against menstruation was to disregard them—not only the taboos of Judaism but also of the Christian middle class; of preindustrial societies; of his sexually repressed female patients, many of them Jewish. He thus contradicted one of the basic tenets of his theory of sexuality: for the sexual denial explicit in these regulations is irreconcilably opposed to the psychoanalytic argument that sexual repression encourages neurotic symptoms. Freud, as well as other analysts, believed that the rejection of sexual intercourse could have particularly dangerous consequences for hysterical or neurotic women; as early as 1897 he wrote to Fliess that "the discharge of sexual excitation for the most part removes the possibility of hysteria." [20] It follows that a woman acting in compliance with menstrual injunctions would be more prone to anxiety; yet Freud as analyst never questioned the prevalent menstrual regulations, which were potentially damaging to a woman's libidinal economy (and to that of the man who kept vigil during the days of restriction). In resisting an examination of the psychological problems generated by menstrual regulations, Freud, as doctor and analyst, inadvertently fostered their continuation.

## The Odor of Blood

Freud's best-known analysis of the menstrual taboo concerned mankind's repression of olfactory odor in favor of visual stimuli. This speculation, suggested in his remarks on Lady Macbeth (1895), appeared as well in a paper delivered at a meeting of the Vienna Psychoanalytic Society in 1909.[21] In that paper he talked of a patient who got pleasure from the "strong-smelling secretion" between his toes, a pleasure that would include anal, vaginal, and, I assume, menstrual odor. "Many get enjoyment from the vagina's odor," he remarked, while at the same time asserting the opposite reaction—that for others the odor is "unbearable." This attraction to smell, which "belongs among those impulses which are for the most part repressed," is related to "*nose eroticism*," a charged term that to my knowledge Freud used only this one time, and one with strong Fliessian innuendos.[22]

Although Freud alluded to the theory of the repression of smell in a number of texts, it received its fullest treatment in *Civilization and Its Discontents* (1930), where nasal stimuli are explicitly associated with menstruation. As in *Totem and Taboo*, so in *Civilizations and its Discontents*, the notion of the "unclean" fired Freud's imagination. In a two-page footnote he narrated his menstrual parable of why men now walk on two feet.[23] According to the fable, men once took pleasure in the intense odors of menstruating women; but as society matured, they stood up, replacing nasal stimuli with more permanent, visual ones.[24] This "organic repression" resulted in the taboo on menstruation, which was "a defense against a phase of development that has been surmounted" (*SE* 21:99n). It was only after men walked upright, at a distance from their genitals, that the olfactory stimuli weakened and civilization, endowed with a sense of the hygienic, began.[25] Freud then walked on, still in the footnote, to the offensive smell of *excreta;* the menstrual taboo was left behind. His neglect of the menstrual taboo placed him in a similar stance to the fabled Upright Man; like his ancestor, he too rejected the originary appeal of vaginal/menstrual odor as he psychoanalytically charted the evolution of human development from smell to sight.[26] Freud's parable of early men turning their noses away from the putrid genitalia strangely parallels his having turned away from Emma Eckstein's nose and from Fliess's theory of the nose and its relationship to the female genitals. Further, the Myth of the Upright Man replicates the structure of a number of his dream interpretations—the Dream of Irma's Injection, the Dream of the Red Bath, the Dream of the Red-Nosed Nun. Freud approached the female, contemplated the aroma, then moved on/up to other (male/intellectual) matters.

*The Blood of Defloration*

Freud's most striking appraisal of the menstrual taboo appeared in "The Taboo of Virginity" (1910), an essay in which he analyzed the ritual of defloration: the ceremonial rupturing of the hymen, usually at puberty, by someone other than the intended bridegroom. The virginal blood under discussion is thus twofold: the blood from the broken hymen and the blood of menstrual discharge. Since menstrual blood is itself taboo, the blood of defloration in certain cultures would also be dangerous because equivalent; the pubescent girl is therefore frequently "deflowered" by some designated functionary who is immune to possible contagion (*The Curse*, 31–32).[27] Many societies do not distinguish between menstrual and hymeneal blood, the age of menarche coinciding with preparations for marriage; according to Paula Weideger, "the classic responses to menarche and to 'losing' one's virginity are so similar that they are virtually identical."[28] Menstruation and defloration tend to reinforce each other, as Karl Abraham suggested in his discussion of female castration: "For both processes are connected with loss of blood and thus resemble an injury; this injury reinforces the castration complex in women."[29] The similarity between menstrual and hymeneal blood is nicely demonstrated in one of Freud's anecdotes about an impotent husband who, on his wedding night, poured red ink on the nuptial linens to deceive the housemaid (*SE* 9:121). It is not clear, though, from Freud's account, whether the man wanted the housemaid to think that he had succeeded in deflowering his bride or that his potency was irrelevant because the bride got her period, preventing consummation.

In "The Taboo of Virginity" Freud took into account (as he did not in the later text, *Totem and Taboo*) the violent and sadistic nature of cultural injunctions against menstruation: "Primitive people cannot dissociate the puzzling phenomenon of this monthly flow of blood from sadistic ideas. Menstruation, especially its first appearance, is interpreted as the bite of some spirit-animal, perhaps as a sign of sexual intercourse with this spirit. Occasionally some report gives grounds for recognizing the spirit as that of an ancestor and then, supported by other findings, we understand that the menstruating girl is taboo because she is the property of this ancestral spirit" (*SE* 11:197). The "monthly flow," Freud acknowledged, is related in preliterate societies to sadism and to the male fear of blood, although he did not explore the implications of this fear but instead reversed his position: "Other considerations, however, warn us not to over-estimate the influence of a factor such as the horror of blood" (*SE* 11:197).[30] No, it is neither uncleanliness nor fear of blood but female sexuality *in general* which men fear, said Freud, in what is perhaps his strongest statement on the mysterious power of women:

> Wherever primitive man has set up a taboo he fears some danger and it cannot be disputed that a generalized dread of women is expressed in all these rules of avoidance. Perhaps this dread is based on the fact that woman is *different* from man, for ever incomprehensible and mysterious, strange and therefore apparently hostile. The man is afraid of being weakened by the woman, infected with her femininity and of then showing himself incapable. . . . In all this there is nothing obsolete, nothing which is still not alive among ourselves. (*SE* 11:198–99, emphasis mine)[31]

In later years Freud was to ask his famous question "What does a woman want?"[32] But the question invoked in "The Taboo of Virginity" is even grander: What does woman *mean?* Characterizing the phylogenetic woman as "mysterious," "incomprehensible," "different," "hostile," Freud seems to have arrived at the notion of female difference through the images of menstruation that serve as prelude to the question of female sexuality: "puzzling," "monthly flow of blood," "sadistic," "bite." His contemplation of an unrepressed, menstruating woman has opened up his discourse, propelled him into a speculation on her abject nature that is rare in his works, rivaled perhaps only in his reports to Fliess about Emma Eckstein.

In "The Taboo of Virginity" Freud perceived women's *difference*, signified by their gendered blood. Primitive man, he speculated, was "infected with her femininity," a phrase that strikingly foreshadows the description of the contagious menstruating woman that will appear without analysis in *Totem and Taboo:* "all *exceptional* states, such as the physical states of menstruation, puberty or birth . . . and what is associated with them through their power of infection or contagion" (*SE* 13:22).[33] But in the virginity piece Freud appeared to be, like his savage ancestors, a bit awestruck by women's difference, admittedly concerned about their capacity to infect, contaminate, defile, perhaps to castrate.[34]

In initially proposing men's horror of blood as an explanation for the menstrual taboo, Freud acknowledged women's difference—only to take it away. Consistent with his avoidance of female sexuality in his interpretation of dreams, he retreated from the question of menstrual difference, apologizing for having strayed from his subject: "The general taboo of women throws no light on the particular rules concerning the first sexual act with a virgin" (*SE* 11:199).[35] Freud thus withdrew from the fear-of-woman hypothesis, shifting to a discussion of female frigidity and "envy for the penis" (*SE* 11:204). The oedipal pattern reasserted its supremacy, engulfing with it the possibility of a separate, female emphasis.

Although Freud, in the 1890s, had on occasion identified with the act of menstruation, recording its patterns among the women of his household, this focus is rare. In his writings on menstruation, he established certain patterns of resistance, repeated frequently enough to reveal a structure of denial—a denial of menstruation, a denial of the seduction theory, a denial of interpretation. In his resistance to Emma Eckstein's bleeding, he blamed Emma for her prolific nasal blood, which in Fliessian theory was analogous to the blood of female periodicity. In his interpretation of dreams, he tended to disregard the menstrual images of redness or fluid in favor of some other, male-oriented reading. In his theories of libido and the death instinct, menstrual structures and associations were more apt to break through—but on a submerged level in which menstruation is not consciously acknowledged—as it is not in his elaborate discussions of primitive taboo.

As we turn, in Part 2, to the theories of male analysts, Freud's neglect of the menstrual/maternal will be to some extent challenged: by Claude Dagmar Daly, Hermann Nunberg, and other men who either expanded upon his concepts or who modified such fundamental theories as castration anxiety and the Oedipus complex in order to incorporate menstruation into their deliberations. Of these male theorists, it was Daly, through his discovery of the menstruation complex, who most aggressively advanced the menstrual cause, claiming that menstruation, a crucial aspect of female sexuality, had been repressed and disclaimed—not only by patients and poets but also by the institution that Freud built.

### Notes

1. Claude Dagmar Daly, "The Psycho-biological Origins of Circumcision," *International Journal of Psycho-analysis* 31 (1950): 233.

2. Peter Gay notes a similar neglect of women in *Totem and Taboo* in Freud's remarks on devouring; see Peter Gay, *Freud: A Life of Our Time* (New York: Norton, 1988), 335. For a discussion of Freud's neglect of the preoedipal mother in *Totem and*

*Taboo,* see Madelon Sprengnether, *The Spectral Mother: Freud, Feminism, and Psycho-analysis* (Ithaca: Cornell University Press, 1990), 86–105.

3. See Freud, "Preface," *Totem and Taboo, SE* 13:xiii. Freud cited two of Wundt's works: *Mythus und Religion* (1906) and *Elemente der Volkerpsychologie* (1912).

4. Pliny, *Natural History,* trans. H. Rackham (Cambridge: Harvard University Press, 1961), book 7:549.

5. Freud frequently quoted Sir James George Frazer's *Taboo and the Perils of the Soul* (London: Macmillan, 1911), and Alfred Ernest Crawley's *The Mystic Rose: A Study of Primitive Marriage* (London: n.p., 1902). Both sources contain detailed discussions of female initiation rites at puberty.

6. These prohibitions cross all geographical and theological boundaries. In *The Koran,* the sacred book of Islam, it is written of menstruating women: "They are a pollution. Separate yourselves therefore from women and approach them not, until they are cleansed"; see the translation by J. M. Rodwell (London: Dent, 1953), 363. Barbara G. Walker cites St. Jerome: "Nothing is so unclean as a woman in her periods; what she touches she causes to become unclean"; in *The Woman's Encyclopedia of Myths and Secrets* (San Francisco: Harper and Row, 1983), 642. In a Catholic handbook for Irish priests, menstruating women are considered to be polluted and "unclean," though not so unclean as to be denied the sacraments, in D. M. Prumner, *Handbook of Moral Theology,* trans. G. W. Sheldon (Cork, Ireland: n.p., 1963), 270. An Indian woman during her periods is *asaucha,* or unclean. Among many communities she is, on the first day of her period, considered "an untouchable pariah." See Benjamin Walker, *Hindu World: An Encyclopedic Survey of Hinduism* (London: Allen and Unwin, 1968), 2:61.

7. See Bronislaw Malinowski, *The Sexual Life of Savages in North Western Melanesia* (London: Routledge and Kegan Paul, 1982), 144.

8. According to William N. Stephens, the greater the taboo, the more attention is given to cleanliness; see "A Cross-cultural Study of Menstrual Taboos," *Genetic Psychology Monographs* 64 (1961): 385–416.

9. Sir James George Frazer, "The Seclusion of Girls at Puberty," *The Golden Bough* (London: Macmillan, 1913), 1:76. Claude Dagmar Daly, in his major anthropological essay, announced his "complete agreement" with Frazer's theory of menstrual taboo and the male fear of blood; see Daly, "The Role of Menstruation in Human Phylogenesis and Ontogenesis," *International Journal of Psycho-analysis* 24 (1943): 156.

10. Frazer, *The Golden Bough,* 1:22–100.

11. Because "The Seclusion of Girls at Puberty" was not published until shortly before *Totem and Taboo,* Freud would not have had access to the extraordinary material on menstrual taboo. He did, however, quote extensively from Frazer's *Taboo and the Perils of the Soul* (1911), a volume that contained the chapter "Women Tabooed at Menstruation and Childbirth." Although Frazer's research was of value to Freud, the two men never acknowledged their similar interests. Frazer "refused to read Freud

or any reviewers of his works"; see John B. Vickery, *The Literary Impact of "The Golden Bough"* (Princeton: Princeton University Press, 1973), 10. Freud, on the other hand, claimed that Frazer "effected little towards elucidating the problems of totemism" (*An Autobiographical Study, SE* 20:67).

12. There are purificatory bathing rituals following menstruation in other cultures as well. See, for example, Devereux's careful account of the elaborate bath required of Mohave women, a bath that in some cases lasted forty days. George Devereux, "The Psychology of Genital Bleeding: An Analysis of Mohave Indian Puberty and Menstrual Rites," *International Journal of Psycho-analysis* 31 (1950): 246–47.

13. For information on menstruation and Judaic law see Louis M. Epstein, *Sex Laws and Customs under Judaism* (New York: Ktav Publishing, 1948); Alice Laffey, *An Introduction to the Old Testament: A Feminist Perspective* (Philadelphia: Fortress Press, 1988); Leonard Swidler, *Women in Judaism* (Metuchen, N.J.: Scarecrow Press, 1976); Arthur Waskow, "Feminist Judaism: Restoration of the Moon," in *On Being a Jewish Feminist,* ed. Susannah Heschel (New York: Schocken, 1983), 261–72; and Isser Yehuda Unterman, "Family Purity: Its Wide Implications," reprinted in *Israel Magazine* 4 (Jan. 1972): 68–74. For information on Freud's Judaic background as it generally affected his psychoanalytic formulations, see David Bakan, *Sigmund Freud and the Jewish Mystical Tradition* (Princeton, N.J.: D. Van Nostrand, 1968); Ken Frieden, *Freud's Dream of Interpretation* (Albany: State University of New York Press, 1990); Theodor Reik, *Pagan Rites of Judaism* (New York: Farrar, Straus, and Giroux, 1964); Emmanuel Rice, *Freud and Moses: The Long Journey Home* (Albany: State University of New York Press, 1991); Marthe Robert, *From Oedipus to Moses: Freud's Jewish Identity,* trans. Ralph Manheim (Garden City, N.Y.: Anchor, 1976); Estelle Roith, *The Riddle of Freud: Jewish Influences on His Theory of Female Sexuality* (London: Tavistock, 1987); and Yosef Hayim Yerushalmi, *Freud's Moses: Judaism Terminable and Interminable* (New Haven: Yale University Press, 1991).

14. Swidler, *Women in Judaism,* 135. Roith quotes a source that defines *niddah* as the "place of rot," in *Riddle of Freud,* 99.

15. Some commentators have looked beyond the negative rituals to those that celebrate menstruation. Arthur Waskow urges the celebration of women's "life-moments"—menstruation, nursing, menopause—as a way to revitalize the feminist element in Judaism. See Waskow, "Feminist Judaism,' " 261–72. See also the interpretation of the Jewish sabbath as a celebration of the menstrual goddess, in Penelope Shuttle and Peter Redgrove, *The Wise Wound: Eve's Curse and Everywoman,* rev. ed. (1978; New York: Grove Press, 1986), 218–22.

16. For a cross-cultural perspective see Stephens, "Menstrual Taboos"; and Karen Ericksen Paige and Jeffery M. Paige, *The Politics of Reproductive Ritual* (Berkeley: University of California Press, 1981). For information on the intercourse taboo in India and in New Guinea, see, respectively, Narendra Nath Bhattacharyya, *Indian Puberty Rites* (1968; Calcutta, India: Munshiram Manoharlal, 1980); and Alma Gott-

lieb, "Menstrual Cosmology among the Beng of Ivory Coast," in *Blood Magic: The Anthropology of Menstruation*, ed. Thomas Buckley and Alma Gottlieb (Berkeley: University of California Press, 1988), 59. For information on a study of 960 Californians, only half of whom had ever experienced sex during menstruation, see Karen Paige, "Women Learn to Sing the Menstrual Blues," *Psychology Today*, Sept. 1973, 43–44. For an overview on the intercourse taboo see *The Curse*, 18–27.

17. Mary Chadwick, *Woman's Periodicity* (London: Noel Douglas, 1933), 143.

18. Swidler, *Women in Judaism*, 133.

19. Helene Deutsch found "the widespread taboos against cohabitation with menstruating women, [and] the Jewish custom of purificatory baths" to be significant in sexual prohibitions. See Helene Deutsch, *The Psychology of Women* (New York: Grune and Stratton, 1944), 1:153. A study done in the 1980s claims that because of the negative attitudes in the larger culture, Jewish women performing the *mikvah* are already predisposed to feelings of menstrual unworth. See Sheila Siegel, "The Effect of Culture on How Women Experience Menstruation: Jewish Women and *Mikvah*," *Women and Health* 10 (1985–86): 63–74.

20. Sigmund Freud, *The Complete Letters of Sigmund Freud to Wilhelm Fliess*, ed. Jeffrey Moussaieff Masson (Cambridge: Harvard University Press, 1985), 275. Freud made similar observations elsewhere. For example, in *Studies in Hysteria* he described a case of "anxiety neurosis which originated from sexual abstinence and had become combined with hysteria" (*SE* 2:260). See also *Three Essays on the Theory of Sexuality* (*SE* 7:162–63).

21. Freud and Breuer (1895) presented Lady Macbeth's hand washing as symptomatic of a compulsion for cleanliness during puberty (*Studies in Hysteria, SE* 2: 245n). In "Some Character Types Met with in Psycho-analytic Work" Freud referred more fully to Lady Macbeth's red bath: "She washes her hands, which are blood-stained and smell of blood, and is conscious of the futility of the attempt" (*SE* 14:319, 324). The 1909 paper on smell was recently discovered by E. James Lieberman and published as "Freud and Fetishism: Previously Unpublished Minutes of the Vienna Psychoanalytic Society," ed. and trans. Louis Rose, *Psychoanalytic Quarterly* 57 (1988): 146–66.

22. Rose, "Freud and Fetishism," 156–57. Freud's essay "Fetishism" (1927) begins with a comment on the nose as fetish: a patient had made a fetish out of the "shine on the nose [*Glanz auf der Nase*]" (*SE* 21:152). See also *Three Essays on the Theory of Sexuality* (1905), where Freud discusses fetishes attached to a foot or shoe, noting that "it is only dirty and evil-smelling feet that become sexual objects" (*SE* 7:155n).

23. Laura Zakarin reads the footnotes as passages that connect for Freud the beginnings of "history" with the repression of menstruation. Drawing parallels among menstrual isolation, the containment of excreta, and Freud's historical periodicity, she suggests that *Civilization and Its Discontents*, in its challenge of the patriarchy, "is

itself a figure for the menstrual," 22. Laura Zakarin, " 'Having Her Time': The Question of Woman, History, and Periodicity in Freud's *Civilization and Its Discontents*," University of California, Irvine, 1991.

24. Freud was to maintain this position concerning the disappearance of menstruation as a sexual stimulus; in his last volume he commented on the evolutionary "transformation in the relationship between female menstruation and male excitation" in "An Outline of Psychoanalysis" (*SE* 23:186). For a treatment of the interconnections among the olfactory, the visual, and modern menstrual taboo, see Ann Treneman, "Cashing in on the Curse," in *The Female Gaze: Women as Viewers of Popular Culture*, ed. Lorraine Gamman and Margaret Marshment (Seattle: Real Comet Press, 1989), 154–55.

25. Ferenczi expressed similar interests in the psychoanalytic effects of olfactory stimuli; see his theory of the connection between smell, upright posture, and the development of capitalism in Sándor Ferenczi, "The Ontogenesis of the Interest in Money," in *First Contributions to Psycho-analysis*, trans. Ernest Jones (1916; New York: Brunner/Mazel, 1980), 319–31.

26. According to Gallop, "Freud links this privilege of sight to the degradation of smell, and ties the whole problematic to sexual difference," an insight she attributes to Michele Montrelay; see Jane Gallop, *The Daughter's Seduction* (Ithaca: Cornell University Press, 1982), 27–28. See also Mary Jacobus, *Reading Women: Essays in Feminist Criticism* (New York: Columbia University Press, 1986), 112. In numerous other instances Freud privileged the eyes: in their response to beauty, they are a major stimulus for adult eroticism (*SE* 7:209); men's terror of Medusa's head is "linked to the *sight* of something" ("Medusa's Head," *SE* 18:273, emphasis mine). I discuss the menstrual implications of the Medusa legend in chapter 8.

27. Elizabeth Gould Davis claims that "the actual reason for premarital defloration, by whomever performed, goes back to man's ancient fear of woman and the shedding of her blood"; *The First Sex* (New York: G. P. Putnam's Sons, 1971), 161.

28. Paula Weideger, *Menstruation and Menopause* (New York: Alfred A. Knopf, 1975), 157. Clellan Stearns Ford has suggested that the frequent concurrence of menstrual and hymeneal bleeding "may afford a common physiological basis for supposing that sexual experience causes menstruation"; see "A Comparative Study of Human Reproduction," *Yale University Publications in Anthropology* 32 (1945–46): 9.

29. Karl Abraham, "Manifestations of the Female Castration Complex," in *Selected Papers on Psychoanalysis* (1922; New York: Basic Books, 1971), 347.

30. Horney criticized Freud for his inadequate explanation of defloration in this essay and for underemphasizing men's "dread of the vagina"; Karen Horney, "The Dread of Women," in *Feminine Psychology*, ed. Harold Kelman (1932; New York: Norton, 1973), 136–37.

31. Freud's application of taboo to women *in general* is similar to a remark made a decade later by Otto Rank: "The primal taboo is the maternal genital which from

the beginning onwards is invested with ambivalent feeling (holy-cursed)." See Otto Rank, *The Trauma of Birth* (1924; New York: Robert Brunner, 1952), 90n.

32. This remark, recorded by Ernest Jones in 1955, is cited in an editor's note (*SE* 19:244n). As late as 1932 Freud was still attesting, as he had in "The Taboo of Virginity," to the incomprehensible nature of women: "If you want to know more about femininity, enquire from your own experiences of life, or turn to the poets, or wait until science can give you deeper and more coherent information" ("Femininity," *SE* 22:135).

33. Although Freud was confining his associations to early peoples, there were among his contemporaries numerous medical and psychological opinions linking menstruation and disease. Krafft-Ebing's inventory of menstrually related diseases included degenerative disorders of the central nervous system, dysmenorrhea, poor circulation, epilepsy, hysteria, menstrual psychosis, and various other infirmities. See Richard Krafft-Ebing, *Psychosis Menstrualis* (Erlangen: Verlag von Ferdinand Enke in Stuttgart, 1902), 1–28.

34. Being "infected" reveals, according to Mary Jacobus, Freud's fear of castration and of sexual difference. She also notes, like Horney, his minimal attention to menstruation and defloration in "Taboo of Virginity." See Jacobus, *Reading Women*, 115–16.

35. Bettelheim comments about this essay: "In view of Freud's subtle analysis of some major taboos, it is regrettable that he paid so little attention to those of menstruation." Bruno Bettelheim, *Symbolic Wounds: Puberty Rites and the Envious Male* (New York: Collier, 1962), 137.

# Part 2

# Male Analysts

# 6

# *The Menstruation Complex*

Although Freud had minimalized the role of menstruation as an aspect of sexual difference, there were contemporaries in the field who loudly proclaimed, as did Fliess, that menstruation was a fundamental factor in female sexuality. Two years after *The Interpretation of Dreams*, the psychoneurologist Richard Krafft-Ebing (1840–1902) published a curious work entitled *Psychosis Menstrualis* (*Menstrual Psychosis*), in which he summarized previous and ongoing theories about menstruation and mental disorders.[1] The survey is interminable, the authors obscure—men such as Goodman and Sigismund and Schlager and Krieger and Kirn—men whose monographs on psychotic periods and menstrual hysteria have long been put to rest. But *Psychosis Menstrualis*, while of little gynecological or psychiatric value, does at least demonstrate that in the half-century before Freud articulated the unconscious, many neurologists—and one will recall that Freud trained as a neurologist—were examining, as best they could, the impact of menstruation on psychic phenomena.[2]

This second part investigates certain attitudes toward menstruation in the works of male analysts after Freud; for Freud, as founder of psychoanalysis, must be the figure to whom his sons and brothers respond—in disagreement, in justification, or in compromise. Because there were no established psychoanalytic formulations about menstruation, these writers tended to approach the topic through fresh interpretations of mythology, anthropology, literature, and theory. Thus a number of second-generation analysts began to offer alternatives to the oedipal paradigm and to a phallocentric symbolism and to view mythology from a more female-centered perspective.

Of these theorists, it was Claude Dagmar Daly (1884–1950) who offered the most complex and cohesive view of the role of menstruation within psychoanalytic thought. His concept of the menstruation complex, which he saw as preceding the Oedipus complex, was revolutionary in its emphasis on female functions and female aggressiveness. While Freud was seeking a universal explanation for the conflict between father and son, Daly was in search of the primal mother onto whom the son displaces his hatred for the father. Freudian analysis, because it is so exclusively concentrated on the masculine, rarely examined the mother except in the context of her effect on the son. Daly, on the other hand, never successfully located his allegory of women's bleeding within the European cultural tradition. Ignored by the psychoanalytic institution of his own day, Daly rests in obscurity, his menstruating mother a forgotten dream.[3] What is more, menstruation itself is forgotten, repressed even by those psychoanalytic feminists currently investigating the politics of the female body.[4]

Daly's first major contribution to the theory of menstruation was "Hindu-Mythologie und Kastrationskomplex," postmarked Quetta, India, and published in 1927 in the leading psychoanalytic journal *Imago;* it is the only work by Daly cited in *The Standard Edition* of Freud's works (*SE* 24:92). In "Hindu-Mythologie," as elsewhere in his essays, Daly's terminology regarding the menstruation complex is ambivalent; at times it is an image of castration, at times a developmental phase prior to castration anxiety—a phase that links incest to punishment not by genital mutilation but by death.[5] These divergent stages can be reconciled by viewing the menstruation complex as the "kernel," or "nucleus," of the Oedipus complex, whose origin is rearticulated in the later phase.

Further motifs connect Daly's menstruating woman to psychoanalytic paradigms. She is the so-called phallic mother, the mother with a fanta-sized penis, a concept several women theorists have taken to task.[6] More loosely, the term denotes a woman with masculine/aggressive characteristics.[7] Daly's menstruating mother, the object of incestuous desire, is masculinized, made phallic, by the son as a defense against this desire;

attracted to but denying his mother's menstrual blood, he "adorns her with a penis in order that he may retain her as a libidinal object." [8] In her critical placement before oedipal symbolization, the menstruating woman resembles the "preoedipal" mother espoused by Melanie Klein, Ruth Mack Brunswick, and others; she is the boy's object of desire during early infancy (what is called the "positive Oedipus complex") but later the object of repulsion (the "negative Oedipus complex"). [9] In her awesome aggressiveness, the menstruating mother is a modification of the *vagina dentata,* the vagina with teeth, while in her "otherness" she anticipates what Julia Kristeva has called the "abject"—the undesired, the defiled. [10] Daly then seems to use the term *menstruation complex* to theorize the mother in a number of ways: phallic, preoedipal, castrated/castrating, the mother/other. His mother is primal but also aggressive, an object of hatred and retaliation, a negative construct finally fixed, despite efforts to feminize her, within Freud's oedipal structure as an object of her son's ambivalent desire. Enticing, pleasurable, the source of pride, the menstruating mother, as a consequence of her desirability, must ultimately assume the role of Repressor and Castrator.

### The Blood of Kali

As Freud had ascribed to Greek theater his analog for the Oedipus complex, so Daly turned to the Hindu goddess Kali for his menstrual paradigm. Scholars have long regarded Kali to be the retributive goddess; like the Third Fate, she is often represented as a tripartite divinity. In her various manifestations she represents the structural "*co-inherence*" of Creation, Preservation, and Destruction. [11] In some artifacts Kali is depicted as having four arms holding emblems of castration—a bloody sword, a severed head. Or she may be imaged as a maternal cannibal, "crouching in a halo of flames, devouring the entrails of her mate Shiva— the guts strung from the corpse to her mouth like an umbilical cord." [12] She is described as a goddess who "delight[s] in the blood of buffaloes" or who, "dressed in blood red," sails "on a sea of blood." [13] In another depiction she decapitates her offenders, drinks their blood, and throws the severed heads to her companions in spirited play. [14] Yet neither in the above descriptions nor in the numerous accounts of Hindu religion that I have consulted is the blood-dark goddess associated with menstruation; on the contrary, historians almost never make a correlation between

Kali and menstrual blood.[15] One must turn to the spiritual feminists for the unorthodox connection between Kali and menstruation, although here too the analogy is uncommon and the material mostly inaccessible. Barbara S. Walker, one of the few scholars to equate Kali with menstrual blood, notes that the goddess symbolizes "the Ocean of Blood at the beginning and end of the world"; her worshipers bathe in and drink her menstrual blood, saving the bloody rags for healing purposes. In her threeness, her white-red-black configuration, Kali recalls the menstrual symbolism of the Great Goddess.[16] It is probable that Kali's menstrual properties were repressed in traditional Hindu cosmology and in so many contemporary texts for the same reasons that menstruation has been repressed almost universally—out of fear or disgust for women's bleeding. The austere taboos against menstruation in Indian culture would support this hypothesis.[17]

It is likely, though, that the Hindu cultic concepts of Kali and blood that Daly confronted during his residency in India were colored by his particular Westernized orientation; the menstruating Kali is a wish that fulfills Daly's vision of the aggressive woman, a wish verified by the dominant themes of blood and retaliation in Hindu mythology.[18] In his quest for psychic meaning, Daly privileged Kali's repressed menstruation, contracting the multiple metaphors of blood into a mythological bleeder whose thighs lay open the secret hidden for epochs.

Daly described Kali as the goddess of death and blood; her "bloody manifestations" emblematize the menstruation trauma and curtail the possibility for happiness: "The black woman of all mythologies and of our dreams, the mother who first arouses all of our love and passion and then through correction, and the bloody manifestations of her periods, erects a barrier against which men (in whom sublimation has failed) may struggle for the remainder of their days, in order to obtain even a minimum of normal happiness."[19] The adjective *black* in this awesome passage refers to the final stage, *yuga*, or "age of darkness," represented by Kali in her phases of Blackness and Time. According to Mircea Eliade, "Time is 'black' because it is irrational, hard, and pitiless; and Kali . . . is the mistress of Time, of all the destinies that she forges and fulfills."[20] Like Eliade, Daly was reflecting the goddess in her most negative cycle or phase—at the Wrong Time of Month. His vision of Kali and "the bloody manifestations of her periods" was a vision of futility, of the impossibility of overcoming the barriers between the menstruating mother and her doomed son. It is the dark aspect of the great goddess to which Daly, in his attentiveness to menstruation, responded; her attributes of mutilation and blood dramatize the psychoanalytic constructions of castration and the prohibition against incest embodied in the negative Oedipus complex.[21]

Allegedly, Daly once showed a picture of Kali to Freud, although I have found no confirmation for this claim.[22] In his analytic thought, Freud had resisted a female mythology; Daly, critical of Freud's neglect of the "mother goddesses," offered instead, through Kali, a *menstrual* paradigm for sexuality and death.[23] By naming the menstruating mother, he lured the goddess from her hiding place, unveiling her pitiless gaze, exposing her menstrual difference. Perhaps, though, Daly felt ill at ease with his cultural model for the menstruation complex, since he never fully conceptualized the Hindu goddess, as Freud did Moses and the king of Thebes. Through the course of Daly's analytic work, Kali eventually became a secondary figure, remolded, revised—closer in kin to Freud's phallic mother than to the "bloodthirsty and blood-curdling Kali" of Hindu mythology.[24] Although he alluded to the goddess Kali from time to time, her menstrual significance diminished to the point that in 1947 he reprinted an extract from a nineteenth-century paper on Kali in which there is no reference to menstruation.[25] Having journeyed to the source of the most virulent of taboos, Daly averted his eyes from Kali's gaze.

### The Pall of Death

In his best-known essay, "The Menstruation Complex in Literature" (1935), Daly used the methodology of applied psychoanalysis to provide "evidence," through selected works by Poe and Baudelaire, of what he had discovered in Hindu mythology and in dreams: the existence of the menstruation complex. The meaning of the menstruation complex gradually surfaced in Daly's explication of menstrual symbols: the black cat, the bleeding eye, the Red Death, the red-lit casement, and other images. When he attempted to verify its meaning, he chose words reminiscent of the poets whom he was analyzing: "the incest *barrier* (= menstruation trauma) descends like a pall of death, shutting out the pre-historic past." [26]

By examining a handful of Baudelaire's poems, Daly hoped to substantiate his thesis that as a child Baudelaire, attracted yet repulsed by his mother's menstruation, repressed his desires for her, desires that reemerged in the poetry, in images of smell, sickness, blood, and castration.[27] Daly described this sickness or infestation in terms of the displacement of a son's guilt onto the mother: "The woman is transformed into a man with a sword (= penis), and the battle represented is that between the mother and the son, who, exasperated by love, rolls into a ravine (= vagina) which is *infested* with lynxes and ounces (= father) [an ounce is a lynx or snow leopard]."[28]

In "The Menstruation Complex in Literature" Daly stressed two stories, "The Black Cat" and "The Fall of the House of Usher," and mentioned several others to demonstrate his theory of the "*menstruation complex being the nucleus of the oedipus complex.*"[29] He believed that the black cat confirmed the existence of a menstruation complex, a repressed desire for the mother's bleeding vagina. In its shift from male to female, the bloody eye of the cat "(= mother)" replicates the structure of the menstruation complex, showing the displacement of the son's hatred from the father to the mother.

In his analysis of "The Fall of the House of Usher," Daly used a more subtle form of sexual equation, comparing the "red-litten windows" to "the loss of joy which results from the menstruation trauma" and the "pestilent and mystic vapor" to the smell of the mother's vagina.[30] The commentary focuses on the effects of the "secondary incest complex," or brother/sister incest, with Roderick's desire for his sister, Madeline, repeating his desire to reenter his mother's womb. But as one looks more closely at his reading of Poe, one observes a veiling of menstruation in Daly's text, a resistance to what he thought he had uncovered in his own analysis.

### Shutting Out Menstruation

Throughout most of "The Menstruation Complex in Literature," menstruating women are peripheral; Daly's primary concern is for male poets and for male sexuality. The bleeding mother is identified less in her own terms than in terms of the incest barrier she erects against the son, the reminder of his castration and death. Daly's neglect of the sister figure, Madeline Usher, is a further example of his resistance to menstruation. Madeline is the victim of some incurable and undiagnosed disease that had confounded her doctors: "a settled apathy, a gradual wasting away of

the person, and frequent although transient affections of a partially cata-
leptical character were the usual diagnosis."[31] The narrator presents the
symptoms as medical hearsay: this was "the usual diagnosis." Yet Daly, a
psychoanalyst, merely quoted the narrator's innuendos, never uncovering
Madeline's female illness but commenting instead on Roderick's male
"identification with his father = destroyer."[32] Daly thus paralleled Freud,
who had passed over Irma's abdominal problems, Camille's consumptive
bleeding, and his flower-patient's menstrual anxiety; the woman's illness
is negligible, to be measured primarily for its effect on the brother/the
male/the victim/the analyst. Madeline's illness, her *fleurs du mal*, have
no relevance on their own. Daly, in his analysis of "The Fall of the House
of Usher," relinquished the opportunity to discuss female difference in
relation to the menstrual process; he seemed instead to listen to the male
voice, taking his cues from Roderick, from the unreliable narrator, and
from his male-centered reading.[33]

"The Menstruation Complex in Literature" concludes with Poe's
"The Masque of the Red Death," a story that "repeats in dramatic form
the terror and despair occasioned in every human being at the sight and
odor of his mother's menstrual bleeding."[34] Here is the place, in a story
so rich in colors and interiors, for Daly to have gained support for his
theory of the menstruation complex. Although much of his interpretation
is convincing, something is missing in this case—additional evidence,
further exploration, a more open reading of the text. As in his analysis of "The Fall of the House of Usher," so here Daly appears to have
masked his reading of menstruation, possibly as a defense against professional rejection. Poe's black room of death calls for a more explicit
menstrual reading—the womb/tomb/room of the Great Mother, of Kali,
of Atropos, of Madeline.[35]

The special power of "The Mask of the Red Death" (the same can
be said for "The Black Cat" and "The Fall of the House of Usher")
resides in Poe's ability to imagine being shut out, shut off, blocked—
which in psychoanalytic theory would correspond to repression. In its
broadest sense, repression is an obstruction: a barrier or defense against
consciousness through which the subject "attempts to repel, or to confine
to the unconscious, representations (thoughts, images, memories) which
are bound to an instinct."[36] Although Daly had accurately identified repression in his discussion of puberty rites, where taboo restrictions served
to defend men from their own desire for women, he neglected or re-

pressed the concept in his reading of "The Mask of the Red Death." The setting and the characters are sealed, enclosed, encapsulated: the castle is "girdled in" by a wall with "gates of iron." There is means "neither of ingress or egress." [37] Yet despite the precautions, the Red Death invades the sanctuary—in a bleeding death mask, unrepressed, disguised as no one but itself: "His vesture was dabbled in *blood*—and his broad brow, with all the features of the face, was besprinkled with the scarlet horror." [38] The scarlet terror has broken the barricade; the repressed matters of sexuality, menstruation, and death have threatened the ego.

Somewhat surprisingly, Daly perceived the Red Death in masculine terms, as "confirmation of the death-bringing attributes" of the prince's father.[39] One could more readily argue that in the ghastly masquerade, even the gender of death is disguised—that the *he* of Poe's story is the destructive woman or phallic mother, freed from her shackles, who, like a bad fairy or a Scud missile, breaks through the defenses of the ego.

The images of repression in Poe's story are reminiscent of the fairy tale "Sleeping Beauty," in which the phallic mother, in the guise of the uninvited fairy, forces herself into the barricaded castle, announcing that on her fifteenth birthday, the princess would prick her finger on a spindle, bleed, and die. To bleed is to menstruate is to die: Sleeping Beauty's menarcheal isolation fulfills the fairy's prophecy. Mary Chadwick, the first analyst to mark the connections between the Grimms' fairy tale and menstrual taboo, interpreted Sleeping Beauty's long sleep as analogous to early rites of seclusion.[40]

In Daly's work the menstruating mother, initially conceived as a dual figure who entices and denies, arouses instead the sense of being a bad fairy with some good moments. She emerges from a Pandora's box of images: she is erotic, the object of desire, but as a consequence of her desirability, she must take on the role of the Repressor, the Red Death. It was Daly's goal to insert menstruation within the Freudian system. Yet in emphasizing the maternal destructiveness of the menstruating woman, he turned a closed eye toward her other side—her potential for nurturance and renewal.

*Notes*

1. See Richard Krafft-Ebing, *Psychosis Menstrualis* (Erlangen: Verlag von Ferdinand Enke in Stuttgart, 1902).

2. Freud does not mention *Psychosis Menstrualis* in his writings. When he does

refer to Krafft-Ebing he usually condescends, finding his ideas about "sexual bond-age" and the medical aspects of hygiene too "simple" and resenting Krafft-Ebing's reputation for having evoked fantasies of perversion among the moral middle class. See *SE* 7:50, 9:184–85, 11:86, 11:193.

3. What little is known about Daly's life is found in an obituary by J. R. (John Rickman), "Claud Dangar Daly (1884–1950)," in the *International Journal of Psycho-analysis* 31 (1950): 290–91. In the title, Daly's first and middle names are misspelled, as if to highlight Daly's obscurity. Daly was a lieutenant-colonel serving in India, and he was a psychoanalyst, having studied with Freud sometime in 1924 and four years later with Sándor Ferenczi. Rickman claims, without substantiation, that during World War II Daly "had the disappointment of seeing his correspondence with Freud on the Menstruation Complex and some of his own MSS. burnt in the Palace Hotel."

4. In recent studies by Shirley Nelson Garner and Madelon Sprengnether, for example, neither author addresses menstruation in the context of Freud's relation-ship with Fliess and Emma Eckstein, although both are concerned with bleeding. See Shirley Nelson Garner, "Freud and Fliess: Homophobia and Seduction," in *Seduction and Theory*, ed. Dianne Hunter (Urbana: University of Illinois Press, 1989), 86–109; and Madelon Sprengnether, *The Spectral Mother: Freud, Feminism, and Psychoanalysis* (Ithaca: Cornell University Press, 1990).

5. Claude Dagmar Daly, "Hindu-Mythologie und Kastrationskomplex," trans. Peter Mendelssohn, *Imago* 13 (1927): 181, 193–95.

6. In an impressive piece of argumentation Karen Horney interprets the phallic mother as "a convulsive attempt to deny the female genitals"; if one projects onto the mother an imagined penis, then it is possible to deny what is really there: the vagina. See Karen Horney, "The Dread of Women," in *Feminine Psychology*, ed. Harold Kel-man (New York: Norton, 1973), 138. Mary Jacobus makes the point that in Freudian theory the phallic mother is an object of fantasy, both for male analyst and for male patient, erected as a defense against the "paralyzing threat" of castration anxiety. See Mary Jacobus, *Reading Women: Essays in Feminist Criticism* (New York: Columbia University Press, 1986), 119.

7. J. Laplanche and J.-B. Pontalis, *The Language of Psycho-analysis*, trans. Donald Nicholson-Smith (New York: Norton, 1973), 311–12.

8. Claude Dagmar Daly, "The Menstruation Complex in Literature," *Psychoana-lytic Quarterly* 4 (1935): 309.

9. See Ruth Mack Brunswick, "The Preoedipal Phase of the Libido Develop-ment," *Psychoanalytic Quarterly* 9 (1949): 293–319.

10. Julia Kristeva, *Powers of Horror: An Essay on Abjection*, trans. Leon S. Roudiez (1980; New York: Columbia University Press, 1982), 71, 99. Norman O. Brown in-corporates menstruation into his description of the *vagina dentata*: the "jaws of the giant cannibalistic mother, a menstruating woman with the penis bitten off, a bleeding trophy." Norman O. Brown, *Love's Body* (New York: Random House, 1966), 63.

11. Wendell Charles Beane, *Myth, Cult, and Symbols in SĀ-kta Hinduism: A Study*

*of the Indian Mother Goddess* (Leiden, Netherlands: E.J. Brill, 1977), 140. Brown stresses Kali's dualism—her positive, maternal aspect as well as her destructive nature; see C. Mackenzie Brown, "Kali: The Mad Mother," in *The Book of the Goddess: Past and Present*, ed. Carl Olson (New York: Crossroad, 1989), 111–13. Neumann claims that "Kali herself, in her positive and non-terrible aspect, is a spiritual figure that for freedom and independence has no equal in the West"; see Erich Neumann, *The Great Mother*, trans. Ralph Manheim, Bollingen Series, vol. 47 (1955; Princeton: Princeton University Press, 1972), 332.

12. Monica Sjöö and Barbara Mor, *The Great Cosmic Mother* (San Francisco: Harper and Row, 1987), 182.

13. Beane, *Myth, Cult, and Symbols*, 121–23; Heinrich Zimmer, "The Indian World Mother," quoted in Neumann, *The Great Mother*, 152.

14. Brown, "Kali, the Mad Mother," 111–13.

15. Kali is in *no way* associated with menstruation in the following: R. C. Hazra, *Studies in the Purá-nic Records on Hindu Rites and Customs* (Delhi, India: Motilal Banarsidass, 1975); Rita M. Gross, "Hindu Female Deities as a Resource for the Contemporary Rediscovery of the Goddess," in *The Book of the Goddess: Past and Present*, ed. Carl Olson (New York: Crossroad Publishing, 1989), 217–30; Emma Jung and Marie-Louise von Franz, *The Grail Legend*, trans. Andrea Dykes (1960; London: Hodder and Stoughton, 1971); Neumann, *The Great Mother*. The term *menstruation* in not indexed in Beane, *Myth, Cult, and Symbols*, although Beane does refer to the menstruation of Mother Earth in a footnote, 128n. Richard A. Shweder, while he notices that certain facial expressions among Indian women resemble pictorial images of Kali, makes no connection between Kali and menstruation. See "Menstrual Pollution, Soul Loss, and the Comparative Study of Emotions," in *Culture and Depression*, ed. Arthur Kleinman and Byron Good (Berkeley: University of California Press, 1985), 187–88. Despite its title, Shweder's article has surprisingly little to say about menstruation.

16. Barbara G. Walker, *The Woman's Encyclopedia of Myths and Secrets* (San Francisco: Harper and Row, 1983), 491–92, 636. Penelope Shuttle and Peter Redgrove make a passing reference to Kali as the Scarlet Woman of menstrual cults, in *The Wise Wound: Eve's Curse and Everywoman*, rev. ed. (New York: Grove Press, 1986), 194. One of Daly's colleagues also saw Kali as a menstrual goddess. In the worshipping of Asana, the Divine Mother, red earth is "used in the worship of the Hindu Goddess Kali, in place of menstrual Blood." See Sarasi Lal Sakar, "A Study of the Psychology of Sexual Abstinence from the Dreams of an Ascetic," *International Journal of Psycho-analysis* 24 (1943): 175.

17. See in particular Narendra Nath Bhattacharyya, *Indian Puberty Rites* (1968; Calcutta, India: Munshiram Manoharlal, 1980).

18. I discussed this absence with Chandra Agrawal, a scholar and feminist who studied Hindi at Lucknow University in India. In Agrawal's experience, Kali is not related to menstruation in *any* region of India; she is not a childbearing mother, and

therefore menstruation is not relevant. Agrawal agreed with my suggestion that Daly had modified Kali's blood for his own theoretical purposes. From an interview with Dr. Chandra Agrawal, Morgan State University, Mar. 1990.

19. Daly, "The Menstruation Complex in Literature," 308.

20. Mircea Eliade *Images and Symbols*, quoted in Beane, *Myth, Cult, and Symbols*, 141.

21. For further discussion of castration and menstruation, see chapter 8.

22. Claude Dagmar Daly, "The Psycho-biological Origins of Circumcision," *International Journal of Psycho-analysis* 31 (1950): 232.

23. See Daly's critique of *Totem and Taboo* and Freud's neglect of the mother goddesses in "The Role of Menstruation in Human Phylogenesis and Ontogenesis," *International Journal of Psycho-analysis* 24 (1943): 164.

24. The double-blooded description of Kali is Carl Jung's, in *The Collected Works of C. G. Jung*, ed. Herbert Read, Michael Fordham, and Gerhard Adler, trans. R. F. C. Hull, Bollingen Series, vol. 20 (Princeton: Princeton University Press, 1979), 10:519. There are two other references to Kali in Jung's works, both having to do with the mother archetype; see vol. 9, part 1, p. 82 and 16:302.

25. Claude Dagmar Daly, "Hindu Treatise on Kali," *Samiksa* (1947): 191–96.

26. Daly, "The Menstruation Complex in Literature," 339.

27. Daly does not associate Baudelaire's famed title *Fleurs du Mal* with menstruation; although it translates as *Flowers of Evil*, one could just as readily interpret the title as *Flowers of (Female) Sickness*, as we did in *The Curse* (191).

28. Daly, "The Menstruation Complex in Literature," 308. See also Marie Bonaparte's *The Life and Works of Edgar Allan Poe: A Psycho-analytic Interpretation*, trans. John Rodker (1933; New York: Humanities Press, 1971). The Bonaparte book was published in 1933, two years before "The Menstruation Complex in Literature," although Daly claims that he was unaware of it when writing his essay; see "The Menstruation Complex in Literature," 340n.

29. Daly, "The Menstruation Complex in Literature," 340.

30. Ibid., 330.

31. Poe, *The Works of Edgar Allan Poe*, ed. Hervey Allen (New York: Walter J. Black, 1927), 278. Catalepsy is a "morbid state in which there is a waxy rigidity of the limbs. . . . The subject is irresponsive to stimuli; the pulse and respiration are slow, and the skin is pale." From *Stedman's Medical Dictionary*, 24th ed. (Baltimore: Williams and Wilkins, 1982).

32. Daly, "The Menstruation Complex in Literature," 329.

33. Numerous critics examine Poe's narrator in "The Fall of the House of Usher"; see, for example, G. R. Thompson, *Poe's Fiction* (Madison: University of Wisconsin Press, 1973); Ronald Bieganowski, "The Self-consuming Narrator in Poe's 'Ligeia' and 'Usher,'" *American Literature* 60 (1988): 175–87; and Daniel Hoffman, *Poe Poe Poe Poe Poe Poe Poe* (1972; New York: Paragon House, 1990), 295–316.

34. Daly, "The Menstruation Complex in Literature," 338.

35. In her reading of "The Masque of the Red Death," Marie Bonaparte pays closer attention than Daly does to menstrual images. The setting of "anal black" drapery and blood-red windows recalls the mother's menstruation, which are linked to blood-spitting and anal eroticism. Bonaparte, *Poe*, 517.

36. J. Laplanche and J.-B. Pontalis, *The Language of Psycho-analysis*, trans. Donald Nicholson-Smith (New York: Norton, 1973), 390.

37. Poe, *Works*, 191.

38. Ibid., 194.

39. Daly, "The Menstruation Complex in Literature," 338.

40. See Mary Chadwick, *Woman's Periodicity* (London: Noel Douglas, 1933), 92. The menstrual implications of "Sleeping Beauty" and other fairy tales were raised again in 1976 in the original edition of *The Curse* and in Bruno Bettelheim's *The Uses of Enchantment: The Meaning and Importance of Fairy Tales* (New York: Vintage, 1976). *The Curse* citations are from *Grimm's Household Tales, with the Authors' Notes*, trans. Margaret Hunt (Detroit: Singing Tree, 1968).

# 7

## *The Menstrual Epoch*

In 1943, at the peak of his argumentative powers, Daly wrote his most dynamic defense of the menstruation complex in a knotted essay entitled "The Role of Menstruation in Human Phylogenesis and Ontogenesis."[1] It was postmarked London, home of Ernest Jones and death place, five years earlier, of Sigmund Freud. Freud's ghost pervades the essay, which is on one level an attempt to "undeceive" Freud of the origins of male ambivalence toward the mother.[2]

The duality of the title—phylogenesis and ontogenesis—is structurally reproduced throughout the essay. The primary duality of evolutionary origins versus individual development resounds through other oppositions: male/female; menstrual/oedipal; part 1/part 2; consciousness/amnesia; odor/repression. Underlying these polarities is son/father or Daly/Freud. For it is only after Freud's death that Daly was able to piece together a consistent defense of the menstruation complex in a field of language that both mirrored and refracted Freud's anthropological works, most specifically his *Totem and Taboo*. That Daly had been analyzed by Freud and that they presumably had corresponded about menstruation would tend to account for the weight given Freud in "The Role of Menstruation in Human Phylogenesis and Ontogenesis." But there is a deeper, personal dissatisfaction in Daly's discourse—his disappointment over Freud's views of female sexuality and his repression of menstruation within the institution of psychoanalysis.

Although Daly had for years viewed his own work as a completion rather than as a critique of Freud, his posture in "The Role of Menstruation in Human Phylogenesis and Ontogenesis" had become progressively antagonistic.[3] Having first admitted his own error (Daly had confused "heat" in animals with menstruation), he then catalogued Freud's, beginning with Freud's misreading, in *Civilization and Its Discontents* (1930), of Daly's theory of the menstrual taboo: "The notes do not convey my personal view nor am I in agreement with them."[4] Still another debate involved Freud's view of menstruating women as passive and potentially traumatized—as opposed to Daly's vision of the menstruating mother as an active influence in the formation of the human psyche. He believed that Freud was closer to the truth about menstruation in "The Taboo of Virginity," where he had associated the male fear of blood with sadistic taboos against menstruating women. Daly struck again and again at what he considered to be the inconsistency of Freud's views of female sexuality, divergent views that "can hardly be reconciled."[5]

Daly, like many other inventive analysts and anthropologists, speculated as to the origins of the menstrual taboos.[6] Freud, as one recalls, had identified the birth of the menstrual taboo with man's standing on two feet, his nose at a safe distance from the genitals. In a phrase that can perhaps be read as sarcastic, Daly called Freud's hypothesis "man's erection from the earth."[7] Consistently maintaining that menstrual odor was a phylogenetic source of pleasure, Daly, in an imaginative reversal of Freud's Upright Theory, traced the origins of the blood taboo not to an evolutionary shift in posture but rather to an inhibition of desire that diffused the erotic impulse—a position he had dramatized in "The Menstruation Complex in Literature" by hypothesizing a community of tabooed women, their enchainment the result of the male need to avoid their "*attractions, olfactory and others.*"[8]

For Daly, Freud's inattention to the blood taboo and its implications signaled a wider error—the neglect of female sexuality itself. Thus Daly attacked *Totem and Taboo* for being "one-sided," too exclusively male; anthropological findings on menstruation, pregnancy, and mothering, he claimed, would also contribute to the theory of the libido. It was Daly's task to correct "the one-sided evolution postulated in *Totem and Taboo* so as to include the role played by female sexuality and the mother goddesses," which, as Freud had admitted, "was there left unexplained." [9]

In his feminization of Freud's myth of the primal horde, Daly reached to the core of sexual difference, placing menstruation at the center of this controversial issue and parodying Freud's famous statement, made in 1932: "We are now obliged to recognize that the little girl is a little man" (*SE* 22:118). On the contrary, Daly charged, boys are boys and girls are girls: "The girl in the positive phase of her Oedipus complex is a little woman just as the boy is a little man, and the fact that she does not menstruate and produce ova is only parallel to the fact that the boy does not produce sperm." [10] Daly demanded a biological distinction between male and female sexuality—little boy is little boy, little girl is little girl—and insisted on a recognition of sexual difference signified by the girl's eventual menstruation.

To correct Freud's one-sidedness Daly retold *Totem and Taboo* in a two-sided narrative where little boys became big boys (they killed the father) and little girls became big girls (they menstruated); thus, he acknowledged but at the same time reconstructed Freud's story of the "primal crime." In Freud's anthropological fantasy, the brothers killed and cannibalistically consumed the father in a ritual that empowered them and enabled them to identify with the father. In their guilt, the sons set up two prohibitions: they banned the killing of the totem-animal, who represented the father; they relinquished "their claim to the women who now had been set free" (*SE* 13:141).

The maleness of Freud's parable is overwhelming. Men murder and commemorate, whereas women are excluded from the mythic totem meal, which does not require a woman's touch. In Freud's phallocentric account of the origin of guilt, women are absent, set apart, suppressed, "set free"; or, as Monique Wittig has observed, social organization for Freud only started after the women had been pushed aside. [11] The women in the myth of the primal crime are eliminated, although we earlier saw how Freud, prompted by menstrual language, portrayed the phylogenetic woman as "incomprehensible and mysterious" ("The Taboo of Virginity," *SE* 13: 198–99).

In a 1932 rewriting of Freud, Daly had tentatively envisioned a female participation in the overthrow of the father. The women, enticed by the younger men of the tribe, "entered the fray and assisted in the downfall of the Primal Leader, joining in the cannibalistic orgy that followed."[12] In "The Role of Menstruation in Human Phylogenesis and Ontogenesis," however, the part played by women is less forceful; although at times they are characterized as being willful or aggressive or castrating, their primary representation is that of victim. Threatened with castration from the father, the men of the prehuman horde isolate their women, starve them, and treat them with "endless cruelty."[13]

Pursuing his debate with Freud, Daly reexamined the role of women in the establishment of the incest prohibition. In *Totem and Taboo* Freud had argued that following the murder of the father, "his" women became sexually vulnerable, the objects of brotherly desire: "Each of them would have wished, like his father, to have all the women to himself" (*SE* 13: 144). What curbed their barbaric lust was the prohibition against incest, a restriction fundamental to the preservation of order within the now leaderless community. Thus the brothers established "the law against incest, by which they all alike renounced the women whom they desired and who had been their chief motive for despatching their father" (*SE* 13: 144). But for how long? How long would it take, despite communal laws against incest, for the first savage brother to rape and brutalize the first "free" sister? In "The Role of Menstruation in Human Phylogenesis and Ontogenesis" Daly raised this very question, conjecturing that Freud's explanation for the incest taboo was developmentally incorrect, that an event that occurred far *later* in prehistory than the primal crime was responsible for the suppression of incest. Like Freud's primal crime, so Daly's menstrual sequel was "necessarily largely hypothetical."[14] Daly speculated that all did not go smoothly for the leaderless brothers: "We assume that with the break-down of the leaders' authority a phase of regression took place and that an increase of rivalry and lust followed these revolutions within the hordes, resulting in a heightening of the aggressive component of the sexual instinct."[15] Rivalry, lust, sexual aggression— Daly's assessment of communal male behavior was far less complacent than Freud's conception of the guilt-ridden totem ritual, meant to recall father-murder and to repress mother-lust.

So dominated by "chemotropic sexual stimuli" were the lustful hordes, alleged Daly, that the very species was threatened with extinction.[16] Control did come, but very slowly, through the collective action the hordes had learned following the primal crime. Thus Daly returned to Freud (to the earlier text and the earlier event), to Freud's primal crime, seeking authorization from and reconciliation with the father in advent of his own remarkable departure: into the female future, into the menstrual epoch.[17]

### Shifting Gender

Toward the middle of "The Role of Menstruation in Human Phylogenesis and Ontogenesis," the structure shifts from male to female; the words that both echo the title and introduce the second half are "the role of female sexuality in human psychic evolution."[18] Crucial to Daly's menstrual argument was the hypothesis of psychic evolution, an idea first formulated in 1922 and developed into a full-scale theory in "Pre-human Psychic Evolution."[19] Daly suggested, "as a hypothesis only," that it was in the prehuman (or posthorde) epoch that menstrual bleeding became an influence on men, arousing their "aggressiveness towards rivals and tenderness and possessiveness towards their females."[20]

He further contended, on rather shaky grounds, that during the horde epoch females reached puberty "about the fourth or fifth year, since there is nothing to show that any interruption in sexual development had so far taken place."[21] Indirectly challenging Freud's theory of a latency period— a cessation of sexual development from the oedipal phase until puberty— Daly was suggesting that in the early evolutionary stages, women, like animals, menstruated from childhood to the menopause, in an uninterrupted stretch.[22] He more plausibly contended that in phylogenetic development, menstruation was the primary factor in the prohibition of incest; initially operative during women's first and most dangerous menstrual period, the menstrual taboo was "gradually extended to include the avoidance of all females at their periods."[23] Although early menstrual taboos have been "lost in racial amnesia," their remnants can be detected in clinical material, particularly in dreams and fantasies related to castration anxiety and the repression of incest.[24]

Unfortunately, Daly's best-crafted essay, "The Role of Menstruation in Human Phylogenesis and Ontogenesis," disintegrates shortly after it reaches the menstrual epoch. Unable to sustain his menstrual vision, Daly returned to male matters, ending with an apology to his readership: "The *digression into the female menstruation complex* in the foregoing paragraphs has led us away from our main object, which was to show the influence which *man's reactions* to female sexuality have had upon human psychic evolution."[25] Reluctant to give the menstruating sisters equal time, he retreated to the brothers and to Freud's "one-sided" view of sexuality; menstruation was no longer to be the "main object" of his research. Daly, who had so stalwartly championed the idea of the menstruation complex, eventually withdrew from a full engagement with that issue.

His last publication, "The Psycho-biological Origins of Circumcision" (1950), reaffirmed his conviction of the menstruation complex, but here subordinated to an investigation of the origins of circumcision. In this final essay Daly seems to have diluted the significance of the menstruation complex, stating, for example, that the ancient custom of being washed in blood before battle did not allude to menstrual blood but to "all blood in the unconscious [that] is associated with oral destruction, aggression, and the fear of being killed, eaten and castrated by the father." [26] The potency of the earlier image of Kali, goddess of menstruation, is diminished in his efforts to de/gender the menstruation complex, in what appears to be a modification of theory designed to placate the psychoanalytic institution.

### Unveiling Menstrual Blood

Regardless of strategy, Daly was unable to convince his colleagues of the relevance of menstruation to female development. Menstruation, with its long cultural history of avoidance and taboo, was a buried topic not only among the "primitive" peoples in Daly's primal myth but also within the psychoanalytic institution. Nor was Daly apt to win supporters with his remark that the idea of the menstruation complex posed a threat to the masculine, homosexual quality of psychoanalytic theory, which has been intellectually limited by the historic repression of women.[27] Because the emerging psychoanalytic movement dismissed or ignored Daly's work, he lacked a discourse community to critique and substantiate his theories.[28]

Despite this rejection by the institution, Daly continued to pursue the wish that is the kernel of "The Menstruation Complex in Literature"—a wish not articulated until the last sentence, in small print, in a footnote: "The aim of the above paper is to show that, when the psychoanalytic inhibitions in relation to the theory of the menstruation complex are overcome, it will be discovered everywhere in literature, art, mythology, etc., by those who are willing and able to see." [29] In his efforts to transcend the cultural inhibitions against menstruation, Daly urged his colleagues to "unveil" rather than to suppress the past, to expose the dread of women that had imprisoned the male psyche: "Perhaps it is the central task of psychoanalysis to unveil [*entschleiern*] the ontogenetic and phylogenetic past, through whose aftereffects the human race is still subjugated."[30] The figurative language that Daly uses to uncover the awesome, menstruating mother (*unveil; lurks; deep level*) is appropriate to both menstruation and psychoanalysis. Menstruation is a process that is deeply hidden or veiled; psychoanalysis is a process that hopes to explore the depths, to lift the veil of repression so long associated with the veiled sexuality of brides and with the hidden faces of Islamic women. Entangled in the dilemma of positioning the menstruating mother within a hostile psychoanalytic structure, Daly ultimately resorted to male theory (the phallic mother) and a male perspective, leaving behind him very few disciples to recast and demasculinize the argument.[31]

Supposedly, Sándor Ferenczi wrote to Daly in 1928, predicting that psychoanalysis would come to recognize the importance of menstruation: "I am sure your work will sooner or later find the appreciation it certainly deserves."[32] Now, more than sixty years later, the psychoanalytic response to Daly remains mute—limited to a footnote here, a few sentences there, and three essays, two of which I have incorporated into this book.[33]

Despite Daly's failure to create a female-focused theory of menstruation, despite his overwhelmingly negative perceptions of menstrual sexuality, he is significant to contemporary feminist and psychoanalytic theory, particularly in his insistence that women's vitality, signaled by their menstruation, has been historically and culturally suppressed. In unveiling the menstruating mother, Daly contributed to an understanding that menstruation is not a periodic psychosis but a biological/psychological process that men, in their fear of female eroticism, have been compelled to deny.

### Notes

1. Claude Dagmar Daly, "The Role of Menstruation in Human Phylogenesis and Ontogenesis," *International Journal of Psycho-analysis* 24 (1943): 151–70.

2. Ibid., 152.

3. See Claude Dagmar Daly, "Hindu-Mythologie und Kastrationskomplex," trans. Peter Mendlessohn, *Imago* 13 (1927): 175, 192–96, in which he proposes to extend rather than to criticize Freud.

4. Daly, "Role of Menstruation," 156. See *Civilization and Its Discontents* for

Freud's two references to Daly's research on the menstruation taboo and the repression of sexual excitement (*SE* 21:99–100, 105–6). For Daly's confusion of estrous ("heat") with menstruation, see in particular "Pre-human Psychic Evolution: A Hypothetical Theory of the Psychological Evolution in Pre-glacial, Glacial, and Early Post-glacial Epochs," *British Journal of Medical Psychology* 12 (1932): 273–86.

5. Daly, "Role of Menstruation," 156.

6. In an intriguing theory that gives women credit for originating the menstrual taboos, Chris Knight speculates that at one time women developed synchrony (menstruating at the same time) and went on a collective "sex strike" (the menstrual intercourse taboo) to regulate the hunting patterns of the community. Chris Knight, *Blood Relations: Menstruation and the Origins of Culture* (New Haven: Yale University Press, 1991).

7. Daly, "Role of Menstruation," 157.

8. Claude Dagmar Daly, "The Menstruation Complex in Literature," *Psychoanalytic Quarterly* 4 (1935): 316. Paula Weideger praises Daly's work on the origins of the menstrual taboo and on his attributing sexual feelings to menstruating women. See Paul Weideger, *Menstruation and Menopause* (New York: Alfred A. Knopf, 1975), 102.

9. Daly, "Role of Menstruation," 164. In the 1920s Otto Rank, like Daly, challenged the Freudians for the neglect of female sexuality within psychoanalysis, which gave "prominence to the man's point of view." Otto Rank, *The Trauma of Birth* (1924; New York: Robert Brunner, 1952), 36–37. Like Rank, Daly was unable to find a safe place within the psychoanalytic hierarchy.

10. Daly, "Role of Menstruation," 167.

11. Monique Wittig, "The Straight Mind" (1980), quoted by Jane Flax in "Mother-Daughter Relationships: Psychodynamics, Politics, and Philosophy," in *The Future of Difference*, ed. Hester Eisenstein and Alice Jardine (New Brunswick: Rutgers University Press, 1985), 26.

12. Daly, "Pre-human Psychic Evolution," 284.

13. Daly, "Role of Menstruation," 163.

14. Ibid., 162.

15. Ibid.

16. Ibid.

17. Daly did not use the term *menstrual epoch*. I have borrowed it from two early theorists, Havelock Ellis and Richard Krafft-Ebing, the latter's German word being *Menstrualepoche*. Both used the phrase to identify the menstrual or premenstrual period but *not* to indicate an evolutionary stage. See Richard Krafft-Ebing, *Psychosis Menstrualis* (Erlangen: Verlag von Ferdinand Enke in Stuttgart, 1902), 1; and Havelock Ellis, *Studies in the Psychology of Sex* (Philadelphia: F. A. Davis, 1910), 1:103.

18. Daly, "Role of Menstruation," 161.

19. In "Pre-human Psychic Evolution" Daly reconstructed prehistory through a five-stage chronology: the preglacial age (with its abundance of food and sexuality);

the glacial period (characterized by hunger and cannibalism); the horde epoch (in which the male became dominant); the posthorde period of aggression, rivalry, and lust; and last, the human epoch.

20. Daly, "Role of Menstruation," 155.

21. Ibid., 163.

22. In "Three Essays on the Theory of Sexuality" (1905), Freud defines latency as a stage of development, beginning in late childhood and ending in puberty, that marks a decrease in sexual activity. Freud attributes Fliess with the term *period of sexual latency* (*SE* 7:176–79, 178n).

23. Daly, "Role of Menstruation," 163.

24. Ibid.

25. Ibid., 168, emphasis mine.

26. Claude Dagmar Daly, "The Psycho-biological Origins of Circumcision," *International Journal of Psycho-analysis* 31 (1950): 234.

27. Claude Dagmar Daly, "Der Kern des Oedipuskomplexes," *Internationale Zeitschrift für Pschoanalyse* 21 (1935): 171.

28. In their assessment of Daly's obscurity, Shuttle and Redgrove contend that Daly's rejection was due to his "doctrinaire psychoanalytic theory," so full of contradictions that his arguments were easily dismissed; Penelope Shuttle and Peter Redgrove, *The Wise Wound: Eve's Curse and Everywoman*, rev. ed. (1978; New York: Grove Press, 1986), 55. Yet for Daly to have initiated an independent theory of menstruation would have been strategically unsound. The only way he could possibly validate the menstruation complex was to work from inside the institution, under the more general issue of female sexuality.

29. Daly, "The Menstruation Complex in Literature," 340n. This prophetic footnote was deleted when, twelve years later, Daly republished "The Menstruation Complex in Literature" under the revised title "The Mother Complex in Literature"; see "The Mother Complex in Literature," *Samiksa* 1 (1947): 177–90. Although the new title implies a deemphasis of menstruation in favor of a more acceptable, sexualized mother, the actual text shows few alterations. A year later he republished "The Mother Complex in Literature" in an expanded version that extended the literary scope of the original to include H. Rider Haggard, John Keats, and other writers. See "The Mother Complex in Literature," enlarged, *Yearbook of Psychoanalysis* 4 (1948): 204–5.

30. Daly, "Der Kern des Oedipuskomplexes," 418.

31. Karen Horney was Daly's strongest supporter but not a disciple. In "The Denial of the Vagina" Horney cited Daly's "Der Menstruationskomplex" in support of her observation that for young girls, menstruation is a sign that a woman's body is extremely vulnerable; in "The Dread of Woman" she mentioned Daly's work on the goddess Kali. See Karen Horney, *Feminine Psychology*, ed. Harold Kelman (New York: Norton, 1973), 159, 134.

32. Cited by John Rickman, "Obituary of Claud Dangar Daly [*sic*]" *International Journal of Psycho-analysis* 31 (1950): 290.

33. See my essays "Claude Dagmar Daly: Notes on the Menstruation Complex," *American Imago* 46 (1989): 1–20; and, with Julia Reinhard Lupton, "Annotated Bibliography of Claude Dagmar Daly (1884–1950)," *American Imago* 47 (1990): 81–91. See also Sarasi Lal Sarkar, "A Study of the Psychology of Sexual Abstinence from the Dreams of an Ascetic," *International Journal of Psycho-analysis* 24 (1943): 170–75. Sarkar applies Daly's concept of the menstruation trauma to explain sexual abstinence in Hindu monasteries. Of the dozen or more authors who refer to Daly, the most significant are Poul M. Faergeman, "Fantasies of Menstruation in Men," *Psychoanalytic Quarterly* 24 (1955): 1–19; Emilio M. Rodrigue, "Notes on Menstruation," *International Journal of Psychoanalysis* 36 (1955): 329–31; Shuttle and Redgrove, *The Wise Wound;* and Weideger, *Menstruation and Menopause*. I wish to apologize for not having mentioned Weideger's discussion of Daly in my essay "Claude Dagmar Daly: Notes on the Menstruation Complex."

# 8

# *The Gaping Wound:*
# *Menstruation and Castration*

Male theorists, in addressing the relationship between castration and menstruation, have invariably focused their sights on the penis. Although in its technical sense castration means the removal of the testicles, as in gelding, the testicles were so insignificant to Freud that the word is not indexed in *The Standard Edition*. It is the valued penis that informs the Freudian narrative of castration anxiety, with sexual difference being determined by its presence or absence. To summarize the psychoanalytic argument: at an early age, the boy has the misfortune of sighting the girl's so-called lack, her penile deficiency.[1] Her lack or gap makes him feel threatened, for it suggests the possibility of being castrated, like a girl. The girl, who from the beginning is missing this elemental organ, symbolically compensates for her loss, or "castration," by desiring to bear a male child, that is, a child with a penis: "She gives up her wish for a penis and puts in place of it a wish for a child; and *with that purpose in view* she takes her father as a love-object" (*SE* 19:256).[2]

In this chapter I will examine the concepts of certain male analysts who related menstruation to castration anxiety in both men and women. Their views seem to rest on several basic assumptions involving sexual difference. In the case of the male, real or imagined exposure to menstruation reinforces castration anxiety and affects male experiences in other bloody arenas, such as circumcision, defloration, and military combat. For the female, the "wound" periodically reminds her of her castrated state and indicates her failure to conceive the wished-for male child, the word *wound* implying at times menstruation but, more generally, all of the dreaded sexual apparatus below the waist. Woman's gaping wound also makes her a primary object of male fantasy: the Castrating Woman, Kali, and in this chapter, the Medusa.

### Castration and the Menarche

Freud's notion of women as castrated, while it derived primarily from his theory of infantile sexuality, also emerged from his clinical work with female adolescents, among whom he encountered certain fantasies that synthesized castration, circumcision, and menstruation. One will recall Emma Eckstein's "scene" of being circumcised and eating a piece of her labia—an imaginary reenactment of female castration.[3] In "The Sexual Theories of Children" Freud confronted the fantasy of a fourteen-year-old girl who believed that marriage was a "mixing of blood" (*SE* 9: 222–23), a ceremony that would parallel the ritual known as the blood covenant: the male mingling of blood in the affirmation of brotherhood.[4] During her period the girl therefore "made an assault" on a menstruating friend to share in "blood-mixing"—although simultaneously she appears to be acting out her lesbian desire.[5]

In "The Wish to Be a Man," Freud's close associate Hanns Sachs presented one of the earliest and most definitive psychoanalytic arguments about menstruation, castration, and sexual guilt, in the abbreviated case history of a young woman who "saw in the sudden flow of blood a punishment for her misuse of her sexual organs."[6] Although the patient was directly referring to her early foreplay with a male cousin, she was also inferring foreplay with herself, or masturbation, an act frequently associated with menstruation in psychoanalytic writing.[7] During the nineteenth and early twentieth centuries it was not extraordinary for male physicians to take female masturbation into their own hands, performing clitoral castration on pubescent girls who had exhibited tendencies toward self-abuse. In 1865, for example, Dr. Gustav Braun had a young female patient who was incessantly rubbing herself against furniture. He treated this masturbatory tendency and its symptoms by amputating her labia and much of her clitoris.[8] One scholar has insinuated Fliess's sexually focused operation on Emma Eckstein's nose to be a "symbolic clitoridectomy."[9]

For Sachs's patient, the first menstruation was reportedly experienced as a symbolic bite or castration; she fantasized that her penis (and not, as in Emma's "scene," the labia) had been chewed off. In his interpretation Sachs was probably recalling Frazer and Crawley in connecting his patient's biting fantasy with the early belief that "a woman in menstruation has been bitten in the genital organs by some demon."[10] For this terrified, menstruating patient—who wanted a penis, wanted male status, wanted to be a man—menstrual blood was the sign of absence or castration. It is this elemental concept of wishing to be a man that a number of analysts (Karen Horney, Ernest Jones, Clara Thompson, and others) were later to contest.[11]

Many analysts, basing their views on Freud's concept of puberty and menopause as trauma, reaffirmed that the first menstruation was a traumatic experience for pubescent girls, one that exacerbated former feelings of being castrated. Sándor Rado, for instance, linked the adult female's absent penis to fantasies of castration traceable to puberty and even to infancy. These fantasies, he insisted, always included "the idea of her own bloody, injured (mutilated) genital organ."[12] More recently, in the 1970s, Samuel Ritvo used language almost identical to Rado's in describing the adolescent girl's menstrual castration. In its regressive phase, the first menstruation "tends to stir up old anal and castration conflicts," while among neurotic girls, the menarche is tied to "old concerns about genital injury and castration and dissatisfaction with the body image."[13] In each of the examples, menstruation represents damage or absence. The analysts emphasize the girl's castration (being a non/male) to the exclusion of her reproductive capacity (being a female). Women's potential for mature sexuality, signified by their menstrual blood, is annihilated by the theory of menstrual castration.

Another important paper on this subject in early psychoanalytic theory was "Manifestations of the Female Castration Complex" by Karl Abraham, a man who analyzed and influenced three of the major women discussed in this book: Melanie Klein, Helene Deutsch, and Karen Horney.[14] Abraham said that the "wound" contributed to the female castration complex: "The primary idea of the 'wound' is re-animated by the impression created by the first and each succeeding menstruation, and then once again by defloration; for both processes are connected with loss of blood and thus resemble an injury; this injury reinforces the castration complex in women." [15] Here Abraham was implying a cyclical and repetitive interplay between menstrual blood, hymeneal blood, and castration, the link being the psychoanalytic concept of women as injured or castrated—what women analysts were to relate to masochism. [16]

In pursuing Freud's theory that women, as castrated, desire a child to replace the absent penis, a number of analysts interpreted menstrual blood as a sign of absence or loss. A lost baby, a lost penis: on a symbolic level they are equivalent. Thus menstruation, a periodic reminder of castration, is also, logically, a periodic sign of infertility. Karen Horney thought the disturbances of the premenstruum were due to a woman's strong desire for a child, struggling against the realization that in a few days menstruation would arrive, proving conception futile. [17] Deutsch, eloquent on the subject of menstruation and pregnancy, wrote that during puberty, "every menstruation signifies the promise and the loss of a child." [18] "There is one thing that is common in all women," she insisted. "With or without intellectual preparation, knowing or only sensing, the young girl connects menstruation with childbirth." [19]

### "As Ill as His Mother"

For men, the concept of castration anxiety is more terrifying than it would be for women, since men have something to lose that does not cyclically reproduce itself, such as an egg or a uterine discharge. Daly took the theoretically unorthodox position that the menstruation complex impacted on the male dread of castration and that the mother's blood, originally enticing, became repulsive to the male child as he retreated from incestuous desire. [20] I find Daly's explanation for the origins of male castration anxiety more credible than Freud's. If castration is so universally frightening an event, then its terror would more likely derive, as Daly had argued, from having smelled or witnessed women's menstrual blood than from having seen her "lack." For what the Freudian view of castration anxiety lacks is an adequate recognition of how menstrual blood contributes to a male child's fear of being genitally mutilated. Imagine the child who sees blood on his mother's nightgown; imagine the horror of discovering her menstruous rags soaking in cold water or, in more modern times, a sanitary napkin protruding from the bathroom wastebasket. Such visible evidence of women's bleeding would be likely to fan the boy's fear of sexual mutilation far more than his glimpse of a playmate's minuscule clitoris.[21]

On at least one occasion, Freud had hinted at the menstrual origins of castration anxiety. His patient the Wolf-Man, perceiving his mother's menstrual blood to be a wound inflicted by the father during intercourse, assumed that all women are castrated; he also feared that he would be "as ill as his mother," that is, castrated (*SE* 17:78). But with a few exceptions, neither Freud nor his followers acknowledged the menstrual origins of the castration complex. Although the theory found some support from Karen Horney and Sándor Ferenczi, it was primarily disregarded by Daly's contemporaries, probably because he was questioning the very foundation of the Oedipus complex: the fear of castration by the father for having desired the mother-object.

### Catastrophic Bleeding in Men

Another vital aspect of male bleeding involves circumcision, a ritual that in its cutting of the penis resembles castration but that in its genital bleeding resembles menstruation. The physical intent of circumcision is to free the penis from its nest, where it has been lying in risk of infection.[22] After circumcision, the penis is no longer hidden or absent; its phallic presence becomes visible, therefore masculine. Yet to achieve its masculinity it must first be made feminine—exposed, vulnerable, bleeding like a vagina.

Although in some societies the removal of the foreskin is deferred until puberty, at which time it is frequently synchronized with the girl's menarche, Freud and his associates tended to focus on Jewish circumcision, performed at infancy. Jewish children, Freud claimed, frequently equate ritual circumcision with castration.[23] In his view, however, a child's fear of these rituals is almost exclusively related to the powers of the father; it is "the symbolic substitute for the castration which the primal father once inflicted upon his sons in the plenitude of his absolute power" (*Moses and Monotheism, SE* 23:122).

Some rituals of bleeding have had the milder function of reinforcing sex role behavior, of making men uncastrated (masculine) and women subservient (feminine). Daly contended that rituals of blood (the removal of the foreskin but also of the clitoris) were designed to stimulate the heterosexual desire anesthetized during the incest taboo; through removal of the "female" part, or foreskin, and the "male" part, or clitoris, the male became more "masculine" and the female more "feminine" in their sexual identities.[24] The most common female mutilations involve infibulation (sewing up the vulva) and clitoridectomy (the removal of the clitoris). Marie Bonaparte noted the close connection between menstruation and female castration (excision) among people of the North Cameroons; they are beaten by old women at their first menstruation and later excised by the same women.[25] One must stress, though, that these rituals exceed the symbolic, inflicting pain on the initiates—as in circumcisions performed in infancy or at puberty, as in painful defloration, as in the unusual ceremony of subincision.[26]

Herman Nunberg was the Freudian who substantiated the importance of the *mother's* menstruation in Judaic rites of circumcision. Like Freud, Nunberg acknowledged the father's role in circumcision; unlike Freud, he posited a formidable female presence in the act of male genital bleeding.[27] Nunberg analyzed a Jewish father who was uncertain about having his infant son circumcised. The indecision helped to recall the patient's own fears of castration, revealed in a series of dreams and fantasies: bleeding nipples (what Nunberg interpreted as aggression against the mother) and a bloody headdress or bandage (what he interpreted as menstrual bleeding). Menstruation, which evokes fears of castration and recollections of circumcision, would be a significant factor in castration anxiety.

Nunberg's patient got sick while witnessing a circumcision: "When I saw this gaping wound around the head of the penis, I thought that the bleeding vagina must look like that."[28] The contemplation of the bleeding genitals prompted reactions of horror and guilt, with the mother representing both desire and punishment. Nunberg observed that in his clinical experience, "patients who had been circumcised in childhood blamed their mother for the operation, hated her and, in turn, felt guilty themselves."[29] Daly was elated by Nunberg's publication, because for the first time "an orthodox Freudian psycho-analyst, of considerable renown, has confirmed the theory I long ago advanced of the part played by the mother's menstruation in the Oedipus complex."[30]

Male genital bleeding, culturally initiated during circumcision, is often reenacted in the ritual of military combat through the catastrophic bleeding of men injured in battle. Freud hinted at this phenomenon in his classification of temporary taboos "attached to certain particular states," such as menstruation and war (*Totem and Taboo, SE* 13:20–21).[31] Extrapolating from Freud's observations on defloration and aggression, George Devereux noted that among the Mohave, a man who "deflowered a virgin had to deny his nausea-reaction to blood by means of a boastful display of his blood-stained penis," much as a warrior first boasts of victory and then cleanses himself.[32] Klaus Theweleit is one of the recent, psychoanalytically inspired theorists to investigate the relationship between war and female genital bleeding. The first volume of *Male Fantasies* gives specific references to menstruation and uses a metaphoric language that emphasizes the war/menstrual function, in sections entitled "Erasing the Stain," "The Red Nurse," "The Red Flood," "Street of Blood," "All That Flows." Theweleit cites a passage from a German drama that connects soldiers' blood and menstrual flow; continuing the analogy, he observes that battle, like menstruation, is "regular" and "violent."[33]

## The Castrating Medusa

Rituals of war, defloration, and circumcision appear to have in common the potential of wounding and of castration—of severe damage to the penis and even to the testicles. Menstruation, in a phallocentric theory, would then represent not only the bloodied ruins of the absent penis but also the instrument of castration: the shears of Atropos, the vagina with teeth, Medusa's head. As men dread the vagina, they would doubly dread the "uncanny, blood-stained" wound of menstruation.[34]

For Daly, the Hindu goddess Kali embodied the fear of castration generated by menstruation—Kali, the maternal cannibal who decapitated her enemies and drank their blood. Yet Daly offered other aggressive menstrual role models as well: Judith of the Old Testament and the Gorgon Medusa of Greek mythology, each of whom exemplify the destructive nature of the castrating female.[35] All three figures, either as perpetrators or as victims, participate in the violent act of decapitation. Both Judith, who beheads her rapist Holofernes, and Perseus, who beheads Medusa, connect with the figure of Kali, who in certain representations decapitates not only her victims but also herself. In one depiction Kali drinks the blood from her own neck after cutting off her head, thus enacting her own menstruation, in a psychic shifting from severed head to bleeding vagina.[36]

Freud, and Ferenczi before him, had seen in the Greek myth of Medusa and her terrifying visage a symbol for "the female genitals devoid of a penis" ("Infantile Genital Organization," *SE* 19:144). In his essay "Medusa's Head" (1922) Freud applied Ferenczi's insight more specifically to castration: "To decapitate = to castrate. The terror of Medusa is thus a terror of castration that is linked to the sight of something" (*SE* 18: 273). Freud compared Medusa to the Goddess Athena, who in legend bore Medusa's head on her shield, thus becoming "a woman who is unapproachable [*unnahbaren*] and repels all sexual desires" (*SE* 18:273).[37] But as Chris Knight has demonstrated, Freud's *unnahbaren* (*unapproachable* or *inaccessible* or *unavailable*), suggests the forbidden or the tabooed, terms universally associated with menstruating women. According to Knight, the word *unavailable*, when it applies to raw meat, translates ethnographically into " 'taboo,' 'totemic,' 'sacrificial,' and so on. It would have stayed taboo for as long as it remained uncooked—just as women remained 'taboo' whilst menstruating."[38] In chapter 2 I drew similar conclusions in my reading of the "neurotic child's" fear of red meat and disgust for blood; the mother's menstruation, her uncooked or bloody state, is not to be approached.

Whereas Freud, in "Medusa's Head," made no allusion to menstrual implications of the goddess, Daly, in his reading of the Perseus myth, traced the son's fear of castration to the awesome bleeding of the menstruous mother, figured in the head of the Medusa. Daly, as if imitating Freud's equation ("to decapitate = to castrate") set up his own formula: Medusa's head "= bloody vagina = menstruating woman."[39] Herman Nunberg found the Medusa legend pertinent to his patient's fear of the "gaping wound" of circumcision; men who viewed her "horrifying genitals" were turned to stone or castrated.[40]

In orthodox Freudian theory, Medusa's head and genitals serve as representations for castration; in a menstrual context they evoke images of woman's potency, of the awesome power residing in her ability to bleed. According to Devereux, "The menstruating woman is dangerous only because she is sacred, and infantile simply because she possesses magical powers."[41] Like the witch, like Kali, so the Medusa, with her capacity to instill terror through her female "wound," emblematizes women's menstrual empowerment.

### Medusa Goes Modern

A recent paper, "CUTTING," by British analyst Christopher Bollas, inventively fuses the themes of castration, bleeding, and menstrual vitality.[42] Readers acquainted with Bollas's books might expect to find in "CUTTING" his usual concerns for the analytic structures of transference and countertransference, his detailed recounting of case history, and his playful extension of object-relations terminology (for example, his term *normotic*, which describes a person who is "abnormally normal").[43] They would never have anticipated the abnormal divergence from the norm represented in "CUTTING," an extraordinary piece of *l'écriture menstruelle* told outside of the analytic environment, from the perspective of the subject "S," a tabooed woman in a mental hospital. It is the narrative of a woman whose pleasure it is to cut herself: "What do I celebrate when I cut? I love the passing of time, the interval between the act, the incision and the arrival of the blood. I must wait. Have I cut deep enough to bring up the blood? Or is this a virgin's cut, no menarche here. I must wait. I am used to such waiting. The cut in my body did not bleed until I was twelve; so I can wait for a cut to bleed." S's self-mutilation is no isolated incident. She belongs to a coven of cutters, more than fifty women in a cutting competition that replicates the menstrual act and challenges the male medical staff, horrifying them with forbidden behavior, unconcealed blood, and the threat of castration: "They can't take this blood, they can't deal with this, our cu/t, that moves around our bodies to new secret places."

The dominant word in the paper, one that I assume Bollas invented, is *cu/t: cunt*, slashed through/castrated by the symbol [/], a frequent technique in Lacanian word play. The (un/speakable) cu/t represents woman's most debased part: the wound, slashed and bloody; the menstruating vagina; the "negative hallucination of an entire civilization." In her abjection, Bollas's subject embodies both the menstrual phase of female sexuality and the threat of sexual difference.

In one satiric passage, S appropriates Lacan's famous mirror: "What does he say of this next mirror stage, when I put a mirror to see my cunt, and there find a gap, a hole, a wound, a ?" Implicit in her question to

Lacan is S's knowledge that Lacan did not say and did not know *her* mirror stage: "He [the male analyst] does not know me. He knows nothing of the sign of my pain" (as Freud "knew nothing" about the patient who dreamed the camellia). In identifying with subject S, Bollas assumes the role of the man who empathetically menstruates, who imitates and articulates the menstruating body. His discourse has been transformed, feminized—much as Freud's language was altered when in "The Taboo of Virginity" he contemplated the unfathomable menstruating woman (*SE* 11:198–99).

What Bollas achieves in "CUTTING" is the vision of psychoanalysis as theater, the acting/speaking emanating not from a polished text but from the body of a mad woman—a Medusa who curses those analysts who know nothing, who think that "a woman is a symptom."[44] S may cut herself, but she also cuts through the jargon, as does Bollas, for whom she becomes the voice of unreason, the antithesis of a linguistically convoluted discourse.

Actually, there is a modest body of writing on the subject of menstruation and the cutting syndrome; according to Louise A. Kaplan, the psychiatric world has been aware of this disorder and of its pertinence to menstruation since 1914, in a case study of self-mutilation reported in *Psychoanalytic Review*.[45] Kaplan describes the disorder called "delicate self-cutting," found among women of all ages but especially among adolescent females, which tends to appear shortly after the menarche. Through self-mutilation the daughter rids herself of the bad mother inside her body, becoming a bleeder in an "identification with the denigrated, castrated, bleeding mother. Moreover, the anticipated passive castration of menstruation is transferred into a controlled active one."[46] The subject of Bollas's study exhibits distinct symptoms of a self-cutting more crass than delicate, an attempt to control her sexuality though a deliberate provocation of bleeding.[47] The term *self-cutting* also seems relevant to Freud's case study of Emma Eckstein's pubescent episodes: "She has always been a bleeder, when cutting herself and in similar circumstances."[48] Although Freud mentions Emma's self-cutting to support the idea that she *wanted* to bleed, he offers no particulars.

Bollas, along with Nunberg, Daly, and a few others, is one of the rare male analysts consciously to engage the menstruating subject, to gaze at Medusa's "red stigmata" without a mirror.[49] A revitalized menstrual consciousness is far less likely to emerge from the analytic sphere, however, than from the media, where advertising, theater, situation comedies, and film have begun to treat menstruation with both openness and humor.[50] It seems fitting to terminate this analysis of menstruation and castration with Robert Altman's film *The Player* (1992), where Whoopi Goldberg, in her role of woman detective, portrays Medusa in one of her latest manifestations. In an image of power that explodes the stereotypes of race and gender, Goldberg lounges at a desk, feet sprawled, and twirls a tampon around and around—like a male cop would twirl his nightstick. In her interrogation of the suspect, Goldberg, for one brief moment, replaces the white man as a figure of authority, much as the tampon replaces the phallus as the source of castration and of sexual difference. Viewers "linked to the sight of something" may have noticed the menstruous grin on Goldberg's face as she violated the most "virulent" of taboos.

## Notes

1. Jane Gallop connects the boy's act of *seeing* to Freud's theory of sexual difference: "The penis, according to Freud, is more visible than what the little girl has. From being more visible, it becomes simply more, in other words better, superior." Jane Gallop, *The Daughter's Seduction* (Ithaca: Cornell University Press, 1982), 27. See also Karen Horney, "On the Genesis of the Castration Complex in Women," in *Feminine Psychology*, ed. Harold Kelman (1922; New York: Norton, 1973). Horney claimed that "just as woman, because her genital organs are hidden, is ever the great riddle for man, so man is an object of lively jealousy for woman precisely on account of the ready visibility of his organ," 40.

2. One critic has made the reasonable point that the male emphasis on female "lack" is really an indication of *his* lack; that the so-called female castration complex is a projection onto women's bodies that functions as a way to avoid or deflect his own fears of being castrated. Margaret Whitford, *Luce Irigaray: Philosophy in the Feminine* (London: Routledge, 1991), 118.

3. Sigmund Freud, *The Complete Letters of Sigmund Freud to Wilhelm Fliess*, ed. Jeffrey Moussaieff Masson (Cambridge: Harvard University Press, 1985), 227.

4. In 1895, only a few years before Freud recorded Emma's circumcision scene, E. Sidney Hartland copiously described the rituals of the blood covenant, which included drinking blood from a common goblet and rubbing together the blood from wounds. Nowhere did Hartland suggest what seems to me obvious—that the rituals of blood bonding are an attempt to appropriate the function of female bleeding as protection against castration. See E. Sidney Hartland, *The Legend of Perseus* (London: Grimm Library, 1895), 2:232–57. Daly referred fleetingly to the blood covenant in a

menstrual context in "The Psycho-biological Origins of Circumcision," *International Journal of Psycho-analysis* 31 (1950): 234–35.

5. Ironically, in Freud's one full study of female homosexuality, he remarked that "there was no obvious deviation from the feminine physical type, nor any menstrual disturbance"—as if lesbianism might be expected to entail menstrual problems. See "A Case of Homosexuality in a Woman" (*SE* 18:154).

6. Hanns Sachs, "The Wish to Be a Man," *International Journal of Psycho-analysis* 1 (1920): 265.

7. See, for example, the associations between the female castration complex and the revival of masturbation during the menarche in Mary Chadwick, *The Psychological Effects of Menstruation* (New York: Nervous and Mental Disease Publishing Company, 1932), 25. According to Deutsch, menstruation excites "genital tension and a need to masturbate" in all girls. Helene Deutsch, *The Psychology of Women* (New York: Grune and Stratton, 1944), 1:57.

8. Gustav Braun, "The Amputation of the Clitoris and Labia Minora: A Contribution in the Treatment of Vaginismus," in *A Dark Science: Women, Sexuality, and Psychiatry in the Nineteenth Century*, ed. Jeffrey Moussaieff Masson (New York: Farrar, Straus, and Giroux, 1986), 126–38. See also Michel Erlich, *La femme blessée: Essai sur les mutilations sexuelles féminines* (Paris: Editions l'Harmattan, 1986); and Elaine Showalter, *The Female Malady: Women, Madness, and English Culture, 1830–1980* (New York: Pantheon, 1985). Alice Walker vividly dramatizes the traumatic consequences for African women submitted to genital mutilation. See Alice Walker, *Possessing the Secret of Joy* (New York: Harcourt Brace Jovanovich, 1992).

9. Lawrence Frank, "Freud and Dora," in *Seduction and Theory*, ed. Dianne Hunter (Urbana: University of Illinois Press, 1989), 113.

10. Sachs, "The Wish to Be a Man," 266.

11. Horney contended that penis envy is not universal, that only during extreme anxiety would it lead to "a revulsion from the subject's own sexual role." See Karen Horney, "On the Genesis of the Castration Complex in Women" (1922), *Feminine Psychology*, 53. Thompson claimed that penis envy is cultural; as the penis is privileged in our culture, so is the male. Clara M. Thompson, *Interpersonal Psychoanalysis: The Selected Papers of Clara M. Thompson*, ed. Maurice R. Green (New York: Basic Books, 1964), 72–73. See also Ernest Jones, "The Early Development of Female Sexuality" (1927); "The Phallic Phase" (1932); and "Early Female Sexuality" (1935), in *Papers on Psychoanalysis* (Boston: Beacon Press, 1961). Bonaparte, on the contrary, wrote that the castration fear, which derives from the mother, is "embodied in woman as the castrated being." Marie Bonaparte, *The Life and Works of Edgar Allan Poe: A Psycho-analytic Interpretation*, trans. John Rodker (1933; New York: Humanities Press, 1971), 481.

12. Sándor Rado, "Fear of Castration in Women," *Psychoanalytic Quarterly* 2 (1933): 433–34.

13. Samuel Ritvo, "Adolescent to Woman," in *Female Psychology*, ed. Harold Blum

(New York: International Universities Press, 1977), 128.

14. Karl Abraham, "Manifestations of the Female Castration Complex," in *Selected Papers on Psychoanalysis*, trans. Douglas Bryan and Alix Strachey (1920; New York: Basic Books, 1971), 338–69. For Abraham's effect on his women analysands, see Edith Kurzweil, *The Freudians: A Comparative Perspective* (New Haven: Yale University Press, 1989), 155–56.

15. Abraham, "Female Castration Complex," 347.

16. I examine the concept of female masochism and its implications for menstruation in chapter 11. Deutsch evidently derived part of her theory about menstrual repetition from her analysis with Abraham.

17. Horney, "Premenstrual Tension" (1931), in *Feminine Psychology*, 106. In the early 1930s, Horney accepted without qualification Freud's belief that a woman's wish for a child was primary. See "Castration Complex," 46.

18. Deutsch, *The Psychology of Women*, 2:459.

19. Ibid., 1:174. One will recall the equation of menstruation with mourning a lost child, in Erik Erikson, "Womanhood and Inner Space," *Identity: Youth and Crisis* (New York: Norton, 1968), 278.

20. See Claude Dagmar Daly, "Hindu-Mythologie und Kastrationskomplex," trans. Peter Mendelssohn, *Imago* 13 (1927): 181, 193–95; and "The Psychology of Man's Attitude Towards Woman" (1930), *Samiksa* 1 (1947): 238. Stephens has made an observation that seems to support Daly's thesis; in certain cultures, a menstruating woman is the most frightening to a man with "intense castration anxiety." See William N. Stephens, *The Oedipus Complex: Cross-cultural Evidence* (New York: Free Press, 1962), 92.

21. Daly had surprisingly little to say about the effect of menstruation on the little *girl*. He did remark that as the menstruation complex affects the boy's castration anxiety, so it would form a "deep basis for neurosis in the case of the little girl, and in the genesis of pathological masochism, penis envy and hysteria." Claude Dagmar Daly, "The Role of Menstruation in Human Phylogenesis and Ontogenesis," *International Journal of Psycho-analysis* 24 (1943): 167. Castration anxiety seems to be the boy's province.

22. As the argument from hygiene has been used to verify the menstrual intercourse taboo, so the same argument has been used to support the need for circumcision. One recent health book suggests, however, that routine circumcision does not necessarily prevent infection and that "most circumcisions today are performed for cultural or religious [rather than hygienic] reasons." One distinct disadvantage of circumcision, according to the resource, is "bleeding that may require a dressing." See the *Mayo Clinic Family Health Book*, ed. David E. Larson (New York: William Morrow, 1990), 32.

23. See in particular *Totem and Taboo* (*SE* 13:153n) and *Moses and Monotheism* (*SE* 23:91, 92n, 122, 190).

24. Daly, "Psycho-biological Origins of Circumcision," 217–22.

25. Marie Bonaparte, *Female Sexuality*, trans. John Rodker (1949; New York: International Universities Press, 1953), 96.

26. Subincision, the splitting of the penis, is the most brutal of male genital ceremonies. As we shall see in the next chapter, this self-inflicted disfigurement, while it is surely an aspect of castration, has been interpreted by anthropologists to be an expression of the man's desire to be a woman. As Poul Faergeman has observed in working with individual male patients, fantasies of bleeding are indications of unconscious castration. "Castration is thus the bloody bridge that leads from masculinity to femininity." Poul M. Faergeman, "Fantasies of Menstruation in Men," *Pschyoanalytic Quarterly* 24 (1955): 18.

27. Anthropology has shown the importance of the maternal presence in some circumcision rites; among the people of the New Hebrides, it is believed that circumcision was women's invention. See Bruno Bettelheim, *Symbolic Wounds: Puberty Rites and the Envious Male* (New York: Collier, 1962), 98.

28. Herman Nunberg, "Circumcision and Problems of Bisexuality," *International Journal of Psycho-analysis* 28 (1947): 171.

29. Ibid., 175. See Daly, "The Psycho-biological Origins of Circumcision," 229.

30. Ibid.

31. In a 1919 introduction to the publication *Psychoanalysis and the War Neuroses*, Freud wrote that the traumas affected by war would involve fear of death and frustration in love (*SE* 17:207–15); he did not, there or elsewhere, connect menstrual blood to the fear of combat or to the ultimate war injury: castration.

32. George Devereux, "The Psychology of Genital Bleeding: An Analysis of Mohave Indian Puberty and Menstrual Rites," *International Journal of Psycho-analysis* 31 (1950): 251.

33. Klaus Theweleit, *Male Fantasies: Women, Floods, Bodies, History*, trans. Stephen Conway, with Erica Carter and Chris Turner (Minneapolis: University of Minnesota Press, 1987), 1:411. Theweleit promises a more extended discussion of menstruation "later" (1:483n). But in the second volume, translated by Erica Carter and Chris Turner (Minneapolis: University of Minnesota Press, 1989), he makes no specific comments on menstrual blood.

34. Karen Horney, "The Dread of Woman" (1932), in *Feminine Psychology*, 136–37. One will recall that in his essay "The Uncanny," Freud had associated that term with the womb. "This *unheimlich* place, however, is the entrance to the former *Heim* [home] of all human beings, to the place where each of us lived once upon a time and in the beginning" (*SE* 17:245).

35. See Mary Jacobus, *Reading Women: Essays in Feminist Criticism* (New York: Columbia University Press, 1986), 115–35, for pictorial illustrations and feminist discussion of the Judith myth. Daly claimed that Andromeda, whom Perseus rescues from captivity, would represent Kali's opposite, Lakshmi, the "ideal mother" of Hindu mythology, in "The Psychology of Revolutionary Tendencies," *International*

*Journal of Psycho-analysis* 11 (1930): 204. Neumann also linked the Medusa to Kali (but not because of menstruation); see Erich Neumann, *The Great Mother*, trans. Ralph Manheim, Bollingen Series, vol. 47 (1955; Princeton: Princeton University Press, 1972), 80.

36. See Benjamin Walker, *Hindu World: An Encyclopedic Survey of Hinduism* (London: Allen and Unwin, 1968), 1:509.

37. Freud, "Das Medusenhaupt," *Gesammelte Werke* (Frankfurt am Main: S. Fischer Verlag, 1968), 17:47. The snake-haired Medusa is compared with the menstrual cult surrounding the Greek goddess Athena in Penelope Shuttle and Peter Redgrove, *The Wise Wound: Eve's Curse and Everywoman*, rev. ed. (New York: Grove Press, 1986), 248–49.

38. Chris Knight, *Blood Relations: Menstruation and the Origins of Culture* (New Haven: Yale University Press, 1991), 39.

39. Daly, "The Psychology of Revolutionary Tendencies," 204. He presented a similar interpretation of Perseus in "Der Kern des Oedipuskomplexes," *Internationale Zeitschrift für Psychoanalyse* 21 (1935): 170–71.

40. Nunberg, "Circumcision and Problems of Bisexuality," 171.

41. Devereux, "The Psychology of Genital Bleeding," 252.

42. Christopher Bollas, "CUTTING," paper written for the Group for the Research and Application of Psychoanalysis and the Psychoses, Paris, 1989. In Bollas's absence, "CUTTING" was read to the audience by Kenneth Reinhard. All further references are to Reinhard's copy, 5–9. I am preserving the capitalized title as it appears in the manuscript.

43. See Christopher Bollas, *The Shadow of the Object* (New York: Columbia University Press, 1987), 135–56. See also his more recent book, *Forces of Destiny: Psychoanalysis and the Human Idiom* (London: Free Association Books, 1991).

44. This phrase, which Bollas does not use, is from Lacan's "Seminar of 21 January 1975," cited in *Feminine Sexuality*, ed. Juliet Mitchell and Jacqueline Rose, trans. Jacqueline Rose (New York: Pantheon, 1985), 168.

45. See the bibliographical note in Louise J. Kaplan, *Female Perversions* (New York: Doubleday, 1991), 553–54. Bollas, although he may have been aware of this material, does not refer to it in "CUTTING." I wish to thank Ellen Lupton for bringing *Female Perversions* to my attention.

46. Kaplan, *Female Perversions*, 382. The mutilated body also relates to the concept of female masochism, discussed in chapter 11.

47. The concept of delicate self-cutting has applications beyond the mental hospital. One observes comparable symptoms in the Grimm brothers' violent version of the Cinderella myth, where Cinderella's witchy stepsisters, umbilically attached to the "real" mother, cut their toes to fit the shoe, in what Bettelheim has interpreted as both menstruation and castration. See Bruno Bettelheim, *The Uses of Enchantment: The Meaning and Importance of Fairy Tales* (New York: Vintage, 1976), 235.

48. Freud, *Letters*, 186.

49. There is no specific reference to Medusa in "CUTTING." Bollas, however, uses the term in a 1979 essay about the poet Sylvia Plath, who thought her mother to be a "Medusa, a red stigmata." There is no specific reference to menstruation in the Plath essay. See Murray M. Schwartz and Christopher Bollas, "The Absence at the Center: Sylvia Plath and Suicide," in *Sylvia Plath: New Views on the Poetry,* ed. Gary Lane (Baltimore: Johns Hopkins University Press, 1979), 198.

50. For discussions of menstruation in popular culture see *The Curse,* 129–37, 151–58. See also Lorraine Kenny, "Are You Sure I'll Still Be a Virgin?" *Camerawork Quarterly* 17 (1990): 8–14; and Ann Treneman, "Cashing in on the Curse," in *The Female Gaze: Women as Viewers in Popular Culture,* ed. Lorraine Gamman and Margaret Marshment (Seattle: Real Comet Press, 1989), 153–65.

# 9

# *The Bleeding Body and Male Desire*

The majority of men, analysts included, have tended to avoid or even abhor sexual intercourse during women's menstrual flow, even when they have witnessed a heightening of female sexual desire during their periods. Wilhelm Reich, whose radical theory of sexual energy brought him notoriety in Europe and later in America, maintained that the libido increased during menstruation, thus increasing women's sexual dissatisfaction. Nonetheless, he enforced the menstrual intercourse taboo among his female patients.[1] The same is true for Wilhelm Stekel; having observed an awakening of libido during menstruation and also during intermenstrual intercourse, Stekel attached to this insight a hasty aside: "(which, incidentally *I never recommend.*)"[2] One historian of psychoanalysis, categorizing any exorbitant desire for intramenstrual sex as a perversion, referred to a "fetishist who could have sexual intercourse only with women who were menstruating." This perversion represents an "unconscious defense against his wish to devour his mother."[3] In a discussion of Lacan, Luce Irigaray points her finger at a different perversion. The infamous Marquis de Sade took pleasure in making women bleed but at the same time observed the intercourse taboo, choosing to penetrate the dry, male anus but not the menstruating vagina: "Excrement, certainly, but blood from a period, no."[4]

Daly, one assumes, would have brushed off such finicky restrictions. In an anthropological speculation more fanciful than historical, he envisioned the enticements of the menstrually hot female, who at the dawn of civilization was "man's greatest source of satisfaction and pride, before the incest barrier descended."[5] His belief in a Primal Menstrual Seduction was confirmed by the intimate confession of a female patient, whose lust for Daly was ignited by her menstrual blood: "A psychotic patient of mine wanted to put her menstrual blood in my bed in order that she might seduce me and bind me to her. . . . The following night she dreamt that she had a child by me."[6]

Other male theorists have noted that for both sexes there is an increase in sexual desire during a woman's period. At the beginning of the century Havelock Ellis fixed the peak of female desire at the menstrual phase, attributing her ardent sexual response at that time to the fact that the blood, a natural lubricant, stimulates coitus.[7] Georg Groddeck, in *The Book of the It* (1923), actually encouraged the release of sexual desire during menstruation: "The right time for this intercourse is when the womb is ardent, during the period. But precisely at this time there breaks in between the wish and its fulfillment a 'No,' which has the force of law in the Hebraic civilization, as well as in many others."[8] Posing as a promiscuous letter writer, Groddeck tantalized his "dear lady" with ideas about menstrual blood, calling it the "magic love philter" and the "deepest enchantment of red love."[9] Like Daly, Groddeck transformed the menstrual taboo into a mythology of desire, with menstruation the original temptation: "Eve tempts Adam; so it was, and is, and ever shall be. She must tempt him, because she is ardent in bleeding, because she herself feels desire."[10] As menstruation arouses female desire, so menstrual blood excites her mate, stimulating his sadistic impulses as he creates erotic fantasies of war, mountain-climbing, and domestic violence. The strength of such eroticism, Groddeck declared, derives from the taboo against intercourse and from the passion aroused in defying it.[11]

### Saignade

In the first part of *Menstruation and Psychoanalysis* I referred to Freud's menstrual migraine, prompted by the menarche of his daughter Mathilde: "At the same time I had a migraine from which I thought I would die. It is the third of this kind and is absolutely awful."[12] The migraine, in its repetition and periodicity, appears to have been a fantasized symptom of male menstruation—a female identification with his daughter's bleeding accompanied by complaints commonly associated with the female period.

In this instance, Freud's migraine lends support to Fliess's theory of a twenty-three-day menstrual cycle in men and to other early speculations on male rhythms.[13] Contemporary studies of factory workers, railway drivers, and other men in the labor force have further suggested a periodic mood swing in men not unlike the menstrual rhythms in women and accompanied by similar feelings: lethargy, inadequacy, withdrawal, irrationality, and so on. While such periodic disturbances are most likely determined by related disorders or by religious, economic, or geographical factors, they nonetheless offer statistical confirmation for Fliess's notion of a male physiological cycle.[14]

For our purposes, though, male menstruation can better be viewed as a psychological response to feelings about gender rather than as a sequence of hormonal fluctuations. As men have revealed a desire to give birth (*couvade*, from the French word *couver*, to hatch) so they have expressed the desire to menstruate, what in *The Curse* we call *saignade*, the imagined menstruation of the male (261, 273). Fantasies of this nature have been observed not only in individual patients but also in certain preliterate societies, in male rituals that involve self-inflicted genital bleeding. The most notorious of these rituals is subincision—the slitting of the underside of the penis so that, in its deformed and bloody state, it resembles a vagina.[15]

By way of subincision, still practiced in remote parts of Australia, Africa, and New Zealand, the man is afforded the opportunity to bleed surgically as the woman bleeds naturally, in a ritual that has been classified as "coarse self-cutting," one far more catastrophic than the "delicate self-cutting" discussed in the previous chapter.[16] Geza Roheim, in an account of this practice so detailed that it filled an entire issue of the *International Journal of Psycho-analysis*, included a series of grisly photographs of men trying to stop the bleeding with firesticks or to reopen the wound with a stone knife.[17] Men's blood is thus a replication of women's blood—the blood of menstruation but also the blood of opening or penetration, preenacted in numerous cultures in rites of deflowering.

Subincision further functions as a hygienic ritual—much as what Freud, in *Totem and Taboo*, had thought was the function of the menstrual taboo (*SE* 13:98). The Wogeo of New Zealand split their penises as a rite of purification, hoping, in simulating menstruation, to cleanse themselves through a "periodic disinfection."[18] For them menstruation is a purgation, an attempt to expel the female "and eventually gain a clear gender identity as a male."[19] At times the genital purgation involves the nose. One recent study records the way in which a New Guinea group combines genital mutilations with nasal mutilation; the subincision rites begin when the leader takes two sharp leaves and, in a manner that suggests both sexual intercourse and vicarious (substituted or displaced) menstruation, "thrusts them up and down his nostrils until blood gushes profusely into the water."[20]

Through his observation of four adolescent patients (two girls, two boys, all suffering from castration anxiety), Bruno Bettelheim learned about the boys' intention to cut their penises each month and mix their blood with the girls' menstrual blood.[21] These fantasies, which reminded him of preliterate puberty rites, led him on an anthropological excursion that resulted in the publication of *Symbolic Wounds,* the psychoanalytic text to have most fully traced the analogy between menstruation and the bleeding penis. In it Bettelheim contended that both subincision and circumcision are symbolic repetitions of menstruation that reveal the male envy of female procreative powers. Among certain Australian groups, circumcision seems to take the place of the menarche, while subincision may be "a second effort to procreate, when the first attempt failed."[22] The man, who envies and desires the woman's reproductive powers, acts out his wishes by imitating her bleeding.

Inverting the Freudian account of sexual difference, Bettelheim proposed that as women wish for a penis, so men, who already have one, wish additionally for a vagina. This male desire is expressed in ceremonial rituals of bleeding: "When men by subincision make themselves *resemble* women, the obvious reason is that they are trying to *be* women."[23] In Bettelheim's view, subincision represents the ritualization of desire that in our postindustrial society is "deeply repressed or else integrated and sublimated," that can be "expressed only in fantasy."[24]

### "The Bloody Bridge"

Like Bettelheim, but without his anthropological perspective, other psychoanalysts, having observed menstrual desire in the repressed fantasies of their male patients, theorize that in suppressing the mother's

blood as a sign of castration, or in retreating from the homosexual implications of bleeding like a woman, the male is often compelled to bleed
from somewhere else, such as the nose or rectum. Wayne Koestenbaum,
in an intriguing exploration of the Freud-Fliess-Eckstein dynamic, argues that male menstruation is a symbolic expression of the desire for
anal intercourse, "a cerebral intercourse whose anal implications Emma's
nosebleed luridly brought to life." [25] One finds support for Koestenbaum's
argument in the anthropological data; among the Chaga, for example,
male initiates insert plugs into their anuses in a symbolism that parodies
the menstrual process: their anuses are "stopped up," whereas the vagina,
in its monthly discharge, is "open." [26]

More often, male fantasies of menstruation take a Fliessian turn, with
nose-bleeding (epistaxis) the metaphorical equivalent of the menstrual
process—as it had been, under different circumstances of gender, for
Emma Eckstein. [27] Douglas Bryan reported the incident of a male patient
whose nose began to bleed on entering his office and persisted through
most of the session, during which the patient kept dabbing his nose until
"his handkerchief became fairly saturated with blood." [28] Although the
patient worked at an interpretation, connecting the event with menstruation, castration, and the fear of pregnancy, the bleeding did not stop until
the analyst pronounced the word *defense* (as in the familiar menstrual
defense against having sexual intercourse). Thus Bryan, who explicated
the patient's bleeding to be a shield against sexual penetration by his
analyst, was able, with one word, to get to the heart of the problem—
the fear that his father (represented in this fantasy by the analyst) would
"bugger" him.[29]

The fullest clinical report about male menstruation is Poul Faergeman's study of seven men with psychopathological conditions ranging
from "severe neurosis to perversion and psychosis." [30] Some of these
patients seemed to have a sardonic, self-conscious attitude toward menstruation; one periodic nosebleeder, for example, asked his analyst why
there was a sanitary pad on the couch. This same man had terrifying
dreams about being soiled on his trousers by his wife's blood and about
giving birth anally. The nosebleeds, and possibly the patient's diarrhea,
represented his castration anxiety, magnified to incorporate the fantasy
of genital bleeding.

Another of Faergeman's patients combined voyeurism with feminine
identification; he had the habit of "going into toilets to seek for women's

pubic hair which he swallowed."[31] The toilet was the site of childhood fantasies stemming from having seen his mother sitting there and from having confused defecation with menstruation. " 'Menstruation," he exclaimed, 'is dirty, disgusting; I hate to see used menstrual pads and also used condoms.' "[32] Faergeman summarized three of this patient's dreams: in one he bleeds from his anus at a racetrack; in the second he kills a horrible insect (vagina); in the third, a dream reminiscent of Freud's Dream of the Red Bath, he discovers his maid's menstrual blood while cleaning the toilet. The majority of Faergeman's case histories encompass some element of nasal or anal identification with menstruation, usually both; in all three of the above studies, in fact, the anal and the nasal components of male menstruation are synthesized.[33]

The bloody nose was to play a crucial role during the Wolf-Man's later years, when, long after his analysis with Freud, he became the patient of Ruth Mack Brunswick. Brunswick was concerned about the Wolf-Man's obsession with a pimple on his nose. Following nasal surgery, he went into "an acute ecstasy" as blood flowed from the wound.[34] Although Brunswick interpreted the bloody opening as "*hallucinated* castration," I would argue, on the basis of his identification with the mother's wound, that his bleeding also represented the achievement of the male desire to menstruate (*saignade*) and that the "acute ecstasy" resulted from the "joy" at having achieved a feminine defense.[35] Earlier I made a similar case for Freud's "flowing Aetna," which imitated Emma Eckstein's "avalanche," her overflowing nose; Freud's nasal symptoms, like the Wolf-Man's, warranted surgery.[36]

From working closely with these male patients, Faergeman discovered the complex interaction between menstruation, castration, and male desire: "Psychoanalytic experience has taught us that when a man bleeds, —in dreams and in fantasies, or actually from his nose or anus, or from a wound—he is unconsciously suffering castration. It is my suggestion that after a man has been psychologically emasculated, he is not simply a castrated man. He has been turned into a woman and bleeds as the woman does; he menstruates, is deflowered, gives birth. Castration is thus the bloody bridge that leads from masculinity to femininity."[37]

The Wolf-Man, the patient with diarrhea, the subincised Wogeo— these disparate individuals have somehow selected to identify symptomatically with women as bleeders. One could even interpret the self-inflicted blindness of Oedipus in this context, with the eyes substituting for the nose as the site of vicarious bleeding. The guilt-ridden son *sees* Jocasta's castration/death, pulls the brooch from her gown, and ritualistically plunges its points into his eyes so that they bleed "like a black/ rain and bloody hailshower."[38] In his imitation of his mother's/wife's menstrual bleeding, Oedipus achieves release from the male (oedipal) sexuality that had signified his doom. Viewed within the Freudian concept of castration anxiety, it would seem that a man who unconsciously desires to menstruate can do so only by symbolically destroying his penis and becoming, like a woman, absent. In bridging the bloody gap between masculinity and femininity, a man who imitates women's bleeding lessens, if only in fantasy, his phallic burden.

Part 3 of *Menstruation and Psychoanalysis* examines the menstrual theories of women analysts affiliated with Freud. In their research and case histories, women analysts emphasized *women's* moods, behavior, and fantasies. Although they described no menstrual ceremony as crippling as the ritual of subincision, some of them regarded the menstrual process itself to be a crippling—a monthly mutilation that offered nothing to desire. One might have expected that women analysts, by virtue of their own experience, would have struggled to eradicate much of the dread surrounding menstruation. That, unfortunately, is not the case, for reasons that I will suggest in the next chapter.

### Notes

1. See Juliet Mitchell, *Psychoanalysis and Feminism* (New York: Pantheon, 1974), 145, 157.

2. Wilhelm Stekel, *Frigidity in Women*, trans. S. Van Teslaar (New York: Horace Liveright, 1929), 1:278, emphasis mine.

3. Ludwig Eidelberg, ed., *Encyclopedia of Psychoanalysis* (New York: Free Press, 1968), 304.

4. Luce Irigaray, cited by Ellie Ragland-Sullivan in *Jacques Lacan and the Philosophy of Psychoanalysis* (Urbana: University of Illinois Press, 1986), 275.

5. Claude Dagmar Daly, "The Menstruation Complex in Literature," *Psychoanalytic Quarterly* 4 (1935): 325.

6. Claude Dagmar Daly, "The Role of Menstruation in Human Phylogenesis and Ontogenesis," *International Journal of Psycho-analysis* 24 (1943): 166. Daly confessed to an attraction for "muffs and furs," whose odor aroused "the deepest desire in me." See Daly, "The Menstruation Complex in Literature," 311. His identification with menstrual odor seems to contradict Faergeman's charge that Daly did not di-

rectly address male fantasies of menstruation. See Poul M. Faergeman, "Fantasies of Menstruation in Men," *Psychoanalytic Quarterly* 24 (1955): 4.

7. Havelock Ellis, *Studies in the Psychology of Sex* (Philadelphia: F. A. Davis, 1931), 1:101, 5:145.

8. Georg Groddeck, *The Book of the It*, trans. V. M. E. Collins (1923; New York: International Universities Press, 1976), 127.

9. Ibid., 124. Groddeck is cited in Daly's "Der Kern des Oedipuskomplexes," *Internationale Zeitschrift für Psychoanalyse* 21 (1935): 185. Roazen claims that Groddeck was "a pioneer in stressing the mother's role in child development"; see Paul Roazen, *Freud and His Followers* (New York: Alfred A. Knopf, 1975), 332.

10. Groddeck, *Book of the It*, 122. Chadwick viewed Eve in the more traditional way, as being "cursed" with menstruation as punishment for her sins. See Mary Chadwick, *Woman's Periodicity* (London: Noel Douglas, 1933), 121. See also *The Curse*, 31, 37.

11. Karl Menninger admired Groddeck's suggestion that menstruation and the inhibitions against intercourse be used as a means for testing the strength of one's desire. See Karl A. Menninger, "Psychogenic Influences on the Appearance of the Menstrual Period," *International Journal of Psycho-analysis* 22 (1941): 64n.

12. Sigmund Freud, *The Complete Letters of Sigmund Freud to Wilhelm Fliess*, ed. Jeffrey Moussaieff Masson (Cambridge: Harvard University Press, 1985), 357.

13. See Ellis, *The Psychology of Sex*, 1:115–21.

14. See Gay Luce, *Biological Rhythms in Psychiatry and Medicine* (New York: Dover, 1970); and Estelle Ramey, "Men's Cycles (They Have Them Too You Know)," *Ms.*, Spring 1972, 8–14. For an overview on male rhythms, see *The Curse*, 267–72.

15. From the large body of psychoanalytic and anthropological studies on subincision, the following seem most valuable: Bruno Bettelheim, *Symbolic Wounds: Puberty Rites and the Envious Male* (New York: Collier, 1962); James Lewton Brain, *The Last Taboo: Sex and the Fear of Death* (Garden City, N.Y.: Anchor Press, 1979); Ian Hogbin, *The Island of Menstruating Men* (Scranton, Pa.: Chandler, 1970); Chris Knight, "Menstrual Synchrony and the Australian Rainbow Snake," in *Blood Magic*, ed. Thomas Buckley and Alma Gottlieb (Berkeley: University of California Press, 1988), 232–55; Ruth W. Lidz and Theodore Lidz, "Male Menstruation: A Ritual Alternative to the Oedipal Transition," *International Journal of Psycho-analysis* 58 (1977): 17–31; M. F. Ashley Montagu, "Physiology and the Origins of the Menstrual Prohibitions," *Quarterly Review of Biology* 15 (1940): 211–20; Theodor Reik, *Ritual: Psycho-analytic Studies*, trans. Douglas Bryan (1931; New York: International Universities Press, 1946); and Geza Roheim, "Psycho-analysis of Primitive Cultural Types," *International Journal of Psycho-analysis* 13 (1932): 1–224.

16. See Louise J. Kaplan, *Female Perversions* (New York: Doubleday, 1991), 369.

17. Roheim, "Primitive Cultural Types," 57–73.

18. Hogbin, *Island*, 88.

19. Lidz and Lidz, "Male Menstruation," 27. See also Daly, "Der Kern des Oedipuskomplexes," 188.

20. Lidz and Lidz, "Male Menstruation," 18.

21. A male friend tells me that "normal" boys participate in comparable rituals, for instance, the cutting of raised (penile) thumbs and the subsequent sharing of the blood. See also the discussion of the blood covenant in E. Sidney Hartland, *The Legend of Perseus* (London: Grimm Library, 1895), 2:232–57.

22. Bettelheim, *Symbolic Wounds*, 108.

23. Ibid., 49.

24. Ibid.

25. Wayne Koestenbaum, "Privileging the Anus: Anna O. and the Collaborative Origin of Psychoanalysis," *Genders* 3 (1988): 74–75. Of the articles cited in this chapter, only Koestenbaum's connects male bleeding to Fliess's theory of the nose and periodicity.

26. Bettelheim, *Symbolic Wounds*, 128–30.

27. Leon Saul is critical of the almost exclusively *male* associations with the nose in the history of psychoanalysis; yet in his correlations between the nose and anal/genital components, Saul does not mention menstruation. Leon Saul, "The Feminine Significance of the Nose," *Psychoanalytic Quarterly* 17 (1948): 51–57.

28. Douglas Bryan, "Epistaxis in a Man Simulating Menstruation," *International Journal of Psycho-analysis* 7 (1926): 80.

29. Ibid., 81. In chapter 11 I will discuss Marie Cardinal's account of an analyst who, like Bryan, is able to stop the flow of blood with a single statement.

30. Faergeman, "Fantasies of Menstruation," 15.

31. Ibid., 9.

32. Ibid., 11. While condoms and menstrual pads may seem like strange bedfellows, they are related in their hygienic functions. The pad protects the environment from menstrual blood, while the condom serves, as one of its uses, to protect the penis during intramenstrual intercourse.

33. There is also an anal component to female menstruation. Bertin Lewin, in an essay entitled "Defecation, Menstruation, and Women's Superego," compared menstrual discharge to the uncontrollable evacuation of feces. So adept had one of his subjects become at containing her menstrual flow that the muscles of her vagina were able to contract much like a sphincter. Cited in Clara M. Thompson, *Interpersonal Psychoanalysis: The Selected Papers of Clara M. Thompson*, ed. Maurice R. Green (New York: Basic Books, 1964), 254. Samuel Ritvo claimed that "the girl first perceives and experiences the onset of menstruation as an excretory phenomenon." See Samuel Ritvo, "Adolescent to Woman," in *Female Psychology*, ed. Harold Blum (New York: International Universities Press, 1977), 128.

34. Ruth Mack Brunswick, "A Supplement to 'History of an Infantile Neurosis,'" in *The Wolf-Man by the Wolf-Man*, ed. Muriel Gardiner (New York: Basic Books, 1971), 273.

35. The Wolf-Man's identification with his mother's "hemorrhage" was discussed in chapter 8. See Freud, "From the History of an Infantile Neurosis" (*SE* 17:78–86).

36. Hemorrhoids are evidently related to Freud's fantasies of menstruation, in an essay that I could not locate. See Didier Anzieu, *L'autoanalyse de Freud* (Paris: Presses Universitaires de France, 1975), 2:553.

 37. Faergeman, "Fantasies of Menstruation," 18.

38. Sophocles, *Oedipus the King*, ed. and trans. Thomas Gould (Englewood Cliffs, N.J.: Prentice-Hall, 1970), ll. 1278–79.

# Part 3

# Women Analysts

# 10

# *Women Analysts, Menstrual Attitudes*

The third part, "Women Analysts," concerns the attitudes toward menstruation formulated by those women Freudians whose ideas or practices specifically pertained to the menstrual process. In their psychoanalytic examination of menstruation, women analysts expressed divergent views. Some denied menstruation altogether, while some granted it a qualified acceptance in their assessment of the female libido. Others revealed an abhorrence of menstruation so internalized that it ultimately suggested a disgust for women as a gender, an attitude that was consolidated under the rubric female masochism. A few viewed menstruation within a broad cultural context, arguing that the anxiety toward the menstrual process resulted from men's flight from the *difference* embodied in menstruating women.

Although there were women working in the analytic field from the beginnings of the movement (Emma Eckstein, for example), they upheld phallic definitions of female sexuality. As advocates of Freud, women analysts often acquiesced in the psychoanalytic denial of the female body and psyche, suppressing pregnancy, menstruation, the menopause, and other essential physiological processes—either in allegiance to Freud or in an attempt to be unobtrusive or in an effort to deny the troublesome nature of their own female sexuality or possibly in fear of the maternal, of their mothers and the mothers in themselves.

It was Freud who had the greatest influence on the theories of both men and women; his commanding intellect and personality touched a number of women analysts between the wars.[1] In their desire to please Freud and to receive the pleasure of his desire, many women accommodated themselves to his expectations of female behavior. Unfortunately, Freud's ideas of the "female sex" were both conservative and patronizing. He thought women should be "ministering angels to the needs and comforts of men"; according to Ernest Jones, Freud had "only one type of sexual object in his mind, a gentle feminine one."[2] Jones quotes a letter Freud wrote to his fiancée in November of 1883, when he was still a medical student: "Nature has determined woman's destiny through beauty, charm, and sweetness. Law and custom have much to give women that has been withheld from them, but the position of women will surely be what it is: in youth an adored darling and in mature years a loved wife."[3]

But Freud was apparently interested in a different type of woman, of a more intellectual and perhaps "masculine" cast: Emma Eckstein, Loe Kann, Lou Andreas-Salome, Joan Riviere, Marie Bonaparte.[4] As a rule, Freud's intellectual female friends sanctioned the concepts of castration anxiety and penis envy, even though these concepts emphasized female passivity and dependency, characteristics with which women analysts would not have personally identified.[5] In their affiliation with Freud they would inevitably have complied with many of his judgments concerning gender—avoiding "female" topics such as menstruation, pregnancy, and childbirth in their theoretical work and setting themselves apart from those women locked in a "female" world of weakness and intellectual inferiority. A woman analyst instructed in Freudian methodology, analyzed by a first-generation Freudian, perhaps by Freud himself, was likely to undervalue menstruation and other special aspects of female difference.

There were, of course, quite legitimate reasons for the downplay of female sexuality and its specific indicator, menstruation. First, to have emphasized menstruation, a process shared by all *women*, would have created an unwanted distinction between the woman analyst and the male professionals who had assimilated her. Women analysts were understandably reluctant either to accentuate their femaleness or to dispute the premises of psychoanalysis once they had become analysts; nor were they likely to challenge the prevailing assumptions about gender within the phallocentric structure.

Women, after all, were not encouraged to be doctors. One of Freud's colleagues, Fritz Wittels, had cautioned the "weaker sex" not to study medicine at all: "Woman could only be happy as woman, as the object of masculine desire."[6] A similar suppression of the female occurred elsewhere, as women entered male-dominated domains like the law and the university.[7] As a matter of survival, women, who had a difficult enough time entering the medical profession, were not in the position to explore the question of menstruation or to emphasize other gender differences between themselves and their male colleagues. According to Mary Chadwick, some women doctors actually denied their menstrual cycles to give the impression that they, as professionals, were not affected by them. Chadwick contended that the formidable sexist attitudes toward women doctors caused many of them to repudiate their menstruation and their femininity, both having long associations with weakness, hysteria, and trauma: "Many women, especially those belonging to the medical profession, will not admit any diminution of vigour or mental balance at this time [menstruation], because to do so would be a tacit confession of inferiority and confirm that it is a hindrance to their profession."[8]

Nor can it be sufficiently stressed that women analysts, like women everywhere, were/are subject to cultural attitudes toward menstruation and to the taboos that still continue to mark women as a class. Most of the analysts under discussion reached puberty before World War I; as primarily Jewish women they were likely, during the menarche, to have introjected the feelings of shame that persisted in the predominantly Judeo-European culture in which they were reared—a culture in which menstruation was hidden from sight and from contact.[9] One must also remember the unthinkable awkwardness surrounding menstruation at the first decades of the century; women of all classes and ages, unable to purchase disposable sanitary napkins, had no choice but to construct, soak, and launder their own—all the while maintaining secrecy so as not offend with the sight of menstrual stains or the smell of blood.[10] The camouflaging of menstruation, coupled with the embarrassment of homemade paraphernalia, could not have helped but infect the theoretical realm, contributing to a repression of menstruation within the psychoanalytic discourse, especially for women, whose centuries of silence could not so immediately be eradicated by a medical degree or some other badge of professionalism.

*Menstruation and Analytic Experience*

As women analysts became self-confident in the field, some began to excel in what might be considered female areas, such as the analysis of the child; and because it dealt with young patients and their mothers, child analysis was able to generate a number of persuasive theories on the menarche, or first menstruation. In the late 1920s and early 1930s there occurred a major departure from Freudian theory, from an almost exclusive emphasis on the father to a recognition of the mother's agency in shaping the personality of the child. As Janet Sayers has demonstrated, many women analysts participated in this theoretical revision, in part made possible because they had incorporated their personal experiences of mothering into their analytic work.[11]

Every woman analyst who wrote about *menstruation* during this period of change integrated into her theories a consideration of the menstruating mother and of her psychological effect on the adolescent daughter. Analytic accounts of the mother's culpability ranged from Annie Reich's study of a mother who sent her daughter to school "without sanitary napkins so that the blood dripped on the floor"[12] to Helene Deutsch's observations on failed communication in the mother-daughter relationship: "Menstruation is very often the one thing that the mother conceals from her children with particular discretion; it is a secret, and the idea of revealing it meets with great psychological resistance on her part. Many mothers find it easier to talk to their daughters about conception, pregnancy, and birth than about menstruation."[13] In an unpublished adolescent diary, Deutsch recalled that when she was fourteen, she had her first period, without any forewarning from her mother.[14] Deutsch's personal recollection thus enabled her to perceive comparable estrangements among her adolescent patients.

Women analysts, perhaps because of their own ambivalent feelings, tended to blame the mother, attributing the daughter's menstrual anxiety to the mother's secrecy or to her personal negligence.[15] In their increasing commitment to female patients, Deutsch and other women analysts were obliged to look to themselves, to their capacity as mothers or daughters, modifying Freudian theories or constructing ones of their own to deal with the unprecedented issues concerning female sexuality that they, as doctors, were facing.

## Menstrual Frameworks

It was Karen Horney, however, who initiated the critique of Freudian theory in those areas that involved female sexuality: penis envy, castration anxiety, and female passivity. These concepts were subjected to scrutiny and examination during the early 1930s, in what is called the Freud-Jones debate. In challenging the phallocentric attitudes toward female sexuality, Jones assimilated the ideas of two leading women analysts, Karen Horney and Melanie Klein.[16] He argued for the recognition of sexual difference, based on his conviction that from the beginning, the little girl is a little girl and not a little boy.[17]

Another circle to have stimulated the psychoanalytic response to menstruation was the International Psycho-analytical Association on Menstruation, also formed in the early thirties, which produced a special issue of *Zeitschrift für psychoanalytische Pädagogik* devoted to menstrual topics.[18] Of the contributors, Karen Horney is still central to the psychoanalytic investigation of female sexuality; the rest—Heinrich Meng, Mary Chadwick, Karl Landauer, Melitta Schmideberg, Claude Dagmar Daly, Karl Pipal—are primarily forgotten.[19] The work of the International Psychoanalytical Association on Menstruation must be seen as innovative, in that Freud and his followers had barely, by the time of the Freud-Jones debate, addressed the issue of female sexuality, let alone that of menstrual blood. To discuss menstruation a theorist would be required, first of all, to insert female sexuality within the phallocentric system and then to talk about menstruation; one could not introduce a theory of menstruation into a framework that had almost entirely ignored those who menstruate. The equivalent would have been to construct the theory of castration anxiety without extensive reference to either penises or to men.

Owing to the debate and to the publications of special interest groups, there emerged a gradual interest in the previously marginalized topic of menstruation. The women's position became in fact so persuasive that Freud, influenced by their arguments, reviewed and partially revised his theory of female sexuality.[20] The women and men who challenged the Freudian underrepresentation of female sexuality did in fact help to open up what had been, with certain exceptions, a one-sided view, dominated by the phallus and unresponsive to women's functions, above all to menstruation.[21]

## Estrangement

Unfortunately, women analysts, in their revision of Freud, did not unify their individual efforts, with the exception of Karen Horney and Clara Thompson, whose friendship was formed in America, outside of Freud's immediate sphere. In the intensity of their commitment to Freud, women analysts were often estranged from each other, possibly because their theories, which tended to identify women as passive, masochistic, or narcissistic, were antithetical to the idea of a female solidarity based on the very biological and cultural issues that had been ignored by the psychoanalytic institution. Helene Deutsch and Marie Bonaparte had each contradictorily labeled female ambition a form of neurosis, while they themselves pursued ambitious, intellectual careers.[22]

While no one has yet fully studied the dynamics of relationship among Freud's women advocates, their association could hardly be called a sisterhood (although their internal conflicts were minor compared to the bitter rivalry between Freud and the "brothers"—Fliess, Rank, Jung, and other dissenters). Deutsch admittedly had problems with women, resenting other women analysts for trying too hard to win Freud's favors.[23] Similar rivalry existed between Anna Freud and Melanie Klein, who competed in caring for the aging Freud and eventually directed competing psychoanalytic schools in England.[24] These personal competitions often invaded the intellectual sphere, preventing the development of a coherent theory of female sexuality to counter the phallic overview. Freud's personal and theoretical influence, then, is evident even among analysts such as Karen Horney, Melanie Klein, and Clara Thompson, all of whom challenged his authoritative conceptualization of female sexuality. Women analysts between the wars, despite their similarities in theory, class, and gender, were unable to create a consistent theory of menstruation, owing to the personal and analytic differences surrounding the larger issue of female sexuality. Rarely was the menstrual experience viewed as an affirmation of the woman-tie among women.

## Menstrual Networking

Yet given the apparent differences among women analysts concerning a psychology of menstruation, there was also a great deal of agreement, a cross-referencing and mutual citation that approached what might be called "menstrual networking": an intricate exchange of ideas among women in their exploration of menstrual similarities/differences and an unusual consensus among them with regard to the menstrual process. Whereas the first two parts of *Menstruation and Psychoanalysis* concentrated on the impact of menstruation on men, in "Women Analysts" the menstrual issue centers around women and their physical/psychological involvement with periodic bleeding. In this and the remaining chapters I examine the connections among those women who most effectively assimilated menstruation into their theories of female sexuality:

Mary Chadwick (dates uncertain)
Marie Bonaparte (1882–1962)
Helene Deutsch (1884–1982)
Karen Horney (1885–1952)
Melanie Klein (1882–1960)
Clara Thompson (1893–1958)
Therese Benedek (1891–1964)

In this part certain interconnecting themes unfold regarding the menstrual process, among them motherhood, female masochism, and the "wound." There is also a discussion of the most prominent theories about menstruation to have come from women analysts, including the menstrual case history and the increasingly acknowledged premenstrual syndrome. Although none of the analysts under review, except perhaps Helene Deutsch, was to construct a definitive theory about women's bleeding, they all helped to lift the silence surrounding menstruation. Admittedly, their ideas were firmly grounded in male-centered Freudian concepts such as castration anxiety and trauma; yet women analysts were generally quite willing to leave castration to the men. They substituted in its place the more female concept of masochism, in which the genital mutilation is internal rather than external. Appropriately, they went inside, to the uterus, to that hidden place that had so perplexed Freud but to women felt more homelike. It was ultimately their personal knowledge of women's biology that led women analysts to the menstrual core of female sexuality.

As forewarning, much of the menstrual theory articulated by women analysts is intolerably negative, as it is in general analytic writing, where "the positive aspect of menstruation has been considerably neglected."[25]

To a contemporary readership, accustomed to the advances of menstrual technology but more removed from the psychic immediacy of the menstrual process, such attitudes would be especially alienating. During the period between the wars, menstruation was usually perceived as trauma or dysfunction, a theory inherited from Freud and assimilated by women analysts, who often augmented Freud's concept of menstruation as psychic upheaval to include their patients' vivid fantasies of fecal staining, social humiliation, self-torture, cannibalism, and other intramenstrual excesses. A depressing view of female difference lies, then, before us, one fraught with concepts of masochism and mutilation. But female Freudians, while their attitudes toward menstruation tend to be pessimistic, are significant for having placed menstruation within psychoanalytic discourse as part of the female psyche/cycle. In recognizing the role of menstruation within psychoanalytic experience, women analysts contradicted the silence and repression inherent in Freudian theory and, to a partial degree, diminished its secrecy.

## Notes

1. For discussions of Freud's influence on women analysts see in particular Paul Roazen, *Freud and His Followers* (New York: Alfred A. Knopf, 1975); and Estelle Roith, *The Riddle of Freud: Jewish Influences on His Theory of Female Sexuality* (London: Tavistock, 1987). See also the following surveys of women analysts: Janine Chasseguet-Smirgel, *Female Sexuality* (Ann Arbor: University of Michigan Press, 1970), 4–38; Luce Irigaray, *This Sex which Is Not One*, trans. Catherine Porter (1977; Ithaca: Cornell University Press, 1985), 46–66; Ruth Moulton, "Early Papers on Women: Horney to Thompson," *American Journal of Psychoanalysis* 35 (1975): 207–23; and Janet Sayers, *Mothers of Psychoanalysis* (New York: Norton, 1991). These surveys refer briefly to menstruation. For fuller discussions of *menstruation* in the writings of women analysts, see *The Curse*, 73–82.

2. Ernest Jones, *The Life and Work of Sigmund Freud* (New York: Basic Books, 1953), 2:421. Paul Roazen's account of Freud and women is strikingly similar to Jones's; see *Freud and His Followers*, 468–74; and Roith, *The Riddle of Freud*, 35–60.

3. Jones, *Life and Work* 1:176. Freud wrote this letter when he was a mere twenty-seven, but its sentiments are representative of his lifelong conviction that women were fragile and adored.

4. This list of friends is from Jones, *Life and Work* 2:241. Of these five women, only Bonaparte contributed to a theory of menstruation.

5. Lou Andreas-Salome, Freud's correspondent and close friend, was constantly

identified by her relationships to great men (Freud, Tolstoy, Rilke, and others); her writings generally represent women as having weak intellects and masochistic patterns. See Roith, *Riddle of Freud*, 40–49.

6. Fritz Wittels, *Freud and His Times* (New York: Liveright, 1931), 147. Freud evidently reprimanded Wittels for this comment: for his discourtesy, not for his sexual bias. See Roith, *Riddle of Freud*, 37.

7. It has been argued that women analysts had fewer difficulties entering the profession because of Freud's personal affection for women. See Lucy Freeman and Herbert S. Strean, *Freud and Women* (New York: Continuum, 1987), 100.

8. Mary Chadwick, *Difficulties in Child Development* (New York: John Day, 1928), 394.

9. See Leonard Swidler, *Women in Judaism* (Metuchen, N.J.: Scarecrow Press, 1976). Each of the following Jewish women analysts was born near the end of the nineteenth century: Helene Deutsch, Ruth Mack Brunswick, Melanie Klein, Anna Freud, and Marie Bonaparte (born in France of Jewish ancestry). See Roazen, *Freud and His Followers*, 420–88.

10. In World War I, French nurses realized that the cellulose used in bandages would be excellent for sanitary napkins. Although Kimberly-Clark (Kotex) and Johnson and Johnson (Modess) manufactured and marketed their products in America in the 1920s, they were not easily accessible in Europe until many years later. See *The Curse*, 138–39.

11. Sayers, *Mothers of Psychoanalysis*, 3–4. Sayers overestimates the mothering effect in claiming that "once patriarchal and phallocentric, it [psychoanalysis] is now almost entirely mother-centered," 3. For an excellent reading of the mother (and of her absence) in psychoanalysis, see Madelon Sprengnether, *The Spectral Mother: Freud, Feminism, and Psychoanalysis* (Ithaca: Cornell University Press, 1990).

12. Annie Reich, "Analysis of a Case of Brother-Sister Incest," in *Annie Reich: Psychoanalytic Contributions* (1932; New York: International Universities Press, 1973), 14.

13. Helene Deutsch, *The Psychology of Women* (New York: Grune and Stratton, 1944), 1:152.

14. Deutsch, quoted in Paul Roazen, *Helene Deutsch: A Psychoanalyst's Life* (Garden City, N.Y.: Anchor Press/Doubleday, 1985), 24. In her memoir, Deutsch makes no reference to menstruation. See Helene Deutsch, *Confrontations with Myself* (New York: Norton, 1973).

15. Clara Thompson, for example, theorized a causation between the secretive mother and a girl's painful menstruation: "self-conscious, sexually unoriented mothers," of whom there are a "shockingly large number," often delay talking to their daughters about menstruation or threaten them with punishment or even death should pregnancy occur. See *Interpersonal Psychoanalysis: The Selected Papers of Clara M. Thompson,* ed. Maurice R. Green (New York: Basic Books, 1964), 306. Mary Chad-

wick claimed that the girl's adolescent fears are exacerbated by her mother's menstruation, the girl having been exposed throughout childhood to her mother's menstrual irritability, her "negligence in personal cleanliness or in the disposal of stained clothing," and her "strange odor" (the latter having a greater impact on boys than on girls). Mary Chadwick, *The Psychological Effects of Menstruation* (New York: Nervous and Mental Disease Publishing Company, 1932), 28.

16. Jones's attention to the dread of the vagina shows Horney's influence, while his views of early vaginal sensation, the importance of the breast, and the developmental sequence from the girl's oral gratification to her oral relationship with the penis shows the particular influence of Melanie Klein. See Juliet Mitchell, *Psychoanalysis and Feminism* (New York: Pantheon, 1974), 121.

17. See Ernest Jones, *Papers on Psychoanalysis* (Boston: Beacon Press, 1961). One is uncertain, though, about Jones's attitude toward menstruation as difference, since none of the papers that he presented during the debate refer to women's periodicity.

18. See Claude Dagmar Daly, "The Psycho-biological Origins of Circumcision," *International Journal of Psycho-analysis* 31 (1950): 222n. My awareness of this special issue comes from Daly's account; I have not been able to obtain the original journal.

19. Melitta Schmideberg, the daughter of Melanie Klein, had an article in this special issue that argued that the girl interprets menstrual blood as punishment from both parents for the girl's having had coitus with the father; see Melitta Schmideberg, "Psychoanalytisches zur Menstruation," *Zeitschrift für Psychoanalytisches Pädagogie* 5 (1931). The Schmideberg essay is described in Melanie Klein, *The Psycho-analysis of Children*, trans. Alix Strachey (1932; London: Hogarth Press, 1963), 307.

20. Paul Roazen somewhat overstates the case when he claims that certain publications by Helene Deutsch and Karen Horney in the 1920s "stimulated Freud into writing on femininity, since he did not want to be left behind." Roazen, *Helene Deutsch*, 231.

21. "It is remarkable," wrote Chadwick, "that to the present [1932] there has not been very much psychoanalytic research carried out upon this important subject of the psychological effect of menstruation upon the woman." Chadwick, *Effects*, 8.

22. See Roith, *The Riddle of Freud*, 45, 59.

23. See Deutsch, *Confrontations with Myself*. Deutsch refers specifically to Ruth Mack Brunswick and Jeanne Lampl-de Groot. Nancy Chodorow, from interviews with a number of analysts active between the wars, heard unfavorable comments about Deutsch's relationship with women: "Deutsch just wanted to please Freud or personally disliked women." Nancy J. Chodorow, *Feminism and Psychoanalytic Theory* (New Haven: Yale University Press, 1989), 205.

24. See Phyllis Grosskurth, *Melanie Klein: Her World and Her Work* (Cambridge: Harvard University Press, 1987), 245–58.

25. Emilio M. Rodrigue, "Notes on Menstruation," *International Journal of Psycho-*

*analysis* 36 (1955): 333. George Devereux makes much the same comment in "The Psychology of Genital Bleeding: An Analysis of Mohave Indian Puberty and Menstrual Rites," *International Journal of Psycho-analysis* 31 (1950): 251.

# 11

# *Born to Bleed:*
# *Menstruation and Masochism*

When Freud identified the three types of masochism—erotogenic, moral, and feminine—he was by no means limiting "feminine masochism" to women; masochistic perversion in men is directly tied to their being placed "in a characteristically female situation."[1] Women analysts such as Bonaparte, Horney, and Deutsch, on the contrary, consistently used the term *masochism* to designate the painful experiencing of *female* functions: menstruation, childbirth, the menopause. In this chapter I will examine the concept of female masochism, in which such folk beliefs as "suffering is destiny" and "women love pain" were validated through the analytic unraveling of women's menstrual fantasies—fantasies of dirt, dismemberment, and mutilation. Inherent in the concept of female masochism is a major paradox in the psychoanalytic writings on menstruation by women: that menstruation represents an injury, disease, or trauma that satisfies all women's inherent desire for pain, and that menstrual pain, meeting this desire, helps to complement their so-called masochistic impulses.

## Dysfunction and Damage

In the breakthrough essays on female sexuality that she wrote in the late 1920s and early 1930s, Karen Horney emphasized the female experience of pain or injury, often augmented during menstruation. Agreeing with Daly's thesis on the consequences of the mother's menstruation, she observed that when a girl is exposed to an adult's menstrual blood, "she sees demonstrated for the first time the vulnerability of the female body"; these feelings are "confirmed and activated again and again through the evidence of menstruation."[2] Explicitly associating menstruation with women's sense of being damaged, Horney contended that menstruation arouses "cruel impulses and fantasies of both an active and a passive nature."[3] One patient described her menstruation in a violent and agonizing way: she felt "as if her insides were torn out."[4]

While many feminists, Luce Irigaray for one, have praised Horney for challenging Freud's position on female sexuality, Horney's position on menstruation was depressingly negative, consisting almost exclusively of fatalistic observations about menstrual cruelty, pain, pathology, and dysfunction.[5] One of her essays, "Psychogenic Factors in Functional Female Disorders," examined some of the unconscious motives behind female disturbances, among them three menstrual problems: dysmenorrhea (painful menstruation); amenorrhea (absent menstruation); and menorrhagia (profuse menstruation). These problems have in common a complexity of emotional preconditions: an imbalance or increase in libidinal tension, a revival of infantile fantasies, an inescapable bond between menstruation and suffering. "These fantasies have, generally speaking, the content that the sex act is something cruel, bloody, and painful."[6] Here, as elsewhere, she described patients who had perceived menstruation as a wound or injury, who felt internally damaged or ripped apart: "The idea of being damaged makes these women resent their own genitals as a sort of wound, and menstruation is therefore emotionally conceived of as a corroboration of this assumption."[7] One current researcher, though, maintains that the masochistic "wound" conceived at the menarche can be physical as well as psychological. A few months after the arrival of the first period some young women begin to practice "delicate self-cutting": a carefully controlled sequence of lacerations that reportedly helps the adolescent deal with trauma. The cutter views menstruation as the "confirmation that her sexual and procreative organs are damaged and vulnerable to other mutilations."[8]

A number of Horney's contemporaries would have interpreted such mutilations as evidence of female masochism. Horney objected, however, to so sweeping a concept; qualifying the popular position, she asserted that the *frequency* of menstrual disorders such as dysmenorrhea must be clearly demonstrated before establishing a masochistic pattern. Her most important point concerning female masochism (and here we begin to see signs of Horney's shift from Freudian to holistic analysis), is that women's pain is not merely a matter of instinctual drives but must be seen in a cultural context: "The problem of feminine masochism cannot be related to factors inherent in the anatomical-physiological-psychic characteristics of woman alone, but must be considered as importantly conditioned by the culture-complex or social organization in which the particular masochistic woman has developed."[9]

## Dismembered from Within

Helene Deutsch devoted chapter 7 of *The Psychology of Women* to the problem of feminine masochism. Applying the Freudian concepts of castration anxiety and penis envy, she maintained that "the absence of an active organ" leads the girl toward masochism, passivity, and narcissism.[10] Although the masochistic tendency enables women to adjust to the pain of their reproductive functions, masochism, if excessive, is likely to drive the woman from her feminine position, to make her "masculine."[11] Menstruation, along with the genital trauma and the female castration complex, "*naturally* contribute[s] to the masochistic character of her sexual functions."[12]

From the various female complications that arose in her practice, Deutsch generalized that "menstrual disorders represent the most important group of genital disturbances in women, and the most common"; almost every neurosis or emotional problem affects the genital function, and this is "most strikingly and objectively apparent in the monthly bleedings."[13] She stressed the psychological impact of the menstrual process, and especially of the *first* bleeding, which "mobilizes psychic reactions so numerous and varied that we are justified in speaking of the 'psychology of menstruation' as a specific problem."[14]

Features of this problem include incontinence, excessive cleanliness, narcissism, vanity, depression, and physical pain—expressly when the girl has not achieved the appropriate degree of psychological maturity. In agreement through most of *The Psychology of Women* with Freud's fundamental views on menstruation, she contended that the menarche is "usually experienced as a trauma," one that stimulates a morbid interest in the interior of the pubescent girl's body.[15] During the period of height-

ened sensitivity surrounding the menarche, a girl is often depressed, even
suicidal. She feels unclean and views her body as "dirty, distasteful."[16]
At its most extreme, menstruation is associated with internal damage,
even dismemberment: "In the anxieties provoked by the sight or imagined presence of blood, the idea of being torn and dismembered internally
plays an extremely important part."[17]

### Mother's Bloody Revenge

Deutsch's negative views on menstruation and internal injury had a
marked effect on Melanie Klein, who agreed with Deutsch's menstrual
position: "My own data fully bears out Helene Deutsch's view that the
disappointments and shocks to her narcissism which the girl receives
when she begins to menstruate are very great."[18] Klein's hypothesis of
internal damage clearly echoed Deutsch's dismembered body, both bar-
barous representations of the menstrual process. It has been argued,
though, that the Kleinian concept of internal injury must be distinguished
from the more passive female masochism theorized by Deutsch: "For
Melanie Klein *female masochism* is woman's sadism turned not against
herself but against her *bad internalized objects*."[19]

In Klein's opinion, menstrual blood had numerous psychoanalytic
interpretations: its identification with excrement, with the loss of the
wished-for child, with castration.[20] Her major speculation, however, concerned the girl's fear of being attacked internally, for which she offered a
complicated network of motivations, centered around the concept of the
preoedipal mother: the mother of early infancy who loves but also de-
vours, who gives the breast but also denies it. This ambivalently perceived
mother is thought to be "imbued with magic power, for all goodness
stems from the breast and the mother also contains the father's penis and
babies."[21]

During the menarche these memories of the preoedipal mother stimulate fantasies that channel the girl's response to her blood; often, she
interprets her first menstruation as a sign of her mother's revenge. At
the same time, she dreads being sadistically attacked by her father. "Her
phantasy that she has introjected her violent parents in the act of performing sadistic coitus and that they are endangering her own inside in
destroying each other there calls out fears of a very acute kind in her."[22]
Klein's depiction of the introjected parents, while provocative, is some-

how ludicrous; one gets the image of an animated womb, inhabited by a tiny mom and dad who are copulating and, simultaneously, kicking at the walls of the daughter's uterus. For the victim of such violence, the menstruating adolescent, her blood is the "sign that all the injuries she has dreaded to receive and all her hypochondriacal fears have come true." [23] One shudders at Klein's conceptualization until one realizes that she is talking about deeply troubled teenagers of the type fantasized by Stephen King in *Carrie* and not about the menarcheal girl next door.[24] Menstrual anxiety, Klein assures us, is *not* a problem for the pubescent girl already established in her femininity; she would view menstruation as proof of her womanhood.[25]

### Unremembered Pain: Menstrual Blood and Excision

In the writings of Marie Bonaparte, one finds similar images of interior mutilation.[26] Convinced that women were born to bleed and that suffering was destiny, Bonaparte argued that masochistic attitudes are irreparably fixed in childhood. Menstruation, a visible sign of masochistic (self-abasing) injury, is proof that "woman is biologically doomed to suffer. Nature seems to have no hesitation in administering to her strong doses of pain, and she can do nothing but submit passively to the regimen prescribed." [27] Bonaparte further maintained that while for men sexual intercourse is pleasurable, for women it is one more painful experience—unless, of course, the "element of suffering, of masochism, is entirely and essentially absent." [28] Within the reproductive process, menstruation and defloration are especially vulnerable to a masochistic response, since they involve "to some degree the shedding of blood." [29] Ultimately, though, Bonaparte thought that the adult menstrual process played only a tangential role in the erotic development of the female, fixed during the passive oedipal phase: "the menstrual flow, passing later through the vagina, will only confirm an erotogenic mode already present." [30]

Bonaparte, so adept at defining internalized masochistic attitudes, also examined the issue of *externally* inflicted pain, in two case studies of women who had been castrated or excised as a matter of Moslem ritual (similar procedures were conducted in Europe and America to cure young women of excessive masturbation, as we observed in chapter 8). The great irony in Bonaparte's situation was that she had masochistically submitted herself to three operations in which her clitoris was moved closer to the vagina so that she might achieve vaginal orgasm.[31] I believe that her own voluntary castration blocked her interpretation of the two case studies of Egyptian women recorded in "Notes on Excision" (1948), making her oblivious to the affinity between periodic and surgical genital bleedings.

In the first of the two studies, Bonaparte described her subject's reactions to the rite of excision, which occurred when Mrs. A. was only six. "The operation took place in a village, being performed by a sort of witch, a wandering fortune-teller round the villages. She remembered the operation; it was intensely painful."[32] Bonaparte reports that when the excised Mrs. A. later lost her hymen, the bleeding was so intense that she consulted a physician. But when Bonaparte mentions the onset of menstrual blood, her tone is remote: "Mrs. A. began to menstruate at fourteen."[33] Bonaparte draws absolutely no connections among the reported bleedings—hymeneal, clitoral, and menstrual—that were likely to have complicated the patient's vaginal sexuality and to have encouraged the feelings of masochism ascribed to female sexual experience. Such a complex network of interrelationships demands more exacting psychoanalytic unraveling, in that one type of genital bleeding so inevitably impinges on the others. Mrs. A.'s menstrual bleeding would undoubtedly have recalled her excision, a mutilation reinforced during her painful defloration and then periodically, at each subsequent menstruation.[34]

In the study of Mrs. B. a more complicated gap occurs, as Bonaparte glides without logical transition from excision to menstruation, the excision being followed by hemorrhage, infection, and fever: "She remembers her bitterness against her mother for delivering her up to the woman. She hated her for depriving her of something precious, for damaging her in some obscure and unjust way. She began to menstruate at twelve, after the excision. There was no pain and she was not frightened by the sight of blood."[35] In the chronology of the above passage, menstruation occurs "at twelve, after the excision," as if in immediate sequence; but from the text we learn that at least a year had elapsed between these two events. Bonaparte as psychoanalyst seems curiously unaware of this condensation, this fusion of bleedings. Nor does she analyze Mrs. B.'s feelings about her mother, feelings that Bonaparte records in pronouns so ambiguous that the reader cannot adequately distinguish between Mrs. B.'s mother and the "horrible black African woman" who removed the clitoris: "She hated her for depriving her of something precious, for damaging her in some obscure and unjust way." The objective pronoun *her* (the mother or the

exciser, we are not sure) is hated for having deprived Mrs. B. of her clitoris; the ambiguity of the pronoun reference indicates that on an unconscious level, Mrs. B. is indicting *both* women for their participation in the
ritual mutilation. Yet in her analysis of Mrs. B., Bonaparte neither solicits the patient's feelings for the mother nor places the mother-daughter
dynamic within a psychoanalytic framework, as she had effectively done
in her earlier work.[36]

Immediately after the word *excision* appears the sentence *"There was no
pain and she was not frightened by the sight of blood."* As the mother and the
African woman are ambiguously interchangeable, so too are menstruation and excision. Is there "no pain" in menstruation? Or in excision?
In the child? Or the mother? How could a child "approaching eleven,"
brutally excised and hemorrhaging and infected, *not* be frightened by
menstrual blood? Marie Bonaparte was one of the leading advocates of
Freud and a theorist herself, someone who had significantly extended
Freud's sparse comments on female sexuality. Yet in "Notes on Excision"
she ignores the double negatives, the displacements of bleedings and persons, of mothers and excisers. Such linguistic confusions are nonetheless
the primary clues in psychoanalytic interpretation. Trained to explore repression, condensation, and projection, Bonaparte fails to ask herself the
most basic of questions, accepting at face value the patient's recollection.

I have emphasized the case study of Mrs. B. in an effort to counter-
point the strange *deemphasis* of menstruation in Bonaparte's account—
her accepting without question Mrs. B.'s version of reality in a manner
that, in its refusal to recognize painful childhood experiences, parallels
Freud's rejected seduction theory. Here, though, the victimization is un-
questionably "real" and authorized by the community. It seems certain
that the mutilated child would have felt both fright and pain by the repetition, at puberty, of bleeding genitalia, so long associated with wounds
and mutilation.[37] The strong, double denial of the narrative ("*no pain,*"
"*not frightened*") reveals an interpretative distortion, much as Freud's
insistence that "the interpretation is not so difficult" had pointed to a denial of menstruation in the Dream of the Red Bath. Despite her clinical
interest in the mutilation of women, Bonaparte was unable, in "Notes
on Excision," to follow through with a certain line of questioning that
Freud had introduced but then evaded in "The Taboo of Virginity":
the inextricable connection in non-Western cultures between defloration, masochism, and menstruation. It appears that Bonaparte skirted the

question of menstruation because it threatened her personal decision to alter her clitoris—a literally painful decision and a prophetic acting out of the concept of female masochism.

Perhaps, by disavowing the confusions in her narrative, she was simultaneously repressing the voluntary excisions she had herself endured. The second operation, performed in May of 1930 when she was almost forty-eight, was accompanied by a hysterectomy.[38] A traumatic event for many women, a hysterectomy was likely to have been extremely problematic for Marie Bonaparte, whose failed surgical approach to vaginal joy was compounded by the simultaneous removal of the uterus and the end of her reproductive function. Like her Egyptian patients, she too must have experienced intense pain, both physical and psychological, as she submitted to the knife that would alter her clitoris and permanently stop the menstrual flow by way of surgical menopause.

### Internal Uproar

One final revelation about menstruation and masochism comes not from an analyst but from a novelist/patient. In *The Words to Say It* (1983), Marie Cardinal lays open her menstrual ambivalence in an array of images that convey an obsessive, masochistic anxiety about menstruation but at the same time a physical engagement with its fluctuations and rhythms. The opening line, a description of the back street where her analyst is located, metaphorically introduces the masochistic body: "The little cul-de-sac was badly paved, full of bumps and holes, bordered by narrow, partly ruined sidewalks."[39] The menstrual landscape thus mirrors the narrator's condition—her menstrual cramps, the internal uproar of her agitation: "I was ashamed of what was going on inside of me, of this uproar, of this disorder, of this agitation; no one should look, no one should know, not even the doctor."[40]

Attentive to the minutest variations in her period, the narrator isolates herself in the bathroom and watches the blood: "It makes me think of the sea and the waves lapping against the shore with a sigh. I think of the planets unchangingly spinning in their orbits."[41] The fluctuating spin of the menstrual cycle is echoed in her rhythmic recollections: "But instead of experiencing the blood as a punishment, I would feel at the base of my calves a powerful sensation, a sort of pinching, tingling on the borderline of pleasure and pain, progressively spreading to my thighs, and invading my stomach."[42] Pleasure versus pain, the unchanging planets versus blood so thick it was like "producing slices of liver": the extremes of the menstrual process punctuate her experience, feed her metaphors.[43]

Cardinal's psychiatrist magically "stops" these sensations when, bundled in diapers, she tells him on her second visit that she is "bled dry." He responds: "Those are psychosomatic disorders. That doesn't interest me. Speak about something else."[44] With those words the menorrhagia vanishes and Cardinal soon achieves regularity. Benefiting from the immediate therapeutic value, she can now dismiss the diapers, the bundles, the prolific stainings to focus on the analytic process of unearthing her primal repression: the "Thing" that the blood is hiding. The menstruous bleeding will recur only in her memory and in her writing.

Although the analytic resolution of Cardinal's menstrual excess seems at first miraculous, the doctor's verbal curettage is executed through the psychoanalytic denial of women's bleeding explored in *Menstruation and Psychoanalysis*: menstruation either doesn't exist or it camouflages more pressing, childhood memories or it's a psychosomatic disorder that's "all in your head."[45] In keeping with such theories of menstruation as trauma or anxiety neurosis, Cardinal's doctor views her bleeding to be a disorder disruptive to the analysis: "Speak about something else." The language of menstruation is thus tamped, dammed up, so that it will not flood its boundaries.

Against such images of containment, Cardinal's *l'écriture feminine* floods forth—like "hot lava," like urine, like libidinal energy. Nouns spill over nouns over verbs as she finds the words to say *menstruation:* "I had stained so many easy chairs, straight-back chairs, sofas, couches, carpets, beds! I had left behind me so many puddles, spots, spotlets, splashes and droplets, in so many living rooms, dining rooms, anterooms, halls, swimming pools, buses, and other places. I could no longer go out."[46] This overflow of menstrual detail reflects not only Cardinal's fascination with the menstrual process but with language itself—with menstruation as women's writing, as speech act. She agrees with co-author Annie Leclerc that *The Words to Say It* is "an adventure which is made through psychoanalysis, an adventure that is made through words."[47] And, I would add, through unveiling her "Thing," associated throughout the text with menstruation and the mother. The "Thing," with its history of psychoanalytic associations, becomes Cardinal's signifier for the unknown terror at the brink of consciousness.[48]

With emphasis on the very same "Thing," Toni Morrison isolates *The Words to Say It* as the key text in introducing her theory of a repressed Africanist presence in American literature. Morrison, who makes no reference to menstruation, contends that the narrator's initial confrontation with the "Thing," provoked during a Louis Armstrong concert, is "a conceptual response to a black, that is, nonwhite, figuration."[49] While Morrison's chronology is precise, I would argue that the Louis Armstrong concert, which occurs when Cardinal is nineteen, is only secondarily an erotic response to black music and primarily a reaction to the freedom experienced in a sexually arousing environment, away from her mother's restrictions. The Armstrong concert, if one reads the scene psychoanalytically, as the text *demands* that one do, initiates an orgasmic terror and retreat, directly followed by Cardinal's first recollection of the strict, Catholic mother whose maternal aggression comprises the basic motif of the analysis. While Morrison's thesis of repressed blackness is generally convincing, it does not work in the context of Cardinal's suffering, where self-punishment overshadows sexual desire, where the freedom of the jazz arena is replaced, one year later, by a confining, bloody bathroom.

The irregular bleeding starts, then intensifies, emblematic of female masochism—punishing the body/self but also punishing the mother. Cardinal's ambivalence toward her mother is central to her distress and at the origins of her fear of the "Thing," which "made itself known every time I displeased my mother or thought I did."[50] During the menarche her mother warns her that menstruation is painless but "dirty" and that "having your period means you can have children."[51] The analysis reveals that the enormous bleeding from Marie's womb is a masochistic revenge against her mother, who had tried unsuccessfully to abort her, although Carolyn A. Durham, in her book on Cardinal, has emphasized the positive, woman-centered treatment of the mother-daughter relationship and "the strength of the bonds of gender."[52] I would suggest that the menorrhagia is itself a show of strength, empowering Cardinal to confront the blood of menstruation (bleeding as excessive potentiality) with the blood of abortion (bleeding as death, in this case her *mother's* cul-de-sac).

In the afterword to *The Words to Say It* Bruno Bettelheim reviews the menstrual theme, claiming that in "developing a symptom that made her feel utterly disgusting," Cardinal was responding to her mother's failed abortion; through her bleeding she fulfilled her mother's former desire for "some bleeding to indicate the loss of the fetus."[53] Bettelheim also men-

tions the analyst's treatment—how a "few words uttered by a psychoanalyst" could have ended a previously untreatable symptom. In Bettelheim's
view an instant cure is not unusual; a person so strongly dominated by her
unconscious can respond "much more than average people to what they
feel are the strong inner convictions of persons of importance to them."[54]
Namely, mothers and analysts. Durham dissects Bettelheim's doubtful
role in *The Words to Say It,* charging him with inconsistencies, with an
authoritative control of Cardinal's narrative, and with too great a faith in
the truth of his own (and the doctor's) interpretations.[55] I would attribute
the dramatic cessation of bleeding to Cardinal's response to professional
(male) authority rather than to what Bettelheim defensively characterizes
as her analyst's "strong inner convictions," hardly conspicuous after one
short office visit. Furthermore, if, on doctor's orders, the menstrual repression had persisted, the condition might have reverted to menstrual
depletion or amenorrhea: the absence of flow, emptiness, no words to
say it.

As I have suggested throughout *Menstruation and Psychoanalysis,* the
menstrual flow that colors women's texts would have life/fertility conno-

tations as well as death/masochism ones. Menstruation, since it represents the body's potential to bear children, would offer Cardinal the
choice to give birth in opposition to her mother's desire to abort. For
the creative writer, the artist, the musician, for women functioning in
privileged cultural environments, menstruation also offers a buildup and
overflow of energy that can be channeled into print and other media. In
Cardinal's case, menstruation becomes both the subject and the instrument of her self-exploration; it is the blood-force, too overwhelming, in
the life and in the recollection of that life, to be silenced. Against doctor's
orders, she reinitiates the unspeakable symptoms, thus achieving pleasure, release, and dis/order—that sense of spinning with the planets and
flowing with the sea that informs her fluid prose.

### Notes

1. See J. Laplanche and J.-B. Pontalis, *The Language of Psycho-analysis,* trans.
Donald Nicholson-Smith (New York: Norton, 1973), 245. Freud connected women's
desire for self-abasement to "the suppression of women's aggressiveness," a condition
that "favours the development of powerful masochistic impulses" (*SE* 22:116).
2. Karen Horney, "The Denial of the Vagina," in *Feminine Psychology,* ed. Harold

Kelman (New York: Norton, 1973), 159; and Horney, "Inhibited Femininity," in *Feminine Psychology*, 76.

3. Horney, "Premenstrual Tension," in *Feminine Psychology*, 99.

4. Horney, "Psychogenic Factors in Functional Female Disorders," in *Feminine Psychology*, 173.

5. Luce Irigaray, *This Sex which Is Not One*, trans. Catherine Porter (1977; Ithaca: Cornell University Press, 1985), 49.

6. Horney, *Feminine Psychology*, 172–73. In a paper written in the same year, Josine Müller, an admirer of Horney, investigated the disorder of delayed menstruation, which in some cases is postponed until the nineteenth year. Delayed menstruation causes chronic depression and is often accompanied by an early and extended menopause. Müller attributes late menstruation to the castration complex and to the repression of vaginal wishes. See Josine Müller, "A Contribution to the Libidinal Development of the Genital Phase in Girls," *International Journal of Psycho-analysis* 13 (1932): 362–68.

7. Horney, "Psychogenic Factors," in *Feminine Psychology*, 172.

8. Louise J. Kaplan, *Female Perversions* (New York: Doubleday, 1991), 389.

9. Horney, "The Problem of Feminine Masochism," in *Feminine Psychology*, 232.

10. Deutsch's observations reframed and amplified Freud's sparing comments on menstruation as trauma into a theory that, while rooted in his schema, became her own distinct contribution to a concept of menstruation and female sexual dynamics. See the thorough discussion of Deutsch's reliance on Freud's metapsychology in Miriam J. Wimpfheimer and Roy Schafer, "Psychoanalytic Methodology in Helene Deutsch's *The Psychology of Women*," *Psychoanalytic Quarterly* 46 (1977): 287–318.

11. In her generous assessment of Deutsch's theory of masochism, Brenda Webster claims that ultimately Deutsch believed that female masochism could be used creatively in the development of the female personality. Like all recent commentaries on Deutsch, Webster's fails to elaborate on the specific problems of the menstrual cycle as they relate to masochistic tendencies. Brenda Webster, "Helene Deutsch: A New Look," *Signs* 10 (1985): 553–71.

12. Helene Deutsch, *The Psychology of Women* (New York: Grune and Stratton, 1944), 1:251, 278, emphasis mine. The word *naturally* implies a biological destiny over which women have no control, as if they were being moved about by the processes and functions that govern them. According to Marcia Cavell, "occasionally [in reading Deutsch] one has the impression that it is genitalia which are being analyzed rather than people." Marcia Cavell, "Since 1924: Toward a New Psychology of Women," in *Women and Analysis*, ed. Jean Strouse (Boston: G. K. Hall, 1985), 164.

13. Deutsch, *The Psychology of Women* 1:182.

14. Ibid., 1:149.

15. Ibid., 1:157. Katherine Dalsimer feels that Deutsch's views on the menarche are representative of the psychoanalytic literature, which has concentrated on

the "negative impact of menstruation—its regressive and anxiety-arousing aspects." Katherine Dalsimer, *Female Adolescence* (New Haven: Yale University Press, 1986), 57.

16. Deutsch, *The Psychology of Women* 1:149, 157–68.

17. Ibid., 1:150.

18. Melanie Klein, *The Psycho-analysis of Children*, trans. Alix Strachey (1932; London: Hogarth Press, 1963), 306.

19. Janine Chasseguet-Smirgel, *Female Sexuality* (Ann Arbor: University of Michigan Press, 1970), 34.

20. Klein, *Psycho-analysis of Children*, 307–8. These powerful insights on menstruation from *Psycho-analysis of Children* are not acknowledged in the index to *The Writings of Melanie Klein*, ed. R. E. Money-Kyrle, with B. Joseph, E. O'Shaughnessy, and H. Segal (London: Hogarth Press, 1975). The only reference to *menstruation* is to her 1936 review of Mary Chadwick's *Woman's Periodicity*.

21. Melanie Klein, "The Oedipus Complex in Light of Early Anxieties," in *Love, Guilt, and Reparation*, ed. Masud R. Khan (London: Hogarth Press, 1945), 413.

22. In "The Dread of Woman" (1932) Horney praises Klein's theory on the sadistic impulses, *Feminine Psychology*, 141.

23. Klein, *Psycho-analysis of Children*, 307.

24. See *The Curse*, 181–82, for the menstrual implications of Steven King's *Carrie* and of Brian de Palma's adaptation into film.

25. Klein, *Psycho-analysis of Children*, 308–9.

26. In her autobiography Deutsch, in referring to Bonaparte, singles out their "mutual interest in female masochism." See Helene Deutsch, *Confrontations with Myself* (New York: Norton, 1973), 139. According to Person, Bonaparte was "a chief architect of the theory of feminine masochism [and] saw it as a necessary concomitant of female sexual development." Ethel Person, "Some New Observations on the Origins of Femininity," in *Women and Analysis*, ed. Jean Strouse (Boston: G. K. Hall, 1985), 252.

27. Marie Bonaparte, "Passivity, Masochism, and Femininity" (1934), in *Female Sexuality*, trans. John Rodker (1949; New York: International Universities Press, 1953), 171.

28. Ibid., 170.

29. Ibid., 169.

30. Bonaparte, "Outline of the Development of Female Sexuality," in *Female Sexuality*, 140.

31. Celia Bertin, *Marie Bonaparte* (New Haven: Yale University Press, 1987), 170. According to Michel Erlich, Bonaparte is "historically the second psychoanalyst (but the first woman) to have conducted the study of feminine sexual mutilations, interesting herself particularly in excision, a subject charged with personal resonances." Michel Erlich, *La femme blessée: Essai sur les mutilations sexuelles féminines* (Paris: Editions l'Harmattan, 1986), 188; translation mine.

32. Bonaparte, *Female Sexuality*, 196.

33. Ibid.

34. In the case of Mrs. A., Helene Deutsch's theory of menstruation as a *repetition* of trauma seems singularly applicable: "The periodic repetition of menstruation every time recalls the conflicts of puberty and reproduces them in a less acute form." See Deutsch, "The Psychology of Woman in Relation to the Functions of Reproduction," paper delivered at the Eighth International Conference in Salzburg and reprinted in *The Psychoanalytic Reader: An Anthology of Essential Papers with Critical Introductions*, ed. Robert Fliess (New York: International Universities Press, 1973), 196.

35. Bonaparte, *Female Sexuality*, 197.

36. See for example the essay "L'identification d'une fille a sa mère morte," *Revue française de psychoanalyse* 2 (1928): 541–65.

37. One social psychologist who interviewed twenty-seven circumcised Sudanese women between 1979 and 1982 found that in almost every case, the subject described her first menstruation as painful, for example, "The menses were exceedingly painful, with much clotting." Hanny Lightfoot-Klein, *Prisoners of Ritual* (New York: Harrington Park Press, 1989), 262.

38. Bertin, *Marie Bonaparte*, 170–81.

39. Marie Cardinal, *The Words to Say It*, trans. Pat Goodheart (Cambridge: Van Vactor and Goodheart, 1983), 1.

40. Ibid., 3.

41. Ibid., 23.

42. Ibid., 101.

43. Ibid., 31.

44. Ibid., 31–32.

45. Even Clara Thompson expressed an "all-in-your-head" attitude when she wrote that for many adolescent girls, menstrual discomfort has psychic origins: "Actual malaise, severe pain, headaches, nausea, vomiting, and complete prostration may occur without demonstrable cause. Certainly, very often these symptoms are conversion phenomena, i.e., expressions in somatic symptoms of emotional states." See Clara M. Thompson, *Interpersonal Psychoanalysis: The Selected Papers of Clara M. Thompson*, ed. Maurice R. Green (New York: Basic Books, 1964), 305.

46. Cardinal, *The Words to Say It*, 4. A similar image appears in Nadine Mac Donald's poem, "On Menstruating in the Middle of a Lecture on the Fall of the Roman Empire." She describes staining her "yellow taffeta" and leaving her mark on a white velvet chair. Mac Donald relates her staining to the "cradle of civilization." See *The Curse*, 189.

47. "Une aventure qui se fait a travers la psychoanalyse, une aventure qui se fait a travers les mots." Marie Cardinal and Annie Leclerc, *Autrement Dit* (Paris: Bernard Grasset, 1977), 85.

48. Kenneth Maurice Reinhard brilliantly glosses the term the *Thing*, through its

roots in Hegel and Heidegger, considering its significance for Freud (*das Ding* or "something else"), and Lacan (*La chose Freudienne*, a "hole in the real"). According to Reinhard, the "Lacanian Thing reveals its origin in Freud's writing at the maternal gap where primal repression and foreclosure [the unwillingness to divide the self] converge." Melanie Klein's primordial mother influenced Lacan in his formulation of the maternal gap. See Kenneth Maurice Reinhard, "Allegories of Mourning: Henry James, Psychoanalysis, and Representation" (Ph.D. diss., Johns Hopkins University, 1989), 166–73, 253–65. The Lacanian view seems to apply to Cardinal's situation: to her repression of the "Thing" and to her loss of the maternal.

49. Toni Morrison, *Playing in the Dark: Whiteness and the Literary Imagination* (Cambridge: Harvard University Press, 1992), vi, viii.

50. Cardinal, *The Words to Say It*, 143–44.

51. Ibid., 112.

52. Carolyn A. Durham, *The Contexture of Feminism: Marie Cardinal and Multicultural Literacy* (Urbana: University of Illinois Press, 1992), 232.

53. Cardinal, *The Words to Say It*, 303–4.

54. Ibid.

55. See Durham, *Contexture of Feminism*, 247–52. I wish to thank Carolyn Durham for sharing with me her discussion of Bettelheim while it was in its prepublication stage.

# 12

# *Constructing Menstruation*

*Menstruation and Psychoanalysis* had its beginnings in the turmoil of the Freud-Fliess relationship—in their misconception that the nose dominated the genitalia and in their negligent surgery on Emma Eckstein. It concludes with an overview of the theoretical approaches taken by women analysts as they attempted to interpret the phenomenon of menstruation and its effect on female psychology. Although like most second-generation Freudians, they adhered to much of the fundamental theory laid out by the founder of psychoanalysis, women analysts were very much persuaded by what they had been discovering about menstruation in their clinical practice—in the intimate sessions with female patients who complained about their premenstrual anxiety or who revealed their menarcheal fantasies. From their analytic sessions, women analysts constructed convincing theories concerning the impact of the menstrual process on the psychic lives of women, contributions that have yet to be acknowledged. This chapter examines the most significant of these theories and/or methodologies: the premenstrual syndrome, cultural theory, vicarious menstruation, the menstrual analogue of witch, menstrual repetition, and the menstrual case study.

## PMS

The now-familiar term premenstrual syndrome (PMS) probably originated with Karen Horney, although earlier analysts had also observed a change in female behavior at the approach of menstruation.[1] In psychoanalytic terms, PMS is a phase preceding the menstrual period in which a woman may experience certain behavioral, even pathological problems: depression, irritability, and distress are terms commonly used to describe its symptoms. Otto Fenichel, who used the term *pre-menstrual body feeling* instead of *premenstrual tension,* said that the symptoms, if the woman is disturbed, can suggest "tension, retention, (sometimes pregnancy), dirt, pregenitality, hatred."[2]

In her 1931 essay "Premenstrual Tension," Horney claimed that "feelings of self-depreciation" and irritability occur premenstrually among "otherwise healthy women," feelings that subside at the onset of menstruation.[3] Although Horney referred to hormonal fluctuation within the cycle, her basic approach was psychoanalytic; she related the premenstruum to women's sense of being injured, as she had done in "Inhibited Femininity" (1926–27), and further observed, from her analysis of women, that menstruation evokes "cruel impulses and fantasies of both an active and a passive nature."[4] In the few days before menstruation these feelings intensify, and at times the dreams of the premenstruum predict the blood: "A patient T spontaneously reported that prior to her period her dreams were always sensuous and red, that she felt as though under the pressure of something wicked and sinful and that her body felt heavy and full. With the onset of menstruation she would immediately have a feeling of relief."[5] Horney attributed this fullness to certain psychological factors: her patient had a "domineering and quarrelsome" mother but a devoted father; the patient had a disappointing sexual life and an early hysterectomy; she had always wanted a child.

The wish to have a child, corroborated by other case studies, governed Horney's theory of the premenstrual syndrome: "*Without exception* and completely independent of the rest of the neurotic structure," premenstrual tension occurs when a woman greatly desires to have a child but when "there is such a strong defense against it that its realization has never been even a remote possibility."[6] In other words, the greater the desire for a child, the more distressed the woman becomes when, immediately prior to menstruation, she comprehends that conception is impossible. Women whose lives are not caught in this inner conflict would be unlikely to suffer from premenstrual tension.

Horney's discovery of the psychological factors regarding PMS was significant, almost prophetic. Yet her emphasis on the desire for pregnancy seems too simple, given the many other psychological and biochemical factors that have been determined to contribute to premenstrual anxiety: stress within the family or at work; the accumulation of physical discomforts such as bloatedness, sore breasts, constipation; fluctuations of the female gonad hormones and of the cycles—what is called the "hypothalamic-pituitary-gonadal (HPG) system."[7]

### *Menstruation and Cultural Attitudes*

While Horney's work on the premenstrual syndrome is largely unacknowledged, her placement of female sexuality within a social context has been applauded by analysts but especially by cultural feminists: Horney was "among the first to develop in detail a description of some of the effects of cultural pressures in producing neurosis."[8] One sees traces of cultural theory in Horney's early work—in "The Distrust between the Sexes," for example, where she argued that woman is not "inferior, only different, but that unfortunately she has fewer or none of those human or cultural qualities that man holds in such high esteem."[9] After Horney went to Chicago in 1932, she began to extend her cultural critique; at this juncture the topic of menstruation, so significant in her earlier evaluation of penis envy and of the male dread of the vagina disappeared from her analyses, presumably because in her shift from a Freudian to a holistic psychology, the biological/psychological aspects of menstruation had lost their specific relevance.[10]

To a greater extent than Horney, Clara Thompson attributed the difficulties surrounding menstruation to factors of culture and gender; she felt that in our society, as in primitive cultures, there are still feelings of shame attached to menstrual blood, a need to hide it from men. Changing times have changed many of these self-deprecatory attitudes as women, in their rebellion against the notion of "femininity," have become increasingly "strong and self-respecting."[11]

In her work with pubescent girls, Thompson found a number of instances where the menarche was difficult not because of physical discomfort but because the girls' formerly active behavior had been curtailed.

One energetic youngster was told, at her menarche, the she was now prohibited from going hiking and camping with her brother. She thus interpreted menstruation as a "sign of her disgrace, the sign that she had no right to be a person." [12] Another girl fixed her resentment of menstruation onto the associated paraphernalia, refusing to accept the sanitary napkin her mother gave her because she felt humiliated, "like a baby with a diaper." [13] In each of these situations, the cultural expectations were that the girl should alter her behavior: the hiker must give up her aggression and become ladylike; the adolescent with the napkin must surrender her former dignity and become a baby girl. This initial resentment toward menstruation is invariably repeated as the girl grows into womanhood. In Thompson's judgment, "many painful menstrual periods are not due to organic difficulties at all but to protests against being female." [14]

### Bleeding Elsewhere

Helene Deutsch, the most theoretical of Freud's female followers, wrote with conceptual force about menstrual issues. She offered the fullest psychoanalytic treatment, to my knowledge, of the quasi-mystical occurrence of vicarious menstruation, a bleeding that by definition circumvents the vagina: *vicarious, from the Latin, meaning substituted.* Vicarious menstruation, which has little apparent relevance to the female cycle, is generally viewed as a male phenomenon, as evidenced in the various studies that associate vicarious menstruation with the male desire to appropriate the menstrual function.[15] Deutsch, though, in considering how vicarious menstruation affects *women,* was exploring virgin terrain that involved innovative but often tenuous speculations.

Deutsch contended that the patient's psyche is responsible for choosing the substituted site (boys favor ear lobes, girls the hair and fingernails). In vicarious bleeding the discharge is usually transferred to an area at a distance from the vagina, like the nose or chin; the choice of the alternate location is "usually psychologically determined." [16] Deutsch described the case of one female patient who at the age of twenty-two had only one menstrual period, in her fifteenth year; "later she suffered from irregular bleedings under the skin of one ear lobe, to which she always reacted with the most violent hypochondriac anxieties." [17] In later years, upon learning that her sister had given birth, the patient developed a lump on her back. The biopsy indicated that there were "a large number of blood-filled cysts in the tissues around the vertebrae," which Deutsch interpreted as "vicarious menstruations that, in conformity with the patient's fantasies, had avoided the genitals and were localized in her back." [18] Rather than viewing these bizarre occurrences as isolated and unlikely events, as they indeed seem to be, Deutsch traced the bleeding to earlier episodes, for instance, the girl's childhood habit of "plucking" her ear to keep from masturbating. Deutsch referred to Andrea, the heroine of Karen Michaelis's story "The Child," who desired to bleed vicariously, "to bleed every day from her nose or the pulse artery of her wrist, so that it [the blood] could be seen." [19] Lest all of these narratives seem hypochondriacal, Deutsch admitted that physiological factors may have influenced the menstrual fantasies.

## *Menstrual Analogue: The Witch*

The most unusual theory to have emerged from women analysts was Mary Chadwick's complex presentation of the menstruating woman as witch, an analogy that resonates through *The Psychological Effects of Menstruation*.[20] The witch flavors the entire text, in one instance representing the menstruous mother; in another the degenerative aspects of the reproductive process; in another the "perversion associated with anal and oral stages of development, cannibalism and poisoning." [21] Like Kali, Judith, and the Medusa, the witch was grounded in the kind of mythological representation that, since Oedipus, had informed psychoanalytic theory.

Chadwick's witch seems to have sprung full-grown from her theory of the menstrual taboo, where she maintained that the cultural isolation of the menstruating woman was a practice initiated by women themselves, to save the community from their contamination.[22] Menstrual restrictions, she surmised, became historically necessary because women's menstrual symptoms were so threatening to early social order that they chose to lock themselves away, containing their feelings of hostility, revenge, and envy so that they were no longer a threat to the community.[23]

Like the menstruating "primitive," the witch threatened the stability of the community, reversing the ordinary patterns of female reproductive and social behavior; instead of acting as midwife, she carried out abortions or sacrificed children in her bloody rituals.[24] In her aberrant behavior, the witch behaved irrationally, like a menstruating woman, an analogy that Chadwick presented again and again: "If we should investigate the characteristics of these persons [female witches], and the symptoms of their menstrual derangements, we find a startling similarity between these and those which make their appearance in women during the menstrual period."[25] Such "menstrual derangements," both normal and psychotic (she rarely distinguishes between the two), accompany the "*monthly neurosis*"; these would include feelings of vengeance and hostility; an impulse to steal, injure, and abuse; an impulse toward suicide; an envy of all things masculine.[26]

In her application of witches to menstruous women, Chadwick regrettably managed to portray one of the most negative readings of menstruation in psychoanalytic theory. With homosexuality as her basic ingredient, she tossed the major mental disorders of the day into the analytic kettle, describing the witch as the "homosexual woman suffering from an obsessional neurosis, a masculinity complex, with envy of the phallus of the father as well as the breasts of the mother, connected with an overwhelming mother-fixation."[27]

What I find most disturbing about Chadwick's thesis is its inference of universality. Like the image of the contaminated woman in early cultures, so the notion of the menstruating witch reflected her disregard for women's rhythms—for her reproductive, emotional, and behavioral constellations. Chadwick made it clear that tabooed women and medieval sorcerers were not all that different from the "modern" women of the 1930s. Each had caroused under the menstrual moon; each had in some way confessed to obsessions and perversions.

Like the witch, her female patients would have faced her psychoanalytic judgment, which was based on a fusion between standard Freudian concepts—hysteria, sadism, penis envy, the obsessional neuroses—and her unique ideas on the psychological effects of the menstrual process. Her writings on witchcraft both reflected and reinforced the common assumptions associated with menstruation, which she substantiated through psychoanalytic diagnosis. A new-day inquisitor, Chadwick was in the practice of "smelling out witches,"[28] hardly conscious that, had she lived in fourteenth-century Europe, she, as a literate medical practitioner, would have been burned at the stake.[29]

### A Play of Repetitions

Wilhelm Fliess had used the word *periodicity* to describe the cyclical rhythms of the female and male cycles and their cumulative effect on the psyche. While Deutsch investigated specific cases and problems related to the menstrual process, her general perspective regarding menstruation, like Fliess's before her, stressed periodicity.[30] Deutsch perceived the menstrual cycle not as an isolated, five-day stage but rather as a series of interconnected responses linking a woman's behavioral patterns, fantasies, and symptoms to earlier phases in development and to phases yet to be: prepuberty, puberty, adolescence, coitus, childbirth, motherhood, the menopause. Menstrual anxiety can invariably be traced to earlier stages of development: to birth, to infancy, to the effect of the mother. Thus the menopause, from Deutsch's perspective, is a play of repetitions in which the climacterium repeats menstruation repeats puberty repeats prepuberty repeats childhood repeats the preoedipal phase repeats the birth trauma—not statically but in a dramatic interplay of traumas, fantasies, and dreams. To repeat is to re/experience. Deutsch went on to argue that the perceptions of the preoedipal phase are restated in "prepuberty" through the emotional reenactment of the daughter-father-mother triangle and through the girl's renunciation of the mother.[31] She consistently made these bio/psychological parallels, as in her argument that "premenstrual symptoms do not take hold until several years after the menarche and . . . are repeated over and over again. This experience teaches women to be sensitive to the preliminary stages of the organic process."[32]

In demonstrating menstruation as periodic repetition, Deutsch proposed a sequence of intertwined analogies; she juxtaposed the climacterium with puberty and the preclimacterium with prepuberty, in a before/after parallelism that is a striking augmentation of Freudian theory. As in prepuberty, so in the menopause the ego is awakened to the major changes in the body. But where puberty signifies the promise of a child, the menopause connotes that the child is forever lost. The menopause is a "second puberty" that, "like the first, is marked by all kinds of oddities of conduct."[33] These are but a few of the parallels that appear with great frequency in both volumes of *The Psychology of Women*, highlighting Deutsch's theory of periodic repetition—beginnings, endings, parallel structures—in a woman's life cycle.

The theory of cyclical repetition also informed the questionable concept of biological servitude, Deutsch's hypothesis that women were destined to serve the species in the task of reproduction. Deutsch claimed that "for woman coitus is above all an act of fecundation, the *beginning* of the reproductive function, which *ends* with the birth of the child."[34] The sex act for woman is fulfilled not in intercourse but in childbirth, the time when she "consummates her individual act in the service of the species."[35] Indispensable to Deutsch's doctrine of servitude was the menstrual function, for it is upon witnessing her blood that the pubescent girl internalizes her servant's status: "For the first time in the girl's development, we are faced with the double function of the female as a sexual creature and as a servant of the species."[36] Woman's role as reproductive servant begins at the first menstruation, continues through each menstrual cycle, climaxes in the orgasm of giving birth, and terminates in the menopause, at which time woman "ends her service to the species."[37]

Through her concept of servitude Deutsch imposed tremendous limitations on women's lives while at the same time detaching herself from the servant's function, much as Chadwick had disassociated herself from the witch. This tendency of women analysts to label and to limit other women for biological reasons is possibly the most irritating aspect of their psychoanalytic theories of menstruation. There is a way, though, to read Deutsch's theory of periodic repetition in a mildly positive way, as it affects menstruation and menopause. One finds in *The Psychology of Women* a coherent sense of women's bio/logical and psycho/logical uniformity; women are distinctive for their cyclical patterns of behavior and, by implication, for their stability within the species.[38] In placing women's menstrual/interior functions within the context of an ordered regularity, Deutsch formulated an image of wholeness that counteracts the more fragmented notions of women as witchy, hysterical, in pieces.[39]

### Tabulating Rhythm

Deutsch gleaned much of her theory from clinical work, from recording the menstrual anxiety of patients such as "Molly" and "Evelyn." It would be imprudent to undervalue such case histories, for in soliciting a reaction to menstrual difficulties, women analysts were opening up the door that Freud had so firmly closed on Emma Eckstein, on "Irma," and on the woman who dreamed the red camellia. Early explorers in the psychoanalytic field had done menstrual case studies, most significantly Krafft-Ebing; in *Psychosis Menstrualis* he described the symptoms of "Marie," a fourteen-year-old patient with a history of childhood disorders stemming from a hydrocephalic condition. Marie had been unable to cope with her early menstruation and her premature sexual development: "The psychic troubles, in conjunction with menstrual events, did not stop."[40] This account, like many of Krafft-Ebing's case studies, ends on an ominous note: "A picture of moral imbecility both before and after."[41]

Mary Chadwick was one of the first analysts to have included an investigation of the patient's cycle within the framework of the analysis. Her case histories were, in comparison to Krafft-Ebing's, encouraging, for she believed that through psychoanalytic treatment of the patient's menstrual symptoms, which are generally connected to melancholia, "they become modified and at last disappear."[42] The appendix to *The Psychological Effects of Menstruation* includes two case histories purportedly meant to demonstrate the connections between girls under treatment and the symptoms of women accused of being witches, although only the first case of "A.B." mentions witchcraft. In each of these cases Chadwick discovered an intensification of emotions, fantasies, and dreams during the ten days that included the menstrual cycle. During her periods, "A.B." had recurrent dreams of "small animals, coming like maggots from her body, feeding upon her, or crawling up and over her legs, biting her."[43] Chadwick's interpretation, given her menstrual viewpoint, is disappointingly orthodox: the girl wanted her brother's phallus, the adult phallus, and a baby. She does not clarify if "A.B." wanted or did not want her periods.

The case of "C.D." involved a nurse who came to analysis because of her "intense affection for other women," which the woman thought was "abnormal."[44] Chadwick traced her patient's sexual preference to her fixation on her mother, a cold woman who had never prepared "C.D." for her first menstruation. During her periods the nurse experienced birth and suicide fantasies, as well as "acute anxiety dreams" in which the symbols were menstrual: "dangerous, overwhelming floods" and "towering waves that threatened to sweep her helplessly away," fantasies that Chadwick connects to the mother-fixation, outwardly expressed in unhappiness, sulking, and an attachment to older women of authority.[45] These case studies, while not particularly innovative in their interpretation of the analytic material, nonetheless represent a breakthrough in menstrual inquiry.

One woman analyst surpassed all others, though, in her use of the case study. Therese Benedek began her psychoanalytic career in Budapest, using the Freudian model, but with immediate modifications such as focusing on female patients and writing about menstruation. In the mid-twenties she treated a patient who protested her "feminine role" by way of a nosebleed and concluded that the nosebleed was to some extent a repetition of the menstrual trauma.[46] This kind of individualized therapeutic encounter subsided in 1942, when Benedek and an endocrinologist at the Chicago Institute for Psychoanalysis, Boris B. Rubenstein, published a monograph for the National Research Council.[47] Gradually, her methodology shifted from the talking cure to the actual, scientific tracking of varying levels of estrogen and progesterone during the sexual cycle. While Benedek viewed her work as providing verification for Freud's theories of female sexuality, her elaborate tabulations of female rhythms seem more akin to Fliess's efforts to link menstruation and psychoanalysis to physiology.

The Benedek-Rubenstein study examined fifteen women for a total of 152 hormonal cycles, intermingling psychoanalytic observation with a record of hormone levels by way of a pap smear. Because individuals were under psychiatric care, there was not a single participant who "had a well-balanced emotional or sexual life," a factor Benedek considered beneficial, since "normal" women would have been unable to highlight the changes as effectively.[48] As methodology, the case histories are invaluable in that the findings are based on a consistent record of psychological and physiological findings. They have a greater continuity than the histories taken by Chadwick and Deutsch because of their intense, day-to-day charting. We learn about menstrual problems and fantasies with amazing clarity from women who are articulating menstruation as part of a cycle of hormonal rise and recession. In most instances menstruation is part of the participant's clinical diary, which Benedek documented with medical detachment, as in case 4 ("Twenty-seven-year-old married white woman"): "When the patient was eleven years of age, she developed a goiter which later disappeared. Her first menstrual flow occurred between her eleventh and twelfth year. She married when she was twenty-one and soon became pregnant. . . . The patient's menstrual cycles were always irregular until the onset of hyperthyroidism, after which the cycles were from 28 to 30 days long and the menstrual flow was abundant. Before the onset of the menstrual flow, her psychosomatic symptoms increased and her anxiety was intensified."[49]

Benedek ran into one unfortunate snag, however, in her efforts to trace the effects of the menstrual process: "Patients were inclined to be especially reluctant to prepare vaginal smears during the menstrual flow. . . . Most of the 152 cycles are therefore not complete because slides for this period are lacking."[50] The menstrual taboo, that notorious barrier against full participation in the life of the community, is here seen in another dimension—as preventing full cooperation in self-administered vaginal smears. Although Benedek did not further discuss this matter, the patients' reticence is felt throughout *Psychosexual Functions in Women;* the blank to be filled under *vaginal smear* is all too regularly answered with the word "*NONE.*"

From the perspective of *Menstruation and Psychoanalysis,* the most valuable findings in Benedek's investigation entail her correlations between dreams and menstruation. As a rule Benedek discussed the dreams from her clinical position, as in her generalization that when progesterone levels are declining, "dreams and fantasies about childbirth, about abortion, or about the impending menstrual flow are the emotional representations of a need for discharge from the genitals."[51] One of the dreams she recorded contained imagery comparable to Freud's Dream of the Red Bath: "Swimming around in a red sea. Part of the water was not red, part of the water was red. I could swim best in the part which was red."[52] In her brief analysis of this dream, Benedek related the watery redness to menstruation, although she also explored other elements, such as infantile sexuality, masturbation, and filth.

In another dream of blood, a patient, jealous of her brother's birth, dreamed of a marble of "red stone," of floods, and of rivers. According to Benedek, the blood is from her mother's giving birth but also represents her own urine, which, like her mother's blood, had soiled the linens. At each premenstrual or menstrual phase, the patient repeated the dream: "She dreams and has fantasies repeatedly about bloody sheets, bloody lakes, floods tinted with blood."[53]

*Psychosexual Functions of Women* was undoubtedly an innovation in the psychoanalytic investigation of the menstrual process, a text in which menstruation, instead of being ignored or disguised, was situated at day one of the analysis. I am suspicious, however, of the overall accuracy of the psychoanalytic components and of their placement within the hormonal calendar. Additionally, the charts, statistics, and tables would tend to alienate readers accustomed to the more informal and interpretive narrative style of classical, psychoanalytic texts. While Benedek retained the meta/economic language of Freudian discourse—*libido, resistances, fixations, superego,* and so forth—gone is the suggestive delight of psychoanalytic reading, the playfulness of metaphor, the multifarious interchange of dream and symbol.[54]

With the growth of clinical psychology, researchers have repeatedly applied Benedek's basic methodology, just one example being a 1984 study of female undergraduates from Indiana University that showed that women in the menstrual and premenstrual phases more frequently watched verbally hostile television programs than at other times.[55] *Psychosexual Functions of Women* has clearly had its effect, over the last five decades, on psychological studies, imposing or trivial, that attempt to correlate menstrual fluctuation and behavioral patterns. Professors and researchers in the universities and laboratories of the world are even now in the process of creating new or modifying old theories concerning the effects of the hormonal cycle on menstruation, premenstrual symptoms, menopausal fluctuations, and innumerable other matters that relate to the female reproductive system. Definitive conclusions: "*NONE.*"

As far as I can judge, the renewed interest in menstruation as part of psychoanalytic theory was more accidental than strategic. There was no deliberate, collective effort among women analysts to construct a theoretics of menstruation; they produced no specialized, menstrual journal like the one published by the International Psycho-analytical Association on Menstruation. As theory, menstruation more or less evolved, a by-product of the great debate and of theoretical insights extrapolated from female patients. Although Deutsch was the foremost of the women theoreticians reviewed in *Menstruation and Psychoanalysis*, I doubt if even she, with her intertwined observations on sexual stages, was conscious of the fact that her very theory, as I have presented it, replicated the regularity and repetition of the menstrual dynamic. Deutsch, Bonaparte, Chadwick, and their colleagues, in their attention to the veiled topic of menstruation, were able to offer the psychoanalytic institution a variety of explanations concerning the periodic aspects of women's behavior. At the same time, in their attempts to articulate their observations, they consistently placed menstruation within a negative, masochistic construction.

### Notes

1. In the same year that Horney presented her observations on PMS, the American gynecologist Robert Frank released his study "The Hormonal Causes of Premenstrual Tension," *Archives of Neurological Psychiatry* 26 (1931): 1053–57. It is Frank, not Horney, who has received the credit for having isolated this highly symptomatic phase of the menstrual cycle. For a turn-of-the-century treatment see Richard

Krafft-Ebing, *Psychosis Menstrualis* (Erlangen: Verlag von Ferdinand Enke in Stuttgart, 1902), 27.

2. Otto Fenichel, *The Psychoanalytic Theory of Neurosis* (New York: Norton, 1945), 240. Helene Deutsch, also writing in the midforties, recognized that "many women suffer menstrual depressions before the menstrual period, and others during it," but found no clear reason for that phenomenon. Helene Deutsch, *The Psychology of Women* (New York: Grune and Stratton, 1944), 1:174. For feminist perspectives on PMS, see *The Curse*, 83–103; and Emily Martin, *The Woman in the Body* (Boston: Beacon Press, 1987), 113–38.

3. Karen Horney, *Feminine Psychology*, ed. Harold Kelman (1931; New York: Norton, 1973), 100. Horney consistently used the word *feelings* rather than *disorders* in describing the premenstruum, a stage she viewed as normal rather than pathological.

4. Ibid., 99.

5. Ibid., 103.

6. Ibid., 104, emphasis mine. Horney presented an identical argument in her discussion of menstrual disorders: "Certainly a temporary amenorrhea will indicate a wish to have a child at any price." See "Psychogenic Factors in Functional Female Disorders," in *Feminine Psychology*, 171.

7. For updated findings on hormonal factors, see Uriel Halbreich and Jean Endicott, "The Biology of Premenstrual Changes: What Do We Really Know?" in *Premenstrual Syndrome: Current Findings and Future Directions*, ed. Howard J. Osofsky and Susan J. Blumenthal (Washington, D.C.: American Psychiatric Press, 1985), 15–24.

8. Clara M. Thompson, *Psychoanalysis: Evolution and Development* (New York: Hermitage House, 1950), 200. According to Chodorow, Horney's concept of the feminine is "the basis, acknowledged or unacknowledged, for most of the recent revisions of psychoanalytic studies of gender." See Nancy J. Chodorow, *Feminism and Psychoanalytic Theory* (New Haven: Yale University Press, 1989), 3.

9. Horney, *Feminine Psychology*, 114.

10. Of the books that Horney published with Norton—*The Neurotic Personality in Our Time* (1937); *New Ways in Psychoanalysis* (1939); *Our Inner Conflicts* (1945); and *Neurosis and Human Growth* (1950)—there is only one brief reference to menstruation. Horney alludes to Deutsch's connections between menstruation and masochism. See Karen Horney, *New Ways in Psychoanalysis* (New York: Norton, 1939), 110.

11. Clara M. Thompson, *Interpersonal Psychoanalysis: The Selected Papers of Clara M. Thompson*, ed. Maurice R. Green (New York: Basic Books, 1964), 267.

12. Ibid., 234–35.

13. Ibid., 72–73. Thompson's analyst, Sándor Ferenczi, had observed similar connections between menstrual humiliations and the recollection of toilet training; see *The Clinical Diary of Sándor Ferenczi*, ed. Judith Dupont, trans. Michael Bálint and Nicola Zarday Jackson (Cambridge: Harvard University Press, 1988), 165.

14. Thompson, *Interpersonal Psychoanalysis*, 234.

15. Earlier in *Menstruation and Psychoanalysis* I addressed vicarious menstruation in reference to Dumas's *Camille* and to the male identification with women's bleeding. See also the discussion of male menstruation in chapter 9.

16. Deutsch, *The Psychology of Women* 1:168–69. An almost identical treatment of vicarious menstruation appears in Helene Deutsch, *Neurosis and Character Types* (New York: International Universities Press, 1965).

17. Deutsch, *The Psychology of Women* 1:168.

18. Ibid., 1:169.

19. Ibid.

20. When Devereux claimed that "the menstruating woman as a witch is, in a sense, the central theme of the psychoanalytic approach to menstruation," he was thinking of Chadwick. See George Devereux, "The Psychology of Genital Bleeding: An Analysis of Mohave Indian Puberty and Menstrual Rites," *International Journal of Psycho-analysis* 31 (1950): 252. Ernest Jones indirectly associated the witch-woman with the menstrual capacity, listing menstrual blood among the ingredients used to prepare the sacred host during the witch's sabbath, in Ernest Jones, *On the Nightmare* (London: Hogarth Press, 1931), 203. See also Shuttle and Redgrove, who contend that witchcraft is "the subjective experience of the menstrual cycle" and that the hunting of witches was probably "one enormous menstrual taboo." Penelope Shuttle and Peter Redgrove, *The Wise Wound: Eve's Curse and Everywoman*, rev. ed. (1978; New York: Grove Press, 1986), 217, 206.

21. Mary Chadwick, *The Psychological Effects of Menstruation* (New York: Nervous and Mental Disease Publishing Company, 1932), 22.

22. Ibid., 48. Theorists other than Chadwick have attributed women with originating the practice of menstrual isolation, but they have tended to interpret it as the creation of a spiritual retreat shared in a company of women. See, for example, Robert Briffault, *The Mothers: A Study of the Origin of Sentiments and Institutions* (1927; New York: Macmillan, 1952), 2:403–6; and Erich Neumann, *The Great Mother*, trans. Ralph Manheim, Bollingen Series, vol. 47 (1955; Princeton: Princeton University Press, 1972), 290. See also the economic theory espoused by Chris Knight in *Blood Relations: Menstruation and the Origins of Culture* (New Haven: Yale University Press, 1991). For an insightful review of male versus female origins of the menstrual taboo, see Adrienne Rich, *Of Woman Born: Motherhood as Experience and Institution* (New York: Norton, 1976), 103–7.

23. Chadwick, *Effects*, 26.

24. Ibid., 15.

25. Ibid., 1. It is surprising that Paula Weideger, one of the few feminists aware of Chadwick's work, does not question the formula menstruating woman = witch. Paula Weideger, *Menstruation and Menopause* (New York: Alfred A. Knopf, 1975), 109–10.

26. *Monthly neurosis* is a term in Harry Campbell, *Differences in the Nervous Organization of Man and Woman* (1891), cited by Chadwick in *Effects*, 11.

27. Chadwick, *Effects*, 22.

28. The term *smelling out witches* was used to describe the action of prosecutors during the witch-hunts. Chadwick connects the phrase to menstrual odor, in *Effects*, 29. The comments on witches and odor also appear, verbatim, in her book *Woman's Periodicity* (London: Noel Douglas, 1933), 79–80.

29. Some feminists have willfully reversed these negative images, reclaiming psychoanalytic concepts of the witch as instruments of personal empowerment. See Hélène Cixous and Catherine Clément, *The Newly Born Woman* (1975; Minneapolis: University of Minnesota Press, 1986), 39. In the 1970s, as an editor of *Women: A Journal of Liberation*, I read many poems submitted by women who identified with witches, embracing their attributes of power, anger, and self-fulfillment.

30. Fliess does not appear in the index to either volume of *The Psychology of Women*.

31. Deutsch, *The Psychology of Women* 1:19–23, 32. Deutsch placed the preoedipal phase at between one and a half and three years old, which would mark a far later separation from the mother than the preoedipal period of infancy established by Melanie Klein and others. See, for example, Ruth Mack Brunswick, "The Preoedipal Phase of the Libido Development," *Psychoanalytic Quarterly* 9 (1949): 293–319.

32. Deutsch, *The Psychology of Women* 1:173–74.

33. Ibid., 2:461.

34. Ibid., 2:91, emphasis mine.

35. Ibid., 2:228.

36. Ibid., 1:172.

37. Ibid., 2:456.

38. Judith Kestenberg, a theorist very much influenced by Deutsch and Klein, developed, in the late 1960s, a theory of female orgasm based on an inside/outside dichotomy. Like Deutsch, Kestenberg stressed the potential of menstrual regularity and repetition in reorganizing the chaotic ego. She further claimed that during puberty, menstruation reestablishes a young woman's body image, "forc[ing] her to accept the existence of the vagina and uterus as feminine organs." See Judith Kestenberg, "Menarche," in *Adolescents: A Psychoanalytic Approach to Problems and Therapy*, ed. Sandor Lorand and Henry Scheer (New York: Harper and Row, 1964), 34.

39. For a fascinating account of medical attitudes toward hysteria, see Ilza Veith, *Hysteria: The History of a Disease* (Chicago: University of Chicago Press, 1965). In the course of her investigation, Veith points out certain misunderstandings about irregular menstruation and hysteria, from Hippocrates to Pinel.

40. "Psychische Storungen, im Zusammenhang mit den menstruelen Vorgangen, stellten sich nicht mehr ein." Krafft-Ebing, *Psychosis Menstrualis*, 20.

41. "Das Bild moralischer Imbecillitat nach wie vor." Ibid.

42. Chadwick, *Effects*, 38.

43. Ibid., 56.

44. Ibid.

45. Ibid., 59.

46. Therese Benedek, "Notes from the Analysis of a Case of Eurythrophobia," *International Journal of Psycho-analysis* 6 (1925): 430–39. Poul M. Faergeman refers to this case in "Fantasies of Menstruation in Men," *Psychoanalytic Quarterly* 24 (1955): 4.

47. The monograph constitutes the first eleven chapters of Therese Benedek, *Psychosexual Functions in Women* (New York: Ronald Press, 1952). Background information is from Benedek's foreword.

48. Ibid., 12.

49. Ibid., 20–21.

50. Ibid., 31.

51. Ibid., 90.

52. Ibid., 66.

53. Ibid., 210.

54. Other reviewers have raised similar objections. Silbermann finds the methodology "too simple and too rigid." See Isodor Silbermann, "A Contribution to the Psychology of Menstruation," *International Journal of Psycho-analysis* 31 (1950): 261. Paula Weideger takes exception to the Freudian value judgments but admires the study for its discovery of ovulatory peaks and other data, in Weideger, *Menstruation and Menopause*, 121–24. Shuttle and Redgrove consider the study to be "an immaculate work" but one that suffers from a "completely stereotyped prejudgement" based on its Freudian biases; see Shuttle and Redgrove, *The Wise Wound*, 87. Less than immaculate themselves, in both editions of *The Wise Wound* they identify Boris Rubenstein as "she."

55. Jeanne Meadowcroft and Dolf Zillman, "The Influence of Hormonal Fluctuations on Women's Selection and Enjoyment of Television Programs," paper presented at the annual meeting of the Association for Education in Journalism and Mass Communication, Gainesville, Fla., Aug. 1984.

# *Postmenstruum*

My purpose in *Menstruation and Psychoanalysis* has been to accentuate the menstrual presence/absence in a number of major psychoanalytic texts written in the first half of this century to illustrate the emergence of a psychology of menstruation, especially in the writings of women. In so doing, I have placed a frame on the diverse yet similar ideas about menstruation that germinated during a period of vigorous release in which female sexuality—and menstruation, its darkest continent—came into the light. Further, in my discussions of Freud, of Bonaparte, of Daly, I have raised a number of questions intended to reintroduce menstruation into contemporary psychoanalytic discourse. What is the significance of menstruation to psychoanalytic theory? If menstruation is absent from a given argument about female sexuality, then why is it absent? Or is it in fact present but veiled? What is the relevance of menstruation to feminist criticism, to female sexuality, to a theory of sexual difference, to the future? From the overwhelmingly subdued treatment of the menstrual process in these vital areas, it seems clear that menstruation still remains a tabooed topic, repressed from discourse, unsympathetic or even hostile to inquiry.

On several occasions I have raised such issues to speakers who had omitted menstruation in their analytic deliberations. The questions I posed to two presenters following their papers at the 1989 Paris–New York Psychoanalytic Workshop provide conclusive examples of their unconscious repression of menstruation. One male analyst read a paper entitled "Voyeurism as Foreplay," about a male social worker in a hospital who enjoyed watching a fifteen-year-old girl masturbate while he and the male nurses looked on. I asked the analyst if his patient, who had a fear of castration, had ever discussed the girl's menstruation, which, since the voyeurism lasted longer than a month, the patient was likely to have observed. "If she had masturbated during her period, wouldn't her blood have reaffirmed his fear of castration?" I asked, to which the analyst responded: "That's interesting, but the patient never mentioned it to me." During another paper, "Women, Shakespeare, Psychoanalysis," the female speaker critiqued Freud's concept of female versus male adjustments at puberty in three areas: changing the parental love object, redirecting female sexuality from the clitoris to the vagina, and accepting a passive role. After the presentation I suggested a fourth, *menstrual*, difference at puberty: that girls, unlike boys, bleed from their sex organs. Although the analyst agreed, she remarked that she wanted to restrict herself to Freud and not "get into anthropology or sociology."

These two quite friendly confrontations led me to believe that neither analyst was antagonistic to the idea of menstruation, but that neither had consciously addressed the potential of menstruation in his or her psychoanalytic theory or practice. The response of the woman analyst implied that menstruation might be of relevance among the inhabitants of Central Agoniland but had little to do with Freud. The male analyst, because he did not assume the victim's menstruation, did not introduce that factor in exploring his patient's castration anxiety.

My third venture into menstrual inquiry occurred at a meeting of the Modern Language Association, where a woman critic, in a paper on Freud, related Emma Eckstein's bleeding to Freud's mouth cancer: "to bleed like her would be an admission of his own castration." When I asked her about the menstrual connotations of Emma's bleeding, she admitted that menstruation was not relevant, either to the paper or to her book. She seemed understandably hostile to my observation that she had repressed menstruation in her text.

There has been, though, at least one major attempt among recent theorists to make use of menstruation as an analytic tool in dealing with the transference phenomenon. Eugenie Lemoine-Luccioni, in an essay titled "A Fable of Blood," writes of Anne-Marie, a patient whose two years of amenorrhea ended when she "put on lipstick, as a physician had advised, and [her] periods came back."[1] Lemoine-Luccioni, who refers to Cardinal's *The Words to Say It* but without questioning the miracle cure, takes a rather different approach than did Cardinal's psychiatrist; she carefully investigates the menstrual symptom within the structure of the analysis rather than suppressing it in order to "speak of something else."[2] "A Fable of Blood" is filled with references to red: red lipstick, red liquid, spattered blood. These associations come not only from the analyst's current patient but are interwoven with other recollections— an amenorrheic girl of twenty, a male analysand—in which dreams are substituted for periods, in which blood clots are suspected in the brain. Of the many interpretations that Lemoine-Luccioni applies to the dream material, one is that the "amenorrhea can be seen as a reaction of fear; a fear of the blood that flows, of inundation, of the terrible sea, of the wave that submerges, and so forth."[3] These dreams reveal a fear of giving birth similar to the dread of a "tidal wave or a wave of blood."[4]

The analysis involves other themes, such as pregnancy, castration, the return to the mother, sexual identification, homosexuality. These motifs receive the lucid attention of Lemoine-Luccioni in her effort to piece together the analytic materials and their relevance to women's bleeding. At case's end, Anne-Marie wants to become an analyst, signaling the potential continuation of menstrual exploration within psychoanalytic discourse.

Sadly, such analytic material is rare. The repression of menstruation, initiated by Freud in his letters to Fliess, has prevailed in the psychoanalytic investigation of male/female sexuality. Few theorists have been "willing or able to see" the importance of female bleeding as it has affected castration, male desire, female masochism, or female fecundity. Claude Dagmar Daly came closest to a revision of Freudian theory with his concept of the menstruation complex and his belief that the repression of menstruation has been perpetrated by the very analysts who should be seeking to uncover it. Unfortunately, Daly was unable to expand his view of the castrating menstrual mother and envision the menstrual process as the most fundamental sign of life and nourishment.

Psychoanalytic attitudes toward menstruation might change, but only through an adjusted perception on the part of the analyst and through a recognition, as one finds in Lemoine-Luccioni's essay, that the presence or absence of menstruation can transform the entire analytic experience. Imagine an analysis in which the menstrual component of castration anxiety and its subsequent symbolism would be remembered, reconstructed, returned from repression. Imagine, as in Lemoine-Luccioni's case study, menstruation functioning as an element in psychoanalytic transference and countertransference—the interrelationship of analyst and analysand in bringing about unconscious processes. Christopher Bollas, writing that the analyst's countertransference is a blank screen on which the patient projects his or her images, makes a list of internalized traits that the analyst brings to the situation: anxiety, anger, and twenty-four others. The emotions of *dread* and *fear*, associated throughout *Menstruation and Psychoanalysis* with the menstruating mother, are absent from his catalog. In a corresponding list of psychoanalytic theories that the analyst should always have mentally available for therapeutic use, not *one* item refers to the mother, despite Bollas's respect for the theories of Melanie Klein.[5]

I believe that within the analytic relationship the analyst, male or female, must be responsive to the impact of menstruation on the patients' childhood fantasies and must previously, through his or her own analysis, have come to "know" menstruation—as the speaker whom I questioned on the voyeur's fear of castration surely did not: "That's interesting but the patient never mentioned it to me." The obvious lack of menstrual communication in this and similar situations indicates a major void in the countertransference-transference phenomenon.

Menstruation as a psychoanalytic concern appears to have immigrated from the analytic session to psychology, to take its place among the stacks of menstrual distress questionnaires and menstrual preference forms; or, ironically, to English and French departments, where scholars engaged in analyzing Freud as literature treat the text as patient. While the close reading of Freudian texts at times elicits a menstrual analysis, as in Mary Jacobus's *Reading Women* and Marie Balmary's *Psychoanalyzing Psychoanalysis*, all too frequently the menstrual reference is avoided, lost.[6] Of the influx of feminist books on the maternal in the past decade, most disregard the fact that mothers menstruate.

As I argued in chapter 4, a menstrual refocusing of Freudian discourse would identify women's blood as preceding the birth trauma or the pre-oedipal mother in a feminine symbolic. What would happen if psychoanalytic and literary explicators acknowledged the value of the endometrium, the first food, made available only through the agency of the menstrual process, discarded, like all food, if it does not get consumed? Menstrual discharge, which has generated exorbitant amounts of fear in "primitive" and "civilized" people and has so rudely offended the senses of sight and smell, is, in the last analysis, good and essential food.

Nourishment, bleeding, fertility: these special powers of women would seem to offer a foundation on which to reconstruct a theory of menstrual difference. Ideally, menstruation's psychic affinity to nurturance, if consciously acknowledged, could strengthen the bonding that originates in the mother/child union. Greater familiarity with the positive aspects of menstrual blood would also reduce the anxiety that men, both phylogenic and sophisticated, have endured. A knowledge of the menstrual process might also assist in reducing the prohibitions against menstruation that have affected contemporary culture, especially in the influential areas of television programming and advertising. It was not until 1972 that the National Association of Broadcasters removed its ban on television advertisements for sanitary hygiene products, and not until 1973 that *All in the Family* became the first program to discuss menstruation on television.[7] The notion that the directors of NAB were keeping menstruation out of *sight*, away from the "viewers," seems a fulfillment of Freud's hypothesis of the Upright Man; men in power, having made the long walk from smell to sight, are anxious to protect their civilized achievements.[8] Women, in this scenario, are still the source of contamination and taboo, with the role of menstruation in perpetuating the species being generally un/seen, dis/regarded.

A theoretics of menstruation has the potential to make some tangible difference, not only in the theory and practice of psychoanalysis but in the social order with which analysis is affiliated. In a responsive worldview, the values of replenishment and renewal embodied in the menstrual process could perhaps reshape the future. "Creative waste," designer Christine Frederick's term for the streamlined disposability of kitchen products, seems an appropriate way to say *menstruation*.[9] "Creative waste": the phrase recapitulates the ambivalence toward women's blood in *Menstruation and Psychoanalysis*, ranging from Carl Jung's "creative mana" to Otto Fenichel's "first pollution."[10] I use it to affirm the menstrual powers, in a world where the spinning planets and the flowing sea are threatened with extinction, and the female values implicit in menstruation are in mourning.

## Notes

1. Eugenie Lemoine-Luccioni, "The Fable of Blood," in *Returning to Freud: Clinical Psychoanalysis in the School of Lacan,* ed. Stuart Schneiderman (New Haven: Yale University Press, 1980), 62. Neither *menstruation* nor *blood* appears in the index.

2. Marie Cardinal, *The Words to Say It,* trans. Pat Goodheart (Cambridge: Van Vactor and Goodheart, 1983), 32.

3. Lemoine-Luccioni, "Fable of Blood," 64.

4. Ibid.

5. Christopher Bollas, *Forces of Destiny: Psychoanalysis and the Human Idiom* (London: Free Association Books, 1991), 101–4. Bollas informs the reader that the twenty-six items (from A to Z), represent only a few of the possibilities. Do the other possibilities include Klein's preoedipal mother or Rank's birth trauma or Daly's menstruation complex?

6. For references to menstruation see Mary Jacobus, *Reading Women: Essays in Feminist Criticism* (New York: Columbia University Press, 1986); and Marie Balmary, *Psychoanalyzing Psychoanalysis,* trans. Ned Lukacher (1979; Baltimore: Johns Hopkins University Press, 1982). A startling menstrual omission is to be found in the recent *Feminism and Psychoanalysis: A Critical Dictionary,* ed. Elizabeth Wright (Cambridge: Basil Blackwell, 1992). *Menstruation* is included neither as a dictionary entry nor in the general index, whereas such terms as *penis envy* and *patriarchy* are adequately represented.

7. For further discussion of the representation of menstruation in advertising and in the media, see *The Curse,* 129–37, 150–56.

8. See *Civilization and Its Discontents, SE* 21:99n. The visual element of Freud's hypothesis was discussed in chapter 5.

9. The concept of "creative waste" is mentioned in Ellen Lupton and J. Abbott Miller, *The Bathroom, the Kitchen, and the Aesthetics of Waste* (Cambridge: MIT List Visual Arts Center, 1992), 68, 71.

10. See Carl G. Jung, *The Collected Works of C. G. Jung,* ed. Herbert Read, Michael Fordham, and Gerhard Adler, trans. R. F. C. Hull, Bollingen Series, no. 20 (Princeton: Princeton University Press, 1979), 16:157; and Otto Fenichel, *The Psychoanalytic Theory of Neurosis* (New York: Norton, 1945), 11.

# Bibliography

Abraham, Karl. *Dreams and Myths.* Trans. William A. White. New York: Journal of Nervous and Mental Disease Publishing Company, 1913.

———. "Father-Murder and Father-Rescue in the Fantasies of Neurotics." 1922. In *The Psychoanalytic Reader: An Anthology of Essential Papers with Critical Introductions.* Ed. Robert Fliess. New York: International Universities Press, 1973: 334–42.

———. "Manifestations of the Female Castration Complex." *International Journal of Psycho-analysis* 3 (1920): 1–29. Reprinted in *Selected Papers on Psychoanalysis.* Trans. Douglas Bryan and Alix Strachey. New York: Basic Books, 1971: 338–69.

Anzieu, Didier. *L'autoanalyse de Freud.* 2 vols. Paris: Presses Universitaires de France, 1975.

Bakan, David. *Sigmund Freud and the Jewish Mystical Tradition.* Princeton, N.J.: D. Van Nostrand, 1968.

Bálint, Michael. "A Contribution to the Psychology of Menstruation." *Psychoanalytic Quarterly* 6 (1937): 346–52.

Balmary, Marie. *Psychoanalyzing Psychoanalysis.* 1979. Trans. Ned Lukacher. Baltimore: Johns Hopkins University Press, 1982.

Beane, Wendell Charles. *Myth, Cult, and Symbols in Śā-kta Hinduism: A Study of the Indian Mother Goddess.* Leiden, Netherlands: E. J. Brill, 1977.

Benedek, Therese. "Notes from the Analysis of a Case of Eurythrophobia." *International Journal of Psycho-analysis* 6 (1925): 430–39.

———. *Psychosexual Functions in Women.* New York: Ronald Press, 1952.

Bertin, Celia. *Marie Bonaparte*. New Haven: Yale University Press, 1987.

Bettelheim, Bruno. *Symbolic Wounds: Puberty Rites and the Envious Male*. New York: Collier, 1962.

———. *The Uses of Enchantment: The Meaning and Importance of Fairy Tales*. New York: Vintage, 1976.

Bhattacharyya, Narendra Nath. *Indian Puberty Rites*. 1968. Calcutta, India: Munshiram Manoharlal, 1980.

*Die Bible: Ober die Schriften des Alten und Neuen Bandes*. Leipzig: F. A. Brodhaus, 1858.

Bieganowski, Ronald. "The Self-consuming Narrator in Poe's 'Ligeia' and 'Usher.'" *American Literature* 60 (1988): 175–87.

Birke, Lynda. *Women, Feminism, and Biology*. New York: Methuen, 1986.

Bollas, Christopher. "CUTTING." Paper written for the Group for the Research and Application of Psychoanalysis and the Psychoses, Paris, 1989.

———. *Forces of Destiny: Psychoanalysis and the Human Idiom*. London: Free Association Books, 1991.

———. *The Shadow of the Object*. New York: Columbia University Press, 1987.

Bonaparte, Marie. *Female Sexuality*. 1949. Trans. John Rodker. New York: International Universities Press, 1953.

———. *The Life and Works of Edgar Allan Poe: A Psycho-analytic Interpretation*. 1933. Trans. John Rodker. New York: Humanities Press, 1971.

Brain, James Lewton. *The Last Tabboo: Sex and the Fear of Death*. Garden City, N.Y.: Anchor Press, 1979.

———. "Male Menstruation in History and Anthropology." *Journal of Psychohistory* 15 (1988): 311–23.

Braun, Gustav. "The Amputation of the Clitoris and Labia Minora: A Contribution in the Treatment of Vaginismus." 1865. In *A Dark Science: Women, Sexuality, and Psychiatry in the Nineteenth Century*. Ed. Jeffrey Moussaieff Masson. New York: Farrar, Straus, and Giroux, 1986: 126–38.

Briffault, Robert. *The Mothers: A Study of the Origin of Sentiments and Institutions*. 1927. 3 vols. New York: Macmillan, 1952.

Brown, C. Mackenzie. "Kali: The Mad Mother." In *The Book of the Goddess: Past and Present*. Ed. Carl Olson. New York: Crossroad, 1989: 110–23.

Brown, John. *A Dictionary of the Holy Bible*. New York: J. and J. Harper, 1829.

Brown, Norman O. *Life against Death*. New York: Vintage, 1959.

———. *Love's Body*. New York: Random House, 1966.

Brunswick, Ruth Mack. "The Preoedipal Phase of the Libido Development." *Psychoanalytic Quarterly* 9 (1940): 293–319.

———. "A Supplement to 'History of an Infantile Neurosis.'" In *The Wolf-Man by the Wolf-Man*. Ed. Muriel Gardiner. New York: Basic Books, 1971: 263–307.

Bryan, Douglas. "Epistaxis in a Man Simulating Menstruation." *International Journal of Psycho-analysis* 7 (1926): 79–81.

Bushman, Richard, and Claudia L. Bushman. "The Early History of Cleanliness in America." *Journal of American History* 74 (1988): 1215–38.

Cardinal, Marie. *The Words to Say It*. Trans. Pat Goodheart. Cambridge: Van Vactor and Goodheart, 1983.

Cardinal, Marie, and Annie Leclerc. *Autrement dit*. Paris: Bernard Grasset, 1977.

Carson, Anne. *Feminine Spirituality and the Feminine Divine: An Annotated Bibliography*. Trumansburg, N.Y.: Crossing Press, 1986.

Cavell, Marcia. "Since 1924: Toward a New Psychology of Women." In *Women and Analysis*. Ed. Jean Strouse. Boston: G. K. Hall, 1985: 162–68.

Chadwick, Mary. *Adolescent Girlhood*. London: Allen and Unwin, 1932.

———. *Difficulties in Child Development*. New York: John Day, 1928.

———. *The Psychological Effects of Menstruation*. New York: Nervous and Mental Disease Publishing Company, 1932.

———. *Woman's Periodicity*. London: Noel Douglas, 1933.

Chasseguet-Smirgel, Janine. *Female Sexuality*. Ann Arbor: University of Michigan Press, 1970.

Chasseguet-Smirgel, Janine, and Béla Grunberger. *Freud or Reich?: Psychoanalysis and Illusion*. Trans. Claire Pajaczkowska. London: Free Association Books, 1986.

Chodorow, Nancy J. *Feminism and Psychoanalytic Theory*. New Haven: Yale University Press, 1989.

Cixous, Hélène. "The Laugh of the Medusa." Trans. Keith Cohen and Paula Cohen. In *New French Feminisms*. Ed. Elaine Marks and Isabelle de Courtivron. New York: Schocken Books, 1981: 245–64.

Cixous, Hélène, and Catherine Clément. *The Newly Born Woman*. 1975. Minneapolis: University of Minnesota Press, 1986.

Clark, Michael. *Jacques Lacan: An Annotated Bibliography*. 2 vols. New York: Garland, 1988.

Coen, Stanley J. "Freud and Fliess: Supportive Literary Relationship." *American Imago* 42 (1985): 385–412.

Crawley, Alfred Ernest. *The Mystic Rose: A Study of Primitive Marriage*. New York: n.p., 1902.

Dalsimer, Katherine. *Female Adolescence*. New Haven: Yale University Press, 1986.

Daly, Claude Dagmar. "Hindu-Mythologie und Kastrationskomplex." Trans. Peter Mendelssohn. *Imago* 13 (1927): 145–98.

———. "Hindu Treatise on Kali." *Samiksa* 1 (1947): 191–96.

———. "Der Kern des Oedipuskomplexes." *Internationale Zeitschrift für Psychoanalyse*, nos. 21, 23 (1935): 165–88, 389–418.

———. "The Menstruation Complex in Literature." *Psychoanalytic Quarterly* 4 (1935): 307–40.

———. "Der Menstruationskomplex." Leipzig: Internationaler Psychoanalatischer Verlag. Reprinted in *Imago* 14 (1928): 11–75.

———. "The Mother Complex in Literature." Reprint of "The Menstruation Complex in Literature." 1935. *Samiksa* 1 (1947): 177–90.

———. "The Mother Complex in Literature." Enlarged. *Yearbook of Psychoanalysis* 4 (1948): 172–210.

———. "Numbers in Dreams." *International Journal of Psycho-analysis* 2 (1921): 68–70.

———. "Pre-human Psychic Evolution: A Hypothetical Theory of the Psychological Evolution of Our Species in Pre-glacial, Glacial, and Early Post-glacial Epochs." *British Journal of Medical Psychology* 12 (1932): 273–86.

———. "Psychic Reaction to Olfactory Stimuli." With R. Senior White. *British Journal of Medical Psychology* 10 (1930): 70–87.

———. "The Psycho-biological Origins of Circumcision." *International Journal of Psycho-analysis* 31 (1950): 217–36.

———. "A Psychological Analysis of Military Moral." *Army Quarterly* (1934): 59–74.

———. "The Psychology of Man's Attitude Towards Woman." *Imago* 10 (1930): 278–88. Reprinted in *Samiksa* 1 (1947): 231–40.

———. "The Psychology of Revolutionary Tendencies." *International Journal of Psycho-analysis* 11 (1930): 193–210.

———. Review of T. Whiffen, "The North West Amazons." *International Journal of Psycho-analysis* 4 (1923): 229–31.

———. "The Role of Menstruation in Human Phylogenesis and Ontogenesis." *International Journal of Psycho-analysis* 24 (1943): 151–70.

———. "A Simple Lapus Linguae." *International Journal of Psycho-analysis* 3 (1922): 46.

———. "Zu meinen Arbeiten über die weiblichen Tabu-Vorschriften." *Zeitschrift für psychoanalytische Pädagogik* 5 (1931): 225–28.

Daly, Mary. *Gyn/ecology: The Metaethics of Radical Feminism.* Boston: Beacon Press, 1978.

Dameron, J. Lasley, and Irby B. Cauthen, Jr. *Edgar Allan Poe: A Bibliography of Criticism, 1872–1967.* Charlottesville: University Press of Virginia, 1974.

Davis, Elizabeth Gould. *The First Sex.* New York: G. P. Putnam's Sons, 1971.

de Beauvoir, Simone. "From an Interview." In *New French Feminisms.* Ed. Elaine Marks and Isabelle de Courtivron. New York: Schocken, 1981: 142–53.

Delaney, Carol. "Mortal Flow: Menstruation in Turkish Village Society." In *Blood Magic.* Ed. Thomas Buckley and Alma Gottlieb. Berkeley: University of California Press, 1988: 75–93.

Delaney, Janice, Mary Jane Lupton, and Emily Toth. *The Curse: A Cultural History of Menstruation.* Rev. ed. Urbana: University of Illinois Press, 1988.

Desautels, Jacques. *Dieux et myths de la Grèce ancienne.* Quebec: Les Presses de l'Université Laval, 1988.

Deutsch, Felix. "A Footnote to Freud's 'Fragment of an Analysis of a Case of Hysteria.'" 1957. In *In Dora's Case: Freud—Hysteria—Feminism*. Ed. Charles Bernheimer and Claire Kahane. New York: Columbia University Press, 1985: 35–43.

Deutsch, Helene. *Confrontations with Myself*. New York: Norton, 1973.

———. *Neurosis and Character Types*. New York: International Universities Press, 1965.

———. *The Psychology of Women*. 2 vols. New York: Grune and Stratton, 1944, 1945. ←

———. "The Psychology of Women in Relation to the Functions of Reproduction." 1925. In *The Psychoanalytic Reader: An Anthology of Essential Papers with Critical Introductions*. Ed. Robert Fliess. New York: International Universities Press, 1973: 192–206.

Devereux, George. "The Psychology of Genital Bleeding: An Analysis of Mohave Indian Puberty and Menstrual Rites." *International Journal of Psycho-analysis* 31 (1950): 237–57.

Dickson, Geri L. "A Feminist Poststructuralist Analysis of the Knowledge of Menopause." *Advances in Nursing Science* 12 (1990): 15–31.

*Dorland's Illustrated Medical Dictionary*. 27th ed. Philadelphia: W. B. Saunders, 1988.

Dumas, Alexandre fils. *Camille*. Trans. Edmond Gosse. New York: New American Library, 1984.

———. *La dame aux camélias*. 1848. Paris: Calmann-Lévy, 1951.

Durham, Carolyn A. *The Contexture of Feminism: Marie Cardinal and Multicultural Literacy*. Urbana: University of Illinois Press, 1992.

Edelson, Jonathan T. "Freud's Use of Metaphor." *Psychoanalytic Study of the Child* 38 (1983): 17–59.

Eidelberg, Ludwig, ed. *Encyclopedia of Psychoanalysis*. New York: Free Press, 1968.

Eisenstein, Hester, and Alice Jardine, eds. *The Future of Difference*. New Brunswick: Rutgers University Press, 1985.

Eissler, K. R. *Talent and Genius: The Fictitious Case of Trausk Contra Freud*. New York: Quadrangle, 1971.

Eliade, Mircea. *Images and Symbols*. Trans. Phillip Mairet. London: Harvill Press, 1961.

Ellenberger, Henri F. *The Discovery of the Unconscious*. New York: Basic Books, 1970.

Ellis, Havelock. *Studies in the Psychology of Sex*. 7 vols. Philadelphia: F. A. Davis, 1930–31.

Epstein, Louis M. *Sex Laws and Customs under Judaism*. New York: Ktav, 1948.

Erikson, Eric. "The Dream Specimen of Psychoanalysis." *Journal of the American Psychoanalytic Association* 2 (1954): 5–56.

———. "Womanhood and Inner Space." In *Identity: Youth and Crisis*. New York: Norton, 1968.

Erlich, Michel. *La femme blessée: Essai sur les mutilations sexuelles féminines*. Paris: Editions l'Harmattan, 1986.

Evans, Martha Noel. "Hysteria and the Seduction of Theory." In *Seduction and*

*Theory*. Ed. Dianne Hunter. Urbana: University of Illinois Press, 1989: 73–85.

Faergeman, Poul M. "Fantasies of Menstruation in Men." *Psychoanalytic Quarterly* 24 (1955): 1–19.

Felman, Shoshana. *Jacques Lacan and the Adventure of Insight*. Cambridge: Harvard University Press, 1987.

Fenichel, Otto. *The Psychoanalytic Theory of Neurosis*. New York: Norton, 1945.

Ferenczi, Sándor. *The Clinical Diary of Sándor Ferenczi*. Ed. Judith Dupont. Trans. Michael Bálint and Nicola Zarday Jackson. Cambridge: Harvard University Press, 1988.

———. "The Ontogenesis of the Interest in Money." 1916. Trans. Ernest Jones. In *First Contributions to Psycho-analysis*. Ed. Judith Dupont. New York: Brunner/ Mazel, 1980: 319–31.

Ferguson, Ann. *Blood at the Root*. London: Pandora, 1989.

Fine, Reuben. *A History of Psychoanalysis*. New York: Columbia University Press, 1979.

Fish, Stanley. "Withholding the Missing Portion: Psychoanalysis and Rhetoric." In *Doing What Comes Naturally*. Durham: Duke University Press, 1989: 525–54.

Flax, Jane. "Mother-Daughter Relationships: Psychodynamics, Politics, and Philosophy." In *The Future of Difference*. Ed. Hester Eisenstein and Alice Jardine. New Brunswick: Rutgers University Press, 1985: 20–40.

Fliess, Wilhelm. *Die Beziehungen zwischen Nase und weiblichen Geschlectsorganen*. Leipzig/Vienna: Deuticke, 1897.

———. *Les relations entre le nez et les organes genitauz de la femme*. Trans. Patrick Ach and Jean Guir. Paris: Editions du Seuil, 1977.

Ford, Clellan Stearns. "A Comparative Study of Human Reproduction." *Yale University Publications in Anthropology* 32 (1945–46): 9–42.

Frank, Lawrence. "Freud and Dora." In *Seduction and Theory*. Ed. Dianne Hunter. Urbana: University of Illinois Press, 1989: 110–32.

Frank, Robert. "The Hormonal Causes of Premenstrual Tension." *Archives of Neurology and Psychiatry* 26 (1931): 1053–57.

Fraser, Nancy, and Sandra Lee Bartky, eds. *Revaluing French Feminism: Essays on Difference, Agency, and Culture*. Bloomington: Indiana University Press, 1992.

Frazer, Sir James George. *The Golden Bough*. Abridged ed. New York: Macmillan, 1953.

———. "The Seclusion of Girls at Puberty." In *The Golden Bough*. London: Macmillan, 1913: 7:1:22–100.

———. *Taboo and the Perils of the Soul*. London: Macmillan, 1911.

Freeman, Erika. *Insights: Conversations with Theodor Reik*. Englewood Cliffs, N.J.: Prentice-Hall, 1971.

Freeman, Lucy, and Herbert S. Strean. *Freud and Women*. New York: Continuum, 1987.

Freud, Anna. *The Ego and the Mechanisms of Defense*. 1932. In *The Writings of Anna*

*Freud*. Trans. Cecil Baines. New York: International Universities Press, 1966.

Freud, Martin. *Sigmund Freud: Man and Father*. New York: Vanguard Press, 1958.

Freud, Sigmund. *The Complete Letters of Sigmund Freud to Wilhelm Fliess*. Ed. and trans. Jeffrey Moussaieff Masson. Cambridge: Harvard University Press, 1985.

———. "Das Medusenhaupt." *Gesammelte Werke*. 18 vols. Frankfurt am Main: S. Fischer Verlag, 1968: 17:47.

———. *The Origins of Psychoanalysis: Letters to Wilhelm Fliess*. Ed. Marie Bonaparte, Anna Freud, and Ernst Kris. Trans. Eric Mosbacher and James Strachey. New York: Basic Books, 1954.

———. *The Standard Edition of the Complete Psychological Works of Sigmund Freud*. 1966. Ed. and trans. James Strachey. London: Hogarth Press, 1986.

———. *Die Traumdeutung: Studienausgabe Band 2*. Frankfurt am Main: S. Fischer Verlag, 1972.

———. "Über neurotische Erkrankungstypen." *Studienausgabe Band 6*. Frankfurt am Main: Fischer Taschenbuch Verlag, 1982.

Frieden, Ken. *Freud's Dream of Interpretation*. Albany: State University of New York Press, 1990.

Gallop, Jane. *The Daughter's Seduction*. Ithaca: Cornell University Press, 1982.

Gallop, Jane, and Carolyn G. Burke. "Psychoanalysis and Feminism in France." In *The Future of Difference*. Ed. Hester Eisenstein and Alice Jardine. New Brunswick: Rutgers University Press, 1985: 106–21.

Garcia, Emanuel. "Johann Weier and Sigmund Freud: A Psychoanalytic Note on Science, Narcissism, and Aggression." *American Imago* 46 (1989): 21–36.

Garner, Shirley Nelson. "Freud and Fliess: Homophobia and Seduction." In *Seduction and Theory*. Ed. Dianne Hunter. Urbana: University of Illinois Press, 1989: 86–109.

Garner, Shirley Nelson, Claire Kahane, and Madelon Sprengnether, eds. *The (M)other Tongue: Essays in Feminist Psychoanalytic Interpretation*. Ithaca: Cornell University Press, 1985.

Gay, Peter. *Freud: A Life of Our Time*. New York: Norton, 1988.

———. *A Godless Jew: Freud, Atheism, and the Making of Psychoanalysis*. New Haven: Yale University Press, 1987.

George, Diana Hume. *Oedipus Anne: The Poetry of Anne Sexton*. Urbana: University of Illinois Press, 1987.

Gottlieb, Alma. "Menstrual Cosmology among the Beng of Ivory Coast." In *Blood Magic: The Anthropology of Menstruation*. Ed. Thomas Buckley and Alma Gottlieb. Berkeley: University of California Press, 1988: 55–74.

Grigg, Kenneth A. "All Roads Lead to Rome: The Role of the Nursemaid in Freud's Dreams." *Journal of the American Psychoanalytic Association* 21 (1973): 108–26.

Grimal, Pierre. *Dictionnaire de la mythologie Grècque et Romaine*. Paris: Presses Universitaires de France, 1958.

*Grimm's Household Tales, with the Authors' Notes.* Trans. Margaret Hunt. Detroit: Singing Tree, 1968.

Grinstein, Alexander. *The Index of Psychoanalytic Writings.* New York: International Universities Press, 1960.

———. *Sigmund Freud's Dreams.* New York: International Universities Press, 1968.

Groddeck, Georg. *The Book of the It.* 1923. Trans. V. M. E. Collins. New York: International Universities Press, 1976.

Gross, Rita M. "Hindu Female Deities as a Resource for the Contemporary Rediscovery of the Goddess." In *The Book of the Goddess: Past and Present.* Ed. Carl Olson. New York: Crossroad, 1989: 217–30.

Grosskurth, Phyllis. *Melanie Klein: Her World and Her Work.* Cambridge: Harvard University Press, 1987.

Gubar, Susan. "'The Blank Page' and Female Creativity." In *The New Feminist Criticism.* Ed. Elaine Showalter. New York: Pantheon, 1985: 292–313.

Guttman, Samuel A., Randall L. Jones, and Stephen M. Parrish, eds. *The Concordance to the Standard Edition of the Complete Psychological Works of Sigmund Freud.* 6 vols. Boston: G. K. Hall, 1980.

Halbreich, Uriel, and Jean Endicott. "The Biology of Premenstrual Changes: What Do We Really Know?" In *Premenstrual Syndrome: Current Findings and Future Directions.* Ed. Howard J. Osofsky and Susan J. Blumenthal. Washington, D.C.: American Psychiatric Press, 1985: 15–24.

Hall, Calvin. *A Primer of Freudian Psychology.* New York: New American Library, 1954.

Hamilton, Edith. *Mythology.* New York: Mentor, 1940.

Hardin, Harry T. "On the Vicissitudes of Freud's Early Mothering." *Psychoanalytic Quarterly* 56 (1987): 628–44, 57 (1988): 72–76, 209–23.

Harding, M. Esther. *Woman's Mysteries.* New York: Pantheon, 1955.

Hartland, E. Sidney. *The Legend of Perseus.* 3 vols. London: Grimm Library, 1895.

Hartman, Frank R. "A Reappraisal of the Emma Episode and the Specimen Dream." *Journal of the American Psychoanalytic Association* 31 (1983): 555–85.

Hastings, James. *A Dictionary of the Bible.* Vol. 2. New York: Scribners, 1899.

Hazra, R. C. *Studies in the Purá-nic Records on Hindu Rites and Customs.* Delhi, India: Motilal Banarsidass, 1975.

Heilbrun, Carolyn G. "Androgyny and the Psychology of Sex Differences." In *The Future of Difference.* Ed. Hester Eisenstein and Alice Jardine. New Brunswick: Rutgers University Press, 1985: 258–66.

Heiman, Marcel. "Sleep Orgasm in Women." In *Female Psychology.* Ed. Harold Blum. New York: International Universities Press, 1977: 285–304.

Hoffman, Daniel. *Poe Poe Poe Poe Poe Poe Poe.* 1972. New York: Paragon House, 1990.

Hogbin, Ian. *The Island of Menstruating Men.* Scranton, Pa.: Chandler, 1970.

*The Holy Bible.* Authorized (King James) Version. Philadelphia: National Bible Press, n.d.

Horney, Karen. *Feminine Psychology.* Ed. Harold Kelman. New York: Norton, 1973.
——. *New Ways in Psychoanalysis.* New York: Norton, 1939.
——. "Review of *Zur Psychologie der weiblichen Sexualfunktionen." International Journal of Psycho-analysis* 7 (1926): 92–100.
Hyman, Stanley Edgar. *The Tangled Bank.* New York: Grosset and Dunlap, 1966.
Irigaray, Luce. *The Irigaray Reader.* Ed. Margaret Whitford. Cambridge: Basil Blackwell, 1991.
——. *Speculum of the Other Woman.* 1974. Trans. Gillian C. Gill. Ithaca: Cornell University Press, 1985.
——. *This Sex which Is Not One.* 1977. Trans. Catherine Porter. Ithaca: Cornell University Press, 1985.
Jacobus, Mary. *Reading Women: Essays in Feminist Criticism.* New York: Columbia University Press, 1986.
Jones, Ernest. *The Life and Work of Sigmund Freud.* 3 vols. New York: Basic Books, 1953.
——. *On the Nightmare.* London: Hogath Press, 1931.
——. *Papers on Psychoanalysis.* Boston: Beacon Press, 1961.
Julkunen, M., J. Koistenen, J. Sjöberg, E. M. Rutanen, T. Wahlström, and M. Seppälä. "Secretory Endometrium Synthesizes Placental Protein 14." *Endocrinology* 118 (1986): 1782–86.
Jung, Carl G. *The Collected Works of C. G. Jung.* 20 vols. Ed. Herbert Read, Michael Fordham, and Gerhard Adler. Trans. R. F. C. Hull. Bollingen Series, no. 20. Princeton: Princeton University Press, 1979.
——. *Psychology of the Unconscious.* Trans. Beatrice M. Hinkle. New York: Moffat, Yard, 1916.
Jung, Emma, and Marie-Louise von Franz. *The Grail Legend.* 1960. Trans. Andrea Dykes. London: Hodder and Stoughton, 1971.
Kaplan, Louise J. *Female Perversions.* New York: Doubleday, 1991.
Kelman, Harold. *Helping People: Karen Horney's Psychoanalytic Approach.* New York: Science House, 1971.
Kenny, Lorraine. "Are You Sure I'll Still Be a Virgin?" *Camerawork Quarterly* 17 (1990): 8–14.
Kerenyi, Karl. *The Gods of the Greeks.* London: Thames and Hudson, 1951.
Kestenberg, Judith. "Menarche." In *Adolescents: A Psychoanalytic Approach to Problems and Therapy.* Ed. Sandor Lorand and Henry Scheer. New York: Harper and Row, 1964.
——. "Outside and Inside, Male and Female." 1968. In *Essential Papers on the Psychology of Women.* Ed. Claudia Zanardi. New York: New York University Press, 1990: 235–77.
King, Lester S. *Growth of Medical Thought.* Chicago: University of Chicago Press, 1969.

Klein, Melanie. "The Oedipus Complex in Light of Early Anxieties." In *Love, Guilt, and Reparation*. Ed. Masud R. Khan. London: Hogarth Press, 1945: 370–419.

———. *The Psycho-analysis of Children*. 1932. Trans. Alix Strachey. London: Hogarth Press, 1963.

———. "Review of *Woman's Periodicity*, by Mary Chadwick." 1936. In *Envy and Gratitude and Other Works 1946–1963*. New York: Delacourte, 1975: 318–19.

———. *The Selected Melanie Klein*. Ed. Juliet Mitchell. Harmondsworth, England: Penguin Books, 1986.

———. *The Writings of Melanie Klein*. Ed. R. E. Money-Kyrle, with B. Joseph, E. O'Shaughnessy, and H. Segal. 4 vols. London: Hogarth Press, 1975.

Knight, Chris. *Blood Relations: Menstruation and the Origins of Culture*. New Haven: Yale University Press, 1991.

———. "Menstrual Synchrony and the Australian Rainbow Snake." In *Blood Magic*. Ed. Thomas Buckley and Alma Gottlieb. Berkeley: University of California Press, 1988: 232–55.

Koestenbaum, Wayne. "Privileging the Anus: Anna O. and the Collaborative Origin of Psychoanalysis." *Genders* 3 (1988): 57–90.

Kofman, Sarah. *The Enigma of Woman: Woman in Freud's Writings*. 1980. Trans. Catherine Porter. Ithaca: Cornell University Press, 1985.

*The Koran*. Trans. J. M. Rodwell. London: Dent, 1953.

Krafft-Ebing, Richard. *Psychosis Menstrualis*. Erlangen: Verlag von Ferdinand Enke in Stuttgart, 1902.

Kris, Ernst. "Introduction." In *The Origins of Psychoanalysis*. Ed. Marie Bonaparte, Anna Freud, and Ernst Kris. Trans. Eric Mosbacher and James Strachey. New York: Basic Books, 1954.

Kristeva, Julia. *Powers of Horror: An Essay on Abjection*. 1980. Trans. Leon S. Roudiez. New York: Columbia University Press, 1982.

———. "Women's Time." In *The Kristeva Reader*. Ed. Toril Moi. New York: Columbia University Press, 1986.

Krüll, Marianne. *Freud and His Father*. 1979. Trans. Arnold J. Pomerans. New York: Norton, 1986.

Kurzweil, Edith. *The Freudians: A Comparative Perspective*. New Haven: Yale University Press, 1989.

Lacan, Jacques. *A Challenge to the Psychoanalytic Establishment*. 1980. In *Television*. Ed. Joan Copec. Trans. Jeffrey Mehlman. New York: Norton, 1990.

———. *The Seminar of Jacques Lacan, Book 2: The Ego In Freud's Theory and in the Technique of Psychoanalysis 1954–1955*. 1978. Trans. Sylvana Tomaselli. Ed. Jacques-Alain Miller. New York: Norton, 1988.

Laffey, Alice. *An Introduction to the Old Testament: A Feminist Perspective*. Philadelphia: Fortress Press, 1988.

Lander, Louise. *Images of Bleeding: Menstruation as Ideology.* New York: Orlando Press, 1988.

Laplanche, J., and J.-B. Pontalis. *The Language of Psycho-analysis.* Trans. Donald Nicholson-Smith. New York: Norton, 1973.

Lederer, Wolfgang. *The Fear of Women.* New York: Grune, 1968.

Lemoine-Luccioni, Eugenie. "The Fable of Blood." In *Returning to Freud: Clinical Psychoanalysis in the School of Lacan.* Ed. Stuart Schneiderman. New Haven: Yale University Press, 1980: 61–74.

Lerman, Hannah. *A Mote in Freud's Eye: From Psychoanalysis to the Psychology of Women.* New York: Springer, 1986.

Lidz, Ruth W., and Theodore Lidz. "Male Menstruation: A Ritual Alternative to the Oedipal Transition." *International Journal of Psycho-analysis* 58 (1977): 17–31.

Lightfoot-Klein, Hanny. *Prisoners of Ritual.* New York: Harrington Park Press, 1989.

Luce, Gay. *Biological Rhythms in Psychiatry and Medicine.* New York: Dover, 1970.

Lupton, Ellen, and J. Abbott Miller. *The Bathroom, the Kitchen, and the Aesthetics of Waste.* Cambridge: MIT List Visual Arts Center, 1992.

Lupton, Julia Reinhard. "Sphinx with Bouquet." Paper delivered at the conference "Freud/Art/History." University of California, Irvine, Nov. 1990.

Lupton, Mary Jane. "Claude Dagmar Daly: Notes on the Menstruation Complex." *American Imago* 46 (1989): 1–20.

———. "Review of *The Wise Wound* and *Images of Bleeding.*" *NWSA Journal* 1 (1989): 749–52.

Lupton, Mary Jane, and Julia Reinhard Lupton. "Annotated Bibliography of Claude Dagmar Daly (1884–1950)." *American Imago* 47 (1990): 81–91.

Malcolm, Janet. *In the Freud Archives.* New York: Alfred A. Knopf, 1984.

Malinowski, Bronislaw. *The Sexual Life of Savages in North Western Melanesia.* London: Routledge and Kegan Paul, 1982.

Mannoni, Octave. *Freud.* Trans. Renaud Bruce. New York: Pantheon, 1971.

Marks, Elaine, and Isabelle de Courtivron, eds. *New French Feminisms.* New York: Schocken Books, 1981.

Martin, Emily. *The Woman in the Body.* Boston: Beacon Press, 1987.

Masson, Jeffrey Moussaieff. *Freud: The Assault on Truth.* New York: Farrar, Straus, and Giroux, 1984.

*Mayo Clinic Family Health Book.* Ed. David E. Larson. New York: William Morrow, 1990.

Meadowcroft, Jeanne, and Dolf Zillman. "The Influence of Hormonal Fluctuations on Womens' Selection and Enjoyment of Television Programs." Paper presented at the annual meeting of the Association for Education in Journalism and Mass Communication, Gainesville, Fla., Aug. 1984.

Menninger, Karl A. "Psychogenic Influences on the Appearance of the Menstrual

Period." *International Journal of Psycho-analysis* 22 (1941): 60–64.

Mitchell, Juliet. *Psychoanalysis and Feminism*. New York: Pantheon, 1974.

Mitchell, Juliet, and Jacqueline Rose, eds. *Feminine Sexuality*. Trans. Jacqueline Rose. New York: Pantheon, 1985.

Montagu, M. F. Ashley. "The Origin of Subincision in Australia." *Oceania* 8 (1937).

———. "Physiology and the Origins of the Menstrual Prohibitions." *Quarterly Review of Biology* 15 (1940): 211–20.

Morrison, Toni. *Playing in the Dark: Whiteness and the Literary Imagination*. Cambridge: Harvard University Press, 1992.

Moulton, Ruth. "Early Papers on Women: Horney to Thompson." *American Journal of Psychoanalysis* 35 (1975): 207–23.

Müller, Josine. "A Contribution to the Libidinal Development of the Genital Phase in Girls." *International Journal of Psycho-analysis* 13 (1932): 362–68.

Neumann, Erich. *The Great Mother*. 1955. Trans. Ralph Manheim. Bollingen Series, vol. 47. Princeton: Princeton University Press, 1972.

*The New English Bible*. Ed. Samuel Sandmel. New York: Oxford University Press, 1976.

Nunberg, Herman. "Circumcision and Problems of Bisexuality." *International Journal of Psycho-analysis* 28 (1947): 145–79.

Nunberg, Herman, and Ernest Federn, eds. *Minutes of the Vienna Psychoanalytic Society*. Trans. M. Nunberg. 4 vols. New York: International Universities Press, 1962–75.

*Oxford NIV Scofield Study Bible: New International Version*. Ed. C. I. Scofield. New York: Oxford University Press, 1984.

Paige, Karen. "Women Learn to Sing the Menstrual Blues." *Psychology Today*, Sept. 1973, 43–44.

Paige, Karen Ericksen, and Jeffery M. Paige. *The Politics of Reproductive Ritual*. Berkeley: University of California Press, 1981.

Person, Ethel. "Some New Observations on the Origins of Femininity." In *Women and Analysis*. Ed. Jean Strouse. Boston: G. K. Hall, 1985: 250–61.

Pike, Judith. "Exquisite Cadavers: Spectacle into Fetish: Or, the Heroine as Still Life in Dumas and Verdi." University of California, Irvine, 1990.

Pliny. *Natural History*. Trans. H. Rackham. Cambridge: Harvard University Press, 1961.

Poe, Edgar Allan. *The Works of Edgar Allan Poe*. Ed. Hervey Allen. New York: Walter J. Black, 1927.

Prumner, D. M. *Handbook of Moral Theology*. Trans. G. W. Sheldon. Cork, Ireland: n.p., 1963.

Rado, Sándor. "Fear of Castration in Women." *Psychoanalytic Quarterly* 2 (1933): 425–75.

Ragland-Sullivan, Ellie. *Jacques Lacan and the Philosophy of Psychoanalysis*. Urbana: University of Illinois Press, 1986.

Ramey, Estelle. "Men's Cycles (They Have Them Too You Know)." *Ms.*, Spring 1972, 8–14.

Rank, Otto. *The Myth of the Birth of the Hero*. 1909. Trans. F. Robbins and Smith Ely Jelliffe. New York: Robert Brunner, 1952.

———. *The Trauma of Birth*. 1924. New York: Robert Brunner, 1952.

Reich, Annie. "Analysis of a Case of Brother-Sister Incest." 1932. In *Annie Reich: Psychoanalytic Contributions*. New York: International Universities Press, 1973: 1–22.

Reik, Theodor. *Pagan Rites of Judaism*. New York: Farrar, Straus, and Giroux, 1964.

———. *Ritual: Psycho-analytic Studies*. Trans. Douglas Bryan. New York: International Universities Press, 1946.

Reinhard, Kenneth Maurice. "Allegories of Mourning: Henry James, Psychoanalysis, and Representation." Ph.D. diss., Johns Hopkins University, 1989.

Reinhard, Kenneth Maurice, and Julia Reinhard Lupton. "Shapes of Grief: Freud, *Hamlet*, and Mourning." *Genders* 4 (1989): 50–67.

Renik, Owen. "An Example of Disavowal Involving the Menstrual Cycle." *Psychoanalytic Quarterly* 53 (1984): 523–32.

Rice, Emmanuel. *Freud and Moses: The Long Journey Home*. Albany: State University of New York Press, 1991.

Rich, Adrienne. *Of Woman Born: Motherhood as Experience and Institution*. New York: Norton, 1976.

Rickman, John. "Obituary of Claud Dangar Daly [*sic*]." *International Journal of Psycho-analysis* 31 (1950): 290–91.

Ritvo, Samuel. "Adolescent to Woman." In *Female Psychology*. Ed. Harold Blum. New York: International Universities Press, 1977: 127–37.

Roazen, Paul. *Brother Animal: The Story of Freud and Tausk*. New York: Knopf, 1969.

———. *Freud and His Followers*. New York: Alfred A. Knopf, 1975.

———. *Helene Deutsch: A Psychoanalyst's Life*. Garden City, N.Y.: Anchor Press/Doubleday, 1985.

Robert, Marthe. *From Oedipus to Moses: Freud's Jewish Identity*. Trans. Ralph Manheim. Garden City, N.Y.: Anchor, 1976.

Rodrigue, Emilio M. "Notes on Menstruation." *International Journal of Psycho-analysis* 36 (1955): 329–31.

Roheim, Geza. "Psycho-analysis of Primitive Cultural Types." *International Journal of Psycho-analysis* 13 (1932): 1–224.

Roith, Estelle. *The Riddle of Freud: Jewish Influences on His Theory of Female Sexuality*. London: Tavistock, 1987.

Rose, Louis, ed. and trans. "Freud and Fetishism: Previously Unpublished Minutes of the Vienna Psychoanalytic Society." Ed. and trans. Louis Rose. *Psychoanalytic Quarterly* 57 (1988): 146–66.

Rothbaum, Barbara O., and Joan Jackson. "Religious Influence on Menstrual Attitudes and Symptoms." *Women and Health* 16 (1990): 63–78.

Rudnytsky, Peter. *Freud and Oedipus*. New York: Columbia University Press, 1987.

Sachs, Hanns. "The Wish to Be a Man." *International Journal of Psycho-analysis* 1 (1920): 262–67.

Sajner, Josef. "The Freiberg Period of the Freud Family." 1968. Trans. Renée Gickhorn. *Journal of the History of Medicine* 24 (1969): 37–43.

Sarkar, Sarasi Lal. "A Study of the Psychology of Sexual Abstinence from the Dream of an Ascetic." *International Journal of Psycho-analysis* 24 (1943): 170–75.

Saul, Leon. "The Feminine Significance of the Nose." *Psychoanalytic Quarterly* 17 (1948): 51–57.

Sayers, Janet. *Biological Politics*. London: Tavistock, 1982.

———. *Mothers of Psychoanalysis*. New York: Norton, 1991.

Schmideberg, Melitta. "Psychoanalytisches zur Menstruation." *Zeitschrift für Psychoanalytisches Pädagogie* 5 (1931).

Schur, Max. *Freud: Living and Dying*. New York: International Universities Press, 1972.

———. "Some Additional 'Day Residues' of the Specimen Dream of Psychoanalysis." In *Psychoanalysis: A General Psychology—Essays in Honor of Heinz Hartmann*. Ed. R. M. Lowenstein, Lottie M. Newman, Max Schur, and A. J. Solnit. New York: International Universities Press, 1966: 45–85.

Schwartz, Murray M., and Christopher Bollas. "The Absence at the Center: Sylvia Plath and Suicide." In *Sylvia Plath: New Views on the Poetry*. Ed. Gary Lane. Baltimore: Johns Hopkins University Press, 1979: 179–202.

Shapiro, Ann-Louise. "Disordered Bodies, Disorderly Acts: Medical Discourse and the Female Criminal in Nineteenth Century Paris." *Genders* 4 (1989): 68–86.

Sharpe, Ella. "An Examination of Metaphor: Psycho-physical Problems Revealed in Language." In *The Psychoanalytic Reader: An Anthology of Essential Papers with Critical Introductions*. Ed. Robert Fliess. New York: International Universities Press, 1973: 306–19.

Showalter, Elaine. *The Female Malady: Women, Madness, and English Culture, 1830–1980*. New York: Pantheon, 1985.

Shuttle, Penelope, and Peter Redgrove. 1978. *The Wise Wound: Eve's Curse and Everywoman*. Rev. ed. New York: Grove Press, 1986.

Shweder, Richard A. "Menstrual Pollution, Soul Loss, and the Comparative Study of Emotions." In *Culture and Depression*. Ed. Arthur Kleinman and Byron Good. Berkeley: University of California Press, 1985: 182–215.

Siegel, Sheila. "The Effect of Culture on How Women Experience Menstruation: Jewish Women and *Mikvah*." *Women and Health* 10 (1985–86): 63–74.

Silbermann, Isodor. "A Contribution to the Psychology of Menstruation." *International Journal of Psycho-analysis* 31 (1950): 258–67.

Sjöö, Monica, and Barbara Mor. *The Great Cosmic Mother.* San Francisco: Harper and Row, 1987.

Sophocles. *Oedipus the King.* Ed. and trans. Thomas Gould. Englewood Cliffs, N.J.: Prentice-Hall, 1970.

Sprengnether, Madelon. *The Spectral Mother: Freud, Feminism, and Psychoanalysis.* Ithaca: Cornell University Press, 1990.

*Stedman's Medical Dictionary.* 24th ed. Baltimore: Williams and Wilkins, 1982.

Stekel, Wilhelm. *Frigidity in Women.* Trans. S. Van Teslaar. 2 vols. New York: Horace Liveright, 1929.

Stephens, William N. "A Cross-cultural Study of Menstrual Taboos." *Genetic Psychology Monographs* 64 (1961): 385–416.

———. *The Oedipus Complex: Cross-cultural Evidence.* New York: Free Press, 1962.

Stewart, Walter. *Psychoanalysis: The First Ten Years 1886–1896.* New York: Macmillan, 1967.

Strouse, Jean, ed. *Women and Analysis.* Boston: G. K. Hall, 1985.

Sulloway, Frank J. *Freud, Biologist of the Mind: Beyond the Psychoanalytic Legend.* New York: Basic Books, 1979.

Swan, Jim. "*Mater* and Nannie: Freud's Two Mothers and the Discovery of the Oedipus Complex." *American Imago* 31 (1974): 1–64.

Swidler, Leonard. *Women in Judaism.* Metuchen, N.J.: Scarecrow Press, 1976.

Tam, W. W., Mo-yin Chan, and P. H. Lee. "The Menstrual Cycle and Platelet 5-HT Uptake." *Psychosomatic Medicine* 47 (1985): 352–62.

Theweleit, Klaus. *Male Fantasies: Women, Floods, Bodies, History.* 2 vols. Vol. 1 trans. Stephen Conway, with Erica Carter and Chris Turner. Vol. 2 trans. Erica Carter and Chris Turner. Minneapolis: University of Minnesota Press, 1987, 1989.

Thompson, Catherine. "Dawn Poems in Blood: Sylvia Plath and PMS." *Tri-Quarterly* 80 (1990–91): 221–49.

Thompson, Clara M. *Interpersonal Psychoanalysis: The Selected Papers of Clara M. Thompson.* Ed. Maurice R. Green. New York: Basic Books, 1964.

———. *Psychoanalysis: Evolution and Development.* New York: Hermitage House, 1950.

Thompson, G. R. *Poe's Fiction.* Madison: University of Wisconsin Press, 1973.

Thornton, E. M. *The Freudian Fallacy.* Garden City, N.Y.: Doubleday, 1984.

Tierney, Helen, ed. *Women's Studies Encyclopedia.* 3 vols. Westport, Conn.: Greenwood Press, 1989.

Tilt, Edward John. *The Change of Life in Health and Disease.* 2d ed. London: n.p., 1857.

Treneman, Ann. "Cashing in on the Curse." In *The Female Gaze: Women as Viewers of Popular Culture.* Ed. Lorraine Gamman and Margaret Marshment. Seattle: Real Comet Press, 1989: 153–65.

Unterman, Isser Yehuda. "Family Purity: Its Wide Implications." *Israel Magazine* 4 (Jan. 1972): 68–74.

Van Herik, Judith. *Freud on Femininity and Faith*. Berkeley: University of California Press, 1982.

Veith, Ilza. *Hysteria: The History of a Disease*. Chicago: University of Chicago Press, 1965.

Vickery, John B. *The Literary Impact of "The Golden Bough."* Princeton: Princeton University Press, 1973.

Vitz, Paul C. *Sigmund Freud's Christian Unconscious*. New York: Guilford Press, 1988.

Walker, Alice. *Possessing the Secret of Joy*. New York: Harcourt Brace Jovanovich, 1992.

Walker, Barbara G. *The Woman's Encyclopedia of Myths and Secrets*. San Francisco: Harper and Row, 1983.

Walker, Benjamin. *Hindu World: An Encyclopedic Survey of Hinduism*. 2 vols. London: Allen and Unwin, 1968.

Wallace, Marjorie. *The Silent Twins*. New York: Prentice Hall, 1986.

Warner, William Beatty. *Chance and the Text of Experience: Freud, Neitzche, and Shakespeare's "Hamlet."* Ithaca: Cornell University Press, 1986.

Waskow, Arthur I. "Feminist Judaism: Restoration of the Moon." In *On Being a Jewish Feminist*. Ed. Susannah Heschel. New York: Schocken, 1983: 261–72.

Webster, Brenda. "Helene Deutsch: A New Look." *Signs* 10 (1985): 553–71.

Weideger, Paula. *Menstruation and Menopause*. New York: Alfred A. Knopf, 1975.

Whitford, Margaret. *Luce Irigaray: Philosophy in the Feminine*. London: Routledge, 1991.

Wimpfheimer, Miriam J., and Roy Schafer. "Psychoanalytic Methodology in Helene Deutsch's *The Psychology of Women*." *Psychoanalytic Quarterly* 46 (1977): 287–318.

Wittels, Fritz. *Freud and His Times*. New York: Liveright, 1931.

Wood, Charles T. "The Doctor's Dilemma: Sin, Salvation, and the Menstrual Cycle in Medieval Thought." *Speculum* 56 (1981): 710–27.

Wright, Elizabeth, ed. *Feminism and Psychoanalysis: A Critical Dictionary*. Cambridge: Basil Blackwell, 1992.

Yerushalmi, Yosef Hayim. *Freud's Moses: Judaism Terminable and Interminable*. New Haven: Yale University Press, 1991.

Zakarin, Laura. " 'Having Her Time': The Question of Woman, History, and Periodicity in Freud's *Civilization and Its Discontents*." University of California, Irvine, 1991.

# Index

MARY JANE LUPTON is the author of the first Feminist Press biography, *Elizabeth Barrett Browning,* and coauthor of *The Curse: A Cultural History of Menstruation.* A professor of English at Morgan State University, she has published widely on literature, psychoanalytic theory, feminism, and African-American women writers.